ACCOUNTING PROCEDURES:

The Recording Process— A Preparer's Perspective

MICHAEL L. WERNER

University of Miami

JEAN B. PRICE

Clemson University

PRENTICE HALL, UPPER SADDLE RIVER, NEW JERSEY 07458

Production editor: Deneise Smith
Acquisitions editor: Annie Todd
Associate editor: Natasha St. Hill
Manufacturing Buyer: Ken Clinton

Printed in the United States of America

10   9   8   7   6

ISBN 0-13-229022-7

Prentice Hall International (UK) Limited, *London*
Prentice Hall of Australia Pty. Limited, *Sydney*
Prentice Hall Canada, Inc., *Toronto*
Prentice Hall Hispanoamericana, S.A., *Mexico*
Prentice Hall of India Private Limited, *New Delhi*
Prentice Hall of Japan, Inc., *Tokyo*
Prentice Hall Asia Pte. Ltd., *Singapore*
Editora Prentice Hall do Brasil Ltda., *Rio de Janeiro*

TABLE OF CONTENTS

The authors and publisher would like to thank the following individuals who served as reviewers for this text:

J. Lawrence Bergin	Winona State University
Richard Fern	Eastern Kentucky University
Leslie B. Fletcher	Georgia Southern University
Barbara Muller	Arizona State University West
Alfonso R. Oddo	Niagara University
Mary Ann M. Prater	Clemson University
Joanne Sheridan	Montana State University-Billings
Jack Zeller	Kirkwood Community College

The authors and publisher would also like to thank the focus group participants for their valuable ideas used in the development of this text and the accompanying software:

Sherri Anderson	Sonoma State University
Alison Drews-Bryan	Clemson University
Richard Fern	Eastern Kentucky University
Maria Mari	Miami Dade Community College
Alfonso R. Oddo	Niagara University
Joanne Sheridan	Montana State University-Billings

In addition, the authors would like to thank Alfonso R. Oddo for his extensive contribution to the assignment materials appearing in this text.

MODULE *1*

EFFECTS OF TRANSACTIONS ON FINANCIAL STATEMENTS

Every business is involved in hundreds, if not thousands of transactions each year. Each transaction has an effect on the financial position of the entities involved. In order to assess the financial progress of a business, data relating to business transactions must be gathered and converted into useful information. This book explores the accounting procedures used to gather, record, and convert transaction data into useful information.

Accounting information in the form of financial statements is the major output of this process. In essence, we are going "behind the scenes" to see how accounting information is actually generated. Before going behind the scenes to see how the output (financial statements) is generated, you should be certain you understand the effects of various transactions on the financial statements.

AMANDA'S TYPING SERVICE — OUR GUIDE TO THE RECORDING PROCESS

Amanda's Typing Service is the company used as the running example throughout most of this book. The business was begun by Amanda Wells and her sister Jessica. After exploring the three major business organizational forms (proprietorships, partnerships, and corporations), Amanda and Jessica chose to form a corporation.

Amanda's Typing Service offers several services and has a variety of customers. The company prepares resumes, papers, and graphical presentations for college students. Several local law firms have contracts and other legal documents prepared by Amanda's. A nearby medical clinic pays the company to transcribe taped medical information recorded by its doctors.

In this module, we will walk through a series of transactions in which Amanda's Typing Service interacts with owners, suppliers, customers and others. Remember, we are viewing the transactions from the company's point of view. Each transaction will be described and explained, with an emphasis on the transaction's impact on the company's financial statements. After each transaction, updated financial statements for the company will be presented. As we will see, the accounting equation, (ASSETS = LIABILITIES + OWNERS' EQUITY), will remain in balance throughout this process.

Because Amanda and Jessica formed a corporation, the financial statement presentations are appropriate for companies using the corporate form of business organization. There would be slight differences in the financial statements if Amanda's Typing Service were a proprietorship or a partnership. These differences will be explained at the end of this module, after all the transactions for Amanda's Typing Service have been explored.

For illustration purposes, we will show financial statements for Amanda's Typing Service after each transaction. Although the company *could* actually prepare financial statements this frequently, it probably would not. Generally, financial statements are prepared monthly, quarterly or annually, and indicate results of hundreds or even thousands of transactions.

TRANSACTION A: On January 1, 1996, the business was begun by an initial investment of $3,000 from the owners.

EXPLANATION: From the company's point of view, cash was received, but in exchange, the company gave an ownership interest in the operations. In a corporation, ownership interest takes the form of shares of common stock. Issuing stock for cash results in an increase in cash and an increase in the equity section of the corporation's balance sheet.

Common stock can either be par value stock or no-par stock. If the stock has a par value, the increase to common stock is limited to the par value of the shares sold. Par value per share is usually set much lower than what the company expects to receive for each share of stock. The additional amount (over and above par value) received by the company is reported as additional paid-in capital or paid-in-capital in excess of par value. For example, if a company issued 2,000 shares of $2 par value stock for $5 per share, it would report:

```
Common Stock                    $ 4,000
Additional Paid-in Capital        6,000
```

The company received a total of $10,000 for the shares, but only the par value (2,000 shares X $2 each) is reported as common stock. The additional amount received (2,000 shares X $3 each) is reported as additional paid-in capital.

If no-par stock is issued, the total amount received by the company for the shares of stock sold is shown as an increase in cash and an increase in common stock.

Amanda's Typing Service began operations on January 1, 1996 by issuing (selling) 1,000 shares of its no-par stock for $3 per share. Amanda bought 600 shares and Jessica bought the remaining 400 shares. The business received a total of $3,000 cash, so assets increased by that amount. The transaction also affected stockholders' equity which is on the other side of the accounting equation. Because the stock has no par value, the entire amount of cash received by the company is reported as common stock.

An investment by owners does not affect the information shown on the company's income statement. It does, however, affect the balance sheet. Amanda's Typing Service's balance sheet prepared immediately after the sale of the stock would look like this:

Amanda's Typing Service Balance Sheet January 1, 1996		
Assets:		**Liabilities:**
		$ 0
Cash	$3,000	**Owners' Equity:**
		Common Stock $3,000
		Total Owners' Equity 3,000
		Total Liabilities and
Total Assets	$3,000	Owners' Equity $3,000

Notice that the accounting equation is in balance:

$$\text{ASSETS} = \text{LIABILITIES} + \text{OWNERS' EQUITY}$$

$$\$3,000 = 0 + \$3,000$$

TRANSACTION B: On January 3, 1996, the owners of Amanda's Typing Service realized their investment in the corporation did not provide enough cash to get the operations of the company started. The company obtained a $5,000 small business loan from First Friendly Bank. Amanda signed a promissory note on behalf of the corporation agreeing to repay the $5,000 principal plus interest in eighteen months.

EXPLANATION: This transaction provided the company with $5,000 additional cash, so total assets rose to $8,000. Amanda's Typing Service now owes $5,000, so liabilities have gone up as well. In most borrowing situations such as this one, the bank requires that a promissory note be signed. Promissory notes are legally binding obligations to repay funds.

After obtaining the loan, Amanda's Typing Service has more cash, but the company owes $5,000 to the bank, so the owners have no greater claim to the assets. Accordingly, owners' equity was not affected by this transaction. The amount the company owes to the bank is shown on its balance sheet as a liability.

Amanda's Typing Service Balance Sheet January 3, 1996		
Assets:		**Liabilities:**
		Notes Payable $5,000
Cash	$8,000	**Owners' Equity:**
		Common Stock $3,000
		Total Owners' Equity 3,000
		Total Liabilities and
Total Assets	$8,000	Owners' Equity $8,000

Even with the impact of the loan, the accounting equation is still in balance:

$$ASSETS = LIABILITIES + OWNERS' \; EQUITY$$

$$\$8,000 = \$5,000 + \$3,000$$

TRANSACTION C: On January 5, 1996, Amanda's Typing Service purchased office supplies from Rebecca's Office Supplies. Amanda's Typing Service opened an account with Rebecca's, and charged $300 of supplies. In business, a common way of saying that goods or services were charged to a charge account is to say that they were "purchased on account". In other words, Amanda's Typing Service purchased $300 of supplies on account.

EXPLANATION: The supplies the company has acquired will be shown as an asset because they will provide future benefit to the company. The supplies will be used to support the business activity over the next several months.

Because Amanda's Typing Service did not pay for the supplies when they were purchased, cash was not affected. Rather, the company agreed to pay for the items within 60 days. Amanda's Typing Service has incurred another liability — accounts payable. Now, the company owes Rebecca's for the supplies and First Friendly Bank for the business loan. The obligation to the bank is evidenced by a promissory note, and therefore is shown as notes payable. There is no such note for the obligation to Rebecca's and, therefore, the obligation is shown as accounts payable as opposed to notes payable. On the company's balance sheet, both of these debts will be shown as liabilities. However, in order to provide more information to the users of the financial statements, the two liabilities will be shown in different categories.

Current liabilities are those debts that are expected to require payment within a period of one year or the company's operating cycle, whichever is longer. As a company operates, it spends funds to either: (1) purchase raw materials to make products to sell (manufacturer), (2) buy products for resale (merchandiser), or (3) perform services for the customer (service company). Then the company sells the products or services, and eventually receives cash from its customers. A company's **operating cycle** is defined as the time that generally passes between the expenditure of cash to buy the raw materials or products, or perform the services, and the point at which the company actually collects cash from its customers. Most businesses' operating cycles are much shorter than a year. However, for companies involved in operations such as the production of tobacco products or lumber, operating cycles may be longer than a year. For companies in these industries, the operating cycle defines the criteria for classification of liabilities.

Again, current liabilities are those debts that are expected to require payment within one year or the company's operating cycle, whichever is longer. Certainly, the accounts payable amount Amanda's Typing Service owes Rebecca's Office Supplies will need to be paid within a year and thus, is classified as a current liability.

Those liabilities *not* expected to require payment during the next year or operating cycle (whichever criteria the company is using to determine its current liabilities) are classified as **long-term liabilities**. For Amanda's Typing Service, the note payable is due in eighteen months, and thus, qualifies as a long-term liability.

After the purchase of supplies on account, the balance sheet for Amanda's Typing Service would appear as follows:

Amanda's Typing Service Balance Sheet January 5, 1996			
Assets:		**Liabilities:**	
		Current Liabilities:	
		Accounts Payable	$ 300
Cash	$8,000	Long-term Liabilities:	
Supplies	300	Notes Payable	5,000
		Total Liabilities	$5,300
		Owners' Equity:	
		Common Stock $3,000	
		Total Owners' Equity	3,000
		Total Liabilities and	
Total Assets	$8,300	Owners' Equity	$8,300

Classification of liabilities into current and long-term will not affect the accounting equation:

$$\text{ASSETS} = \text{LIABILITIES} + \text{OWNERS' EQUITY}$$

$$\$8,300 = \$5,300 + \$3,000$$

TRANSACTION D: Amanda's Typing Service purchased an insurance policy to cover the business in case of lawsuits from clients or any other type of liability. On January 7, the company paid $1,200 for one year of insurance coverage.

EXPLANATION: The company spent money, so the amount of cash reported on the balance sheet should go down. However, what did the company get for its $1,200? Amanda's Typing Service obtained a one-year insurance policy. The insurance coverage will protect the company for the next year, so the policy will provide the company with future benefits.

As you know, an item expected to provide future benefits is an asset. Because it is expected to provide a future benefit to the company, the insurance paid in advance is reported as an asset, prepaid insurance. As time passes, the insurance is "used up" as more and more of the insurance coverage is associated with the past, and less is associated with the future. As this happens, the cost of the insurance associated with the past should be taken out of the asset classification and added to the expense classification. In other words, as time passes, the cost associated with the insurance policy will be converted from an asset to an expense. This process can be used for any expenses paid in advance, such as rent or advertising. Expenses paid in advance are assets called prepaid expenses.

As indicated below, payment of expenses in advance only affects the asset section of the balance sheet. Neither liabilities nor owners' equity is affected.

```
            Amanda's Typing Service
                 Balance Sheet
                January 7, 1996

Assets:                          Liabilities:
                                  Current Liabilities:
                                   Accounts Payable      $   300
   Cash              $6,800       Long-term Liabilities:
   Supplies             300        Notes Payable           5,000
   Prepaid Insurance   1,200        Total Liabilities     $5,300

                                 Owners' Equity:
                                  Common Stock     $3,000
                                 Total Owners' Equity       3,000
                                 Total Liabilities and
Total Assets         $8,300         Owners' Equity        $8,300
```

After payment of expenses in advance, Amanda's Typing Service has less cash, but now has prepaid expenses. The amount of total assets remains the same. Notice that the accounting equation remains the same as before the purchase of the insurance:

$$ASSETS = LIABILITIES + OWNERS' \ EQUITY$$

$$\$8,300 = \$5,300 + \$3,000$$

TRANSACTION E: On January 9, 1996, Amanda's Typing Service paid cash for a desk, three chairs, a small table and a file cabinet for the office. Total spent — $2,500.

EXPLANATION: The company paid cash, so the amount reported as cash must go down. What did the company get for its money? It received a number of specific items, each of which could be listed on the company's balance sheet. Because the details of specific items is not likely to provide additional information, Amanda's Typing Service can simply show the items purchased as office furniture. The office furniture will provide the company with future benefits, so would be properly shown as an asset.

This transaction and the previous one are somewhat similar. In both cases, Amanda's Typing Service gave up cash in exchange for another asset. However, there is a basic difference between the prepaid insurance and the office furniture. The prepaid insurance will be "used up" a year from now; the office furniture is expected to benefit the company for several years.

Differences in the basic nature of the two assets can be disclosed by classifying them differently on the company's balance sheet. The balance sheet below divides the company's assets into two groups (classifications) to provide additional information to financial statement users. The two categories of assets are defined using the criteria of time in a manner similar to the distinction between current and long-term liabilities. **Current assets** are those that are either: (1) cash; (2) expected to become cash within the next year or operating cycle, whichever is longer; or (3) expected to be used up in the next year or operating cycle, whichever is longer. As you can see in the balance sheet for Amanda's Typing Service (presented below), the company's cash, supplies, and prepaid insurance are shown as current assets. Other examples of current assets include accounts receivable and inventory.

Long-term assets are those that are expected to last longer than a year or operating cycle, whichever criteria the company is using to determine its current assets. In the case of the office furniture purchased by Amanda's Typing Service, the company expects to benefit from this item for more than a year, so it should be classified as a long-term asset. Other examples of long-term assets include buildings, equipment, and vehicles. Classifying assets into current and long-term provides additional information to financial statement readers. This type of information about the assets of Amanda's Typing Service can be seen on the balance sheet below:

```
                    Amanda's Typing Service
                         Balance Sheet
                       January 9, 1996

Assets:                            Liabilities:
 Current Assets:                    Current Liabilities:
  Cash              $4,300           Accounts Payable      $   300
  Supplies             300          Long-term Liabilities:
  Prepaid Insurance  1,200           Notes Payable           5,000
    Total Current Assets  $5,800       Total Liabilities    $5,300

 Long-term Assets:                 Owners' Equity:
  Office Furniture   $2,500         Common Stock      $3,000
                                    Total Owners' Equity      3,000
    Total Long Term Assets  2,500
                                   Total Liabilities and
Total Assets              $8,300     Owners' Equity          $8,300
```

The assets held by Amanda's Typing Service are quite different than when the company first started, but the accounting equation is still in balance:

$$ASSETS = LIABILITIES + OWNERS' \ EQUITY$$

$$\$8,300 = \$5,300 + \$3,000$$

TRANSACTION F: On January 11, Amanda's Typing Service bought a complete computer system from Carl's Computers for $7,000. A down payment of $2,000 was made, and Carl's Computers allowed Amanda's Typing Service to open a charge account with the store and charge the balance.

EXPLANATION: The company has a new asset — the computer system. Because the system is expected to benefit the company for more than one year, it is considered a long-term asset.

Amanda's Typing Service spent money on the down payment, causing the amount of cash shown on the balance sheet to go down. The remaining $5,000 is still owed, increasing accounts payable.

```
                    Amanda's Typing Service
                         Balance Sheet
                       January 11, 1996

Assets:                          Liabilities:
 Current Assets:                  Current Liabilities:
  Cash              $2,300         Accounts Payable      $ 5,300
  Supplies             300        Long-term Liabilities:
  Prepaid Insurance  1,200         Notes Payable           5,000
    Total Current Assets  $ 3,800   Total Liabilities    $10,300

 Long-term Assets:               Owners' Equity:
  Office Furniture  $2,500         Common Stock      $3,000
  Computer System    7,000       Total Owners' Equity     3,000
    Total Long Term Assets  9,500
                                 Total Liabilities and
Total Assets             $13,300   Owners' Equity        $13,300
```

Even though the company's purchase of the computer system impacted three items on the balance sheet, the accounting equation is still in balance:

$$ASSETS = LIABILITIES + OWNERS' \ EQUITY$$

$$\$13,300 = \$10,300 + \$3,000$$

TRANSACTION G: On January 13, Amanda's Typing Service paid a portion of the amount it owed to Rebecca's Office Supplies. Although the total amount owed was $300, Amanda's Typing Service decided to pay only $200. This transaction is referred to as a payment on account.

EXPLANATION: The company paid cash, causing the amount of cash shown on the balance sheet to go down. What did the company receive for the cash spent? The supplies bought on account were shown on the balance sheet when they were purchased. Amanda's Typing Service is not receiving an asset when it finally pays for the supplies. Rather, it is reducing the amount owed to Rebecca's Office Supplies.

As shown in the balance sheet below, the payment on account causes a decrease in the amount of cash and a decrease in the amount of accounts payable.

```
                    Amanda's Typing Service
                         Balance Sheet
                        January 13, 1996

Assets:                         Liabilities:
 Current Assets:                 Current Liabilities:
  Cash              $2,100        Accounts Payable      $ 5,100
  Supplies             300       Long-term Liabilities:
  Prepaid Insurance  1,200        Notes Payable           5,000
   Total Current Assets $ 3,600    Total Liabilities    $10,100

 Long-term Assets:              Owners' Equity:
  Office Furniture $2,500         Common Stock      $3,000
  Computer System   7,000       Total Owners' Equity      3,000
   Total Long Term Assets  9,500
                                Total Liabilities and
Total Assets            $13,100   Owners' Equity          $13,100
```

The company's payment on account reduces total assets as well as total liabilities, but the accounting equation is still in balance:

$$ASSETS = LIABILITIES + OWNERS' \ EQUITY$$

$$\$13,100 = \$10,100 + \$3,000$$

The transactions we have examined thus far only impacted items on Amanda's Typing Service's balance sheet. They had no effect on the company's income statement or statement of retained earnings. Business activities involving the earnings process impact all three financial statements, and distributions to owners impact both the statement of retained earnings and the balance sheet. To illustrate the effects of revenues, expenses, and dividends on a company's financial statements, we will examine several transactions at one time. The following five transactions took place during Amanda's Typing Service's first month of operations.

TRANSACTION H: During the month, Amanda's Typing Service performed $800 of services for customers who paid cash upon completion of the work.

TRANSACTION I: Amanda's Typing Service performed $2,100 of work during January for customers who were billed, with the understanding they will pay for the work next month.

TRANSACTION J: Amanda's has two part-time workers who keyboard documents and help in the office. During the month, the company paid these employees a total of $1,100.

TRANSACTION K: Speedy Delivery Service picks up completed jobs from Amanda's Typing Service and delivers them to customers. On January 30, Amanda's Typing Service received a bill from Speedy for $100, reflecting the deliveries made during the month. Amanda's expects to pay the bill early next month.

TRANSACTION L: On January 31, the owners of Amanda's Typing Service determined the company had sufficient cash and retained earnings to pay a dividend. A $500 cash dividend was paid to the stockholders.

EXPLANATION: During the month, Amanda's Typing Service performed services for a number of customers. Some customers paid cash for the jobs performed. Other customers set up accounts with the company and agreed to pay for the work next month. Whether or not the customers paid Amanda's Typing Service right away has no impact on the fact that the company earned revenue.

Under accrual accounting, the company's income statement for the month shows all revenues EARNED during the period, regardless of whether any cash has been received. Generally, revenue is considered earned when the company has a legally enforceable claim to the associated cash. In other words, a company should recognize revenue when the associated obligation to the customer has been met. For some companies, recognizing revenue requires that the product sold is delivered to the customer; in a service business, revenue should be recognized when the service for the customer has been performed.

In the example of Amanda's Typing Service, the $800 associated with services performed for customers who paid cash (TRANSACTION H) is reflected as increased revenue on the income statement and an increase in cash on the balance sheet. The $2,100 associated with services performed for customers who were billed (TRANSACTION I) is shown as increased revenue on the income statement and an increase in accounts receivable on the balance sheet. For these revenues, Amanda's Typing Service did not receive cash, but did receive a current asset in the form of accounts receivable, which is the customers' promise to pay.

The work performed by the two part-time employees of Amanda's Typing Service helped to generate the revenues earned during January. For that reason, the wages paid to the company's employees (TRANSACTION J) are expenses for the period. Payment of the wages resulted in a $1,100 expense shown on the income statement and a $1,100 decrease in the amount of cash shown on the balance sheet.

Like the work of the company's employees, the delivery services performed by Speedy (TRANSACTION K) helped to generate revenues in January. Therefore, the $100 cost of the delivery service is an expense for the period. The fact that Amanda's Typing Service has not yet paid for the delivery services does not affect the presentation of this amount as an expense on the income statement. It does, however, cause a $100 increase in accounts payable shown on the balance sheet.

Cash dividends are amounts distributed to owners. Dividends are *not* an expense. Dividends are a *distribution of income* — not a cost of earning income. Because they are not expenses, dividends paid are never included on the income statement. These distributions reduce owners' equity. Thus, payment of a dividend (TRANSACTION L) has no impact on Amanda's income statement. Cash dividends cause a reduction of retained earnings, as shown on the statement of retained earnings and a reduction in the amount of cash shown on the balance sheet.

The combined effects of TRANSACTIONS H, I, J, K, and L are reflected in the company's financial statements shown below:

```
                    Amanda's Typing Service
                       Income Statement
                  For the Month of January, 1996

         Service Revenue                           $2,900
         Less:
           Wages Expense            $1,100
           Delivery Expense            100
             Total Expenses                          1,200
         Net Income                                 $1,700
```

```
                    Amanda's Typing Service
                  Statement of Retained Earnings
                  For the Month of January, 1996

         Retained Earnings   January 1, 1996      $     0
         Add Net Income                             1,700
                                                   $1,700
         Less Dividends                               500
         Retained Earnings January 31, 1996        $1,200
```

```
                    Amanda's Typing Service
                         Balance Sheet
                       January 31, 1996

Assets:                              Liabilities:
 Current Assets:                      Current Liabilities:
  Cash              $1,300             Accounts Payable      $ 5,200
  Accounts Receivable 2,100           Long-term Liabilities:
  Supplies             300             Notes Payable           5,000
  Prepaid Insurance  1,200             Total Liabilities     $10,200
    Total Current Assets  $ 4,900
                                     Owners' Equity:
 Long-term Assets:                    Common Stock    $3,000
  Office Furniture  $2,500            Retained Earnings 1,200
  Computer System    7,000           Total Owners' Equity     4,200
    Total Long Term Assets  9,500
                                     Total Liabilities and
Total Assets            $14,400        Owners' Equity        $14,400
```

The arrows connecting items on the company's financial statements indicate how the financial statements relate to one another. As you can see, net income from the income statement becomes a key component of the statement of retained earnings. Likewise, the ending retained earnings amount from the statement of retained earnings becomes an important component of the balance sheet. This relationship of interdependence among the financial statements is called **articulation**.

The statements above reflect the effects of five different transactions, but the accounting equation still remains in balance:

$$\text{ASSETS} = \text{LIABILITIES} + \text{OWNERS' EQUITY}$$
$$\$14,400 = \$10,200 + \$4,200$$

Now, we have seen the impact of a variety of transactions on the financial statements of a business. We've examined transactions that affected only balance sheet items, and transactions impacting the income statement. We have also seen the effect of dividends on the statement of retained earnings and the balance sheet. In all these illustrations, the company involved, Amanda's Typing Service, was a corporation. What impact does the form of business organization have on how transactions affect financial statements? The next section provides the answer.

FINANCIAL STATEMENTS FOR PROPRIETORSHIPS AND PARTNERSHIPS

Using Amanda's Typing Service as our example, let's explore the impact of organizational form on a company's financial statements. At the beginning of this module, we described the creation of the company. Amanda and Jessica chose to set up a corporation. But what if they had instead created a proprietorship or a partnership? How would the company's financial statements been different?

First, consider the balance sheet. In general, a difference in business organizational form only impacts the equity section of a company's balance sheet. Recall Transaction A in which stock was issued to the owners in exchange for the cash used to start the operation of the business. If Amanda's Typing Service began as either a proprietorship or partnership, no stock would have been issued. Rather, investments by owners are shown in capital accounts. The balance sheets below illustrate the impact of investments by owners in proprietorships and partnerships.

If the company were started as a proprietorship, assume Amanda invested the entire $3,000 herself. The single capital account reflects this investment.

Amanda's Typing Service (Proprietorship) Balance Sheet January 1, 1996			
Assets:		Liabilities:	$ 0
Cash	$3,000	Owner's Equity:	
		A. Wells, Capital $3,000	
		Total Owner's Equity	3,000
		Total Liabilities and	
Total Assets	$3,000	Owner's Equity	$3,000

If the company had been started as a partnership, assume Amanda invested $1,800 and Jessica invested $1,200. Notice the capital accounts reflecting each owner's investment.

```
+-------------------------------------------------------------------+
|            Amanda's Typing Service (Partnership)                  |
|                      Balance Sheet                                |
|                    January 1, 1996                                |
+------------------------------+------------------------------------+
| Assets:                      | Liabilities:                       |
|                              |                              $  0  |
|  Cash             $3,000     | Owners' Equity:                    |
|                              |  A. Wells, Capital $1,800          |
|                              |  J. Wells, Capital  1,200          |
|                              | Total Owners' Equity      3,000    |
| Total Assets      $3,000     | Total Liabilities and              |
|                              |     Owners' Equity        $3,000   |
+------------------------------+------------------------------------+
```

If Amanda's Typing Service had experienced the same transactions as described throughout this module, relatively few other transactions would have been affected by a change in organizational form. In fact, all the other transactions affecting only the balance sheet (Transactions B - G) would have been the same if Amanda's Typing Service had been a proprietorship or a partnership. Thus, after Transaction G, if the company had been established as a proprietorship, a balance sheet reflecting those first seven transactions would have appeared as:

```
+-------------------------------------------------------------------+
|          Amanda's Typing Service (Proprietorship)                 |
|                      Balance Sheet                                |
|                    January 13, 1996                               |
+------------------------------+------------------------------------+
| Assets:                      | Liabilities:                       |
|  Current Assets:             |  Current Liabilities:              |
|   Cash          $2,100       |   Accounts Payable      $ 5,100    |
|   Supplies         300       |  Long-term Liabilities:            |
|   Prepaid Insurance 1,200    |   Notes Payable          5,000     |
|    Total Current Assets      |   Total Liabilities     $10,100    |
|                   $ 3,600    |                                    |
|                              |                                    |
|  Long-term Assets:           | Owner's Equity:                    |
|   Office Furniture $2,500    | A. Wells, Capital $3,000           |
|   Computer System   7,000    | Total Owner's Equity     3,000     |
|    Total Long Term Assets    |                                    |
|                    9,500     | Total Liabilities and              |
|                              |   Owner's Equity        $13,100    |
| Total Assets      $13,100    |                                    |
+------------------------------+------------------------------------+
```

Notice the assets and liabilities of the company are reported exactly as they were when the company was a corporation.

If the business had been established as a partnership between Amanda and Jessica, the assets and liabilities would still have been the same. The company's balance sheet after Transaction G would have been:

```
              Amanda's Typing Service (Partnership)
                         Balance Sheet
                        January 13, 1996

Assets:                               Liabilities:
 Current Assets:                       Current Liabilities:
  Cash                 $2,100           Accounts Payable        $ 5,100
  Supplies                300          Long-term Liabilities:
  Prepaid Insurance    1,200            Notes Payable             5,000
   Total Current Assets  $ 3,600         Total Liabilities      $10,100
                                      Owners' Equity:
 Long-term Assets:                     A. Wells, Capital $1,800
  Office Furniture     $2,500          J. Wells, Capital  1,200
  Computer System       7,000          Total Owners' Equity       3,000
   Total Long Term Assets  9,500
                                      Total Liabilities and
Total Assets              $13,100       Owners' Equity          $13,100
```

After the transactions affecting only the balance sheet were completed, Amanda's Typing Service began recording revenue and expense transactions. The next few transactions (H - K) recorded by Amanda's Typing Service would have been no different if the business had been a proprietorship or a partnership. In fact, the income statement would be the same no matter which organizational form had been chosen. Business form has no impact on the recording of revenues and expenses.

The final transaction, however, would have been different. Recall that Transaction L was the payment of a $500 dividend. Dividends are distributions to stockholders. Since proprietorships and partnerships do not issue stock, they cannot pay dividends. They CAN, however, make distributions to owners. Generally, in a proprietorship or partnership, a distribution to an owner or owners is called a drawing or withdrawal.

Drawings have the same basic impact as dividends. Owners' equity is reduced. However, as dividends are a reduction of a corporation's Retained Earnings, a drawing is a reduction of the owner's Capital account. The bridge statement for a proprietorship or partnership shows the change in owners' Capital accounts. The statement of capital articulates with the income statement and the balance sheet just as the statement of retained earnings did in the corporate setting.

If Amanda had established the business as a proprietorship, and had made a $500 drawing, the company's set of financial statements after all the transactions would appear as:

```
             Amanda's Typing Service (Proprietorship)
                         Income Statement
                   For the Month of January, 1996

           Service Revenue                          $2,900
           Less:
             Wages Expense                 $1,100
             Delivery Expense                 100
               Total Expenses                        1,200
           Net Income                               $1,700
```

```
                   Amanda's Typing Service
                     Statement of Capital
                 For the Month of January, 1996


        Amanda Wells, Capital  January 1, 1996      $  0
             ADD: Investment by Owner               3,000
             ADD: Net Income                        1,700
                                                    $4,700
             LESS: Drawings                           500
        Amanda Wells, Capital  January 31, 1996     $4,200
```

```
                   Amanda's Typing Service
                        Balance Sheet
                       January 31, 1996

Assets:                             Liabilities:
 Current Assets:                     Current Liabilities:
  Cash              $1,300            Accounts Payable      $ 5,200
  Accounts Receivable 2,100          Long-term Liabilities:
  Supplies             300            Notes Payable           5,000
  Prepaid Insurance  1,200            Total Liabilities     $10,200
   Total Current Assets  $ 4,900
                                    Owner's Equity:
 Long-term Assets:                  A. Wells, Capital $4,200
  Office Furniture  $2,500
  Computer System    7,000          Total Owner's Equity     4,200
   Total Long Term Assets  9,500
                                    Total Liabilities and
Total Assets          $14,400        Owner's Equity         $14,400
```

Notice that in a proprietorship, investments by the owner, net income, and distributions to the owner all impact the owner's Capital account. Recall in a corporation, the owners' investments were recorded in a Stock account, while earnings and dividends were reflected in a separate account — Retained Earnings. In a proprietorship, no distinction is made between equity from investment by the owner and equity from earnings. Both impact the Capital account.

If Amanda's Typing Service had been established as a partnership, Amanda and Jessica may have signed a partnership agreement. This legally binding document would outline contractual details, not the least of which would be how profits generated by the company are to be shared. If Amanda and Jessica had established the company as a partnership, and had agreed to share net income in the same proportion as their initial investments, the company's statement of capital would show the net income increasing each partner's Capital account. Recall Amanda's initial investment was $1,800 and Jessica's was $1,200. If net income is shared proportionally to these initial investments, Amanda's Capital account should be increased by 60% ($1,800 / $3,000) of the net income, and Jessica's Capital account should be increased by 40% ($1,200 / $3,000) of the net income. The company's statement of capital reflects allocation of the period's net income to each partner's Capital account in these proportions. (Amanda: 60% X $1,700 = $1,020) (Jessica: 40% X $1,700 = $680)

Additionally, the partnership agreement may outline under what circumstances owners are allowed to make withdrawals. Some partners may not wish to take cash out of the business; they may prefer to allow their equity in the partnership to remain untouched. Assume in our example, that Amanda made a $500 withdrawal, but Jessica took no cash out of the business this period. In that case, the financial statements of Amanda's Typing Service would appear as:

```
                Amanda's Typing Service (Partnership)
                          Income Statement
                    For the Month of January, 1996

             Service Revenue                          $2,900
               Less:
                 Wages Expense              $1,100
                 Delivery Expense              100
                   Total Expenses                      1,200
                 Net Income                           $1,700 ─┐
```

```
                       Amanda's Typing Service
                         Statement of Capital
                    For the Month of January, 1996

       Amanda Wells, Capital  January 1, 1996     $  0
             ADD: Investment by Owner             1,800
             ADD: Net Income                      1,020 ◄───
                                                 $2,820
             LESS: Drawings                         500
       Amanda Wells, Capital January 31, 1996              $2,320
       Jessica Wells, Capital  January 1, 1996    $  0
             ADD: Investment by Owner             1,200
             ADD: Net Income                        680 ◄
       Jessica Wells, Capital  January 31, 1996             1,880
       TOTAL CAPITAL                                       $4,200 ─┐
```

```
                       Amanda's Typing Service
                            Balance Sheet
                          January 31, 1996

Assets:                             Liabilities:
 Current Assets:                     Current Liabilities:
  Cash              $1,300            Accounts Payable      $ 5,200
  Accounts Receivable 2,100          Long-term Liabilities:
  Supplies            300             Notes Payable           5,000
  Prepaid Insurance  1,200             Total Liabilities    $10,200
   Total Current Assets  $ 4,900
                                    Owners' Equity:
 Long-term Assets:                  A. Wells, Capital $2,320 ◄
  Office Furniture  $2,500          J. Wells, Capital  1,880 ◄
  Computer System    7,000          Total Owners' Equity     4,200
   Total Long Term Assets  9,500
                                    Total Liabilities and
Total Assets         $14,400         Owners' Equity         $14,400
```

Notice the net income increases each partner's Capital account, but only Amanda's Capital account shows the impact of a drawing. As was the case with a proprietorship, partnerships do not distinguish between equity from investments by the owners and equity from earnings. Both impact partners' Capital accounts.

LOOKING AHEAD

We have now reviewed how business transactions impact financial statements. With only a few transactions, directly changing the amounts that appear on financial statements to reflect each transaction works well. Real businesses, however, have thousands of transactions each year. With so many transactions to consider, directly changing the amounts on financial statements would not provide adequate documentation of individual transactions and would likely lead to serious recording errors. Businesses, therefore, use a more formal recording process designed to carefully record each individual business transaction so that its effect will be properly indicated in the amounts that appear on financial statements.

In the next module, we will begin to explore this process of gathering, recording, and processing transactions data to provide the valuable information provided in financial statements.

APPLY WHAT YOU HAVE LEARNED

1-1. (Effect of Transactions on Financial Statement Items)
Anderson Engineering began operations in January 1995. During its first month of operations the following transactions occurred:

a. Sold 1,000 shares of no-par common stock for cash of $10,000.

b. Borrowed $12,000 from Money-To-Go Bank. A promissory note was signed stating that the loan plus 12% interest would be repaid in 18 months.

c. Purchased $500 worth of office supplies for cash.

d. Purchased equipment costing $11,000, paying $2,000 down with the balance on account.

e. Received cash of $7,500 for services performed during January.

f. Billed customers $9,000 for services performed during January.

g. Paid $2,500 rent for January 1995.

h. Paid $500 for utilities for January 1995.

i. Paid $900 to part-time employees for wages.

j. Paid a cash dividend to shareholders in the amount of $500.

Required: In the table below, indicate the effect of each transaction on the financial statement items listed. Indicate whether the item is increased or decreased by entering a "+" or a "—".

Financial Statement Item	Transaction a	b	c	d	e	f	g	h	i	j
Cash										
Supplies										
Equipment										
Accounts Receivable										
Notes Payable										
Accounts Payable										
Common Stock										
Dividends										
Service Revenue										
Rent Expense										
Utilities Expense										
Wage Expense										

1-2. (Effect of Transactions on Accounting Elements)

Refer to the transactions listed in Problem 1-1.

Required:

In the table below, identify which accounting elements are affected by each transaction. Indicate whether the accounting element is increased or decreased by entering a "+" or a "—". If the transaction causes an increase *and* a decrease in a single accounting element, place both a "+" and a "-" in the appropriate box.

Accounting Element	Transaction a	b	c	d	e	f	g	h	i	j
Assets										
Liabilities										
Equity										
Revenues										
Expenses										

1-3. (Effect of Transactions on Financial Statements)

Refer to the transactions listed in Problem 1-1.

Required: In the table below, indicate with an "X" which financial statements are affected by the transactions listed.

Financial Statement	Transaction									
	a	b	c	d	e	f	g	h	i	j
Income Statement										
Statement of Retained Earnings										
Balance Sheet										

1-4. (Preparation of a Balance Sheet based on Transactions)

Maupin Western Wear began operations in September 1995. During its first month of operations, the following transactions occurred:

a.   Sold 3,000 shares of $3 par common stock for cash of $30,000.

b.   Purchased $1,000 worth of store supplies for cash.

c.   Borrowed $20,000 from Money-To-Go Bank. A promissory note was signed stating that the loan plus 12% interest would be repaid in 18 months.

d.   Purchased equipment costing $11,000, paying $5,000 down with the balance on account.

Required:

1.   In the space provided, prepare a balance sheet dated September 30, 1995 which reflects the above transactions.

_____

_____

_____

_____

_____

_____

_____

_____

_____

_____

_____

_____

_____

_____

_____

_____

_____

_____

2. On the top line of the space provided below, state the accounting equation in
    words. On the bottom line, enter the appropriate dollar amounts from the
    balance sheet prepared in part 1. above.

    _____ = _____ + _____

    $_____ = $_____ + $_____

1-5. (Financial Statement Preparation)

General Cleaning Service began operations in January 1995. After recording several transactions, the following balance sheet was prepared.

```
                         General Cleaning Service
                              Balance Sheet
                             January 5, 1995

Assets:                                  Liabilities:
 Current Assets:                          Current Liabilities:
  Cash                    $ 9,000          Accounts Payable        $ 2,000
  Supplies                  1,000         Long-term Liabilities:
  Prepaid Insurance         2,000          Notes Payable             3,000
    Total Current Assets  $12,000           Total Liabilities      $ 5,000

 Long-term Assets:
  Cleaning Equipment        4,000         Owners' Equity:
  Shelving                  1,000          Common Stock            $12,000
    Total Long Term Assets $ 5,000           Total Equity          $12,000

                                         Total Liabilities and
Total Assets              $17,000          Equity                  $17,000
```

The items listed below are General Cleaning Service's first revenue and expense transactions.

a.   Received cash of $8,000 for cleaning services performed during January.

b.   Billed customers $10,000 for services performed during January.

c.   Paid $1,000 warehouse rent for January 1995.

d.   Received a $100 utility bill for the electricity used in January 1995. The bill will be paid in February.

e.   Paid $12,000 to employees for wages.

Required:

Prepare an income statement, a statement of retained earnings, and a revised balance sheet as of January 31, 1995 to reflect the transactions listed above.

1-6. (Accounting Equation)

Required:

Fill in the missing numbers in the accounting equation for each of the items in the following table:

Item	ASSETS	LIABILITIES	OWNERS' EQUITY
a.	10,000	6,000	
b.	15,000		8,000
c.		13,000	24,000
d.	40,000	19,000	
e.		22,000	25,000
f.	26,000		16,000

1-7. (Determining Net Income and Dividends — Corporation)

The following information is available for Mueller Monroe:

	January 1	January 31
Assets	$12,000	$20,000
Liabilities		7,000
Common Stock	8,000	
Retained Earnings	0	5,000

Required:

a. Determine the missing numbers which belong in the boxes above.

b. How much is net income for the month of January if there were no dividends?

$_____

c. How much is net income for the month of January if there were dividends of $4,000?

$_____

d. If net income for the month of January was $11,000, how much were dividends?

$_____

1-8. (Determining Net Income and Drawings — Partnership)

The following information is available for the partnership of Pat & Connie, who share profits and losses equally:

	January 1	January 31
Assets		$50,000
Liabilities	16,000	
Pat, Capital	7,000	12,000
Connie, Capital	13,000	18,000

Required:

a.   Determine the missing numbers which belong in the boxes above.

b.   How much is net income for the month of January if there were no additional investments and no withdrawals?

$_____

c.   How much is net income for the month of January if Pat and Connie each withdrew $3,000?

$_____

d.   If net income for the month of January was $34,000, how much did Pat and Connie withdraw from the partnership during January?

$_____

1-9. (Preparing Financial Statements from Transactions)

Rocco Controls began business in June 1995. The following transactions occurred during the first six months of operations.

a.   Sold 2,000 shares of common stock for $3 per share.

b.   Borrowed $10,000 from Western Trust, and signed a two-year note payable at 10% interest.

c.   Purchased $1,000 of supplies on account.

d.   Purchased computer equipment for $5,000 cash.

e.   Performed services for $14,000 cash.

f.   Performed services of $22,000 for customers on account.

g.   Paid for the supplies purchased in transaction (c).

h.   Collected $6,000 from customers on account.

i.   Paid rent of $12,000.

j.   Paid wages of $15,000.

k.   Paid cash dividends of $3,000.

Required:

Prepare an income statement, a statement of retained earnings, and a balance sheet as of December 31, 1995 to reflect the transactions listed above.

1-10. (Relationships Among Accounting Elements)

Free Wind Travel had the following account balances at the beginning and end of September, 1995:

	September 1	September 30
Total Assets	$100,000	$150,000
Total Liabilities	60,000	100,000

Required:

a.   How much is owners' equity at September 1 and at September 30?

September 1 _____ September 30 _____

b.   How much is net income if the owner made no investments and no withdrawals in September?
        $_____

c.   How much is net income if the owner had withdrawals of $5,000 in September, and no additional investments were made in September?

        $_____

d.   If net income for September was $12,000, and the owner made no additional investments, how much were withdrawals in September?

        $_____

e.   If the owner withdrew $7,000 and invested an additional $10,000 during September, how much was net income for September?

        $_____

1-11. (Preparation of Financial Statements — Corporation)

Ricky began business on June 1, 1995 by selling $10,000 of common stock. Account balances for Ricky, Inc. at June 30, 1995, the end of its first month of operations are:

Accounts Receivable	$ 4,000
Accounts Payable	3,500
Cash	3,000
Common Stock	10,000
Dividends	5,000
Equipment	9,900
Notes Payable (Due 6/1/98)	8,500
Office Furniture	10,500
Prepaid Insurance	1,600
Rent Expense	15,000
Retained Earnings	?
Service Revenue	40,000
Supplies	1,000
Wages Expense	12,000

Required:

Based on the information above, prepare an income statement, a statement of retained earnings, and a balance sheet. Draw arrows to indicate the articulation among the financial statements.

1-12. (Preparation of Financial Statements — Proprietorship)

Tammy Kippler began business on November 1, 1995 by investing $20,000 in her business. Account balances for Kippler Associates at November 30, 1995, the end of her first month of operations are:

Accounts Receivable	$ 8,000
Accounts Payable	7,000
Cash	6,000
Equipment	19,800
Notes Payable (4 years)	17,000
Office Furniture	21,000
Prepaid Insurance	3,200
Rent Expense	30,000
Service Revenue	80,000
Supplies	2,000
Tammy, Withdrawals	10,000
Tammy, Capital	?
Wages Expense	24,000

Required:

Based on the information above, prepare an income statement, a statement of capital, and a balance sheet. Draw arrows to indicate the articulation among the financial statements.

MODULE 2

T-ACCOUNTS AND
THE DEBIT/CREDIT SYSTEM

In Module 1, we saw how transactions affect the financial statements and how the financial statements relate to each other. The effect of each business transaction was shown by directly changing the dollar amounts on the financial statements. For the few transactions we examined, changing the amounts on the financial statements worked well; however, this procedure would not work well for a company having hundreds or thousands of transactions each year. A more formal system is needed to record and keep track of a company's many business transactions.

Now that you are familiar with financial statements and how they are affected by various business transactions, you may be curious as to how accounting systems collect and record data so that it can be assimilated into useful financial information. Module 1 portrayed the process as a kind of black box in which financial statements were directly updated to show the effect of business transactions. Now that you understand the impact of transactions on the accounting elements, it's time for us to look further into the process that allows companies to keep track of their many transactions. We will now focus on how data relating to the hundreds or thousands of business transactions is collected and recorded in formal accounting records to culminate in the useful tools known as financial statements.

THE ACCOUNT — AN INFORMATION STORAGE UNIT

The purpose of accounting is to provide information to economic decision makers. As an information system, accounting must identify and record results of business activity. As each business transaction occurs, its impact is recorded in two or more information storage units known as accounts. The total number of accounts in the information system and the titles of the accounts are based on the information needs of the business. As an example, let's relate this idea to an information system for your personal financial position.

If you were to list the description and cost of each item you owned (your assets), the list would seem to go on forever. The order of the list might appear quite random if you listed the assets as they came to mind. To make the list more useful, it would help to categorize the listed items. The categories you would choose to set up would depend on what information would be useful. You might list your shoes in one category, your shirts in another, and your pants in still another. Instead, you might have more detailed categories titled: dress shoes, casual shoes, and sport shoes rather than having only one category of shoes. Each of these categories or information storage units, is similar to an account used in recording business activity. The level of detail provided by the accounts should be based on the information needs of those using the accounting system.

Whether your personal record keeping system should have accounts called shoes, shirts, and pants, or your records should detail the *types* of shoes, *types* of shirts, and *types* of pants depends on your information needs. In any case, however, if you were to prepare a personal balance sheet depicting these items, the balance sheet might be more useful if several "accounts" were grouped together in a meaningful way. For example, your personal balance sheet might show a single item called clothes. This financial statement item would summarize the information in all the accounts for shirts, shoes, and pants. Again, the final decision about what accounts should be grouped and summarized in your financial statements should be based on the information needs of those using the financial statements.

Accounting information systems for businesses operate in much the same way as our example of your personal financial information. Businesses choose the number of total accounts and their titles based on information needs. For instance, some businesses have one account called "Cash" in which the effects of all transactions increasing or decreasing the total cash of the business are recorded. Other companies might have three cash accounts: an account called "Cash in Checking" for cash in the company checking account, another called "Cash in Savings" for cash in the company savings account, and still another called "Cash on Hand" for the cash stored at the business. As we pointed out, accounts are the basic information storage units. However, the amount (balance) in each individual account may or may not be shown on financial statements. If several cash accounts are utilized, information pertaining to cash can be presented in a detailed, account-by-account form, or summarized into a single amount, depending on how the information is to be used. So, even if you see a company presenting one amount called "Cash" on its balance sheet, the company may have many different cash accounts. The purpose of financial statements is to present information that is detailed enough to be informative, yet not so detailed that it is confusing or otherwise loses its usefulness.

Account names are not formally fixed by accounting rules. They differ from company to company. The only requirement is that each account name should adequately describe the item it represents. In addition to the account name, most companies use account numbers to help identify each account. For instance, in the case of companies with several cash accounts, referring to the **account number** of an account may reduce confusion. There are no accounting rules dictating how accounts are to be numbered.

A list of all the accounts used by the company is called a **chart of accounts**. The chart of accounts does not show any dollar amounts. It is a reference list that shows the account name and the corresponding account number, if numbers are used. A chart of accounts for Amanda's Typing Service is shown below.

```
                Amanda's Typing Service
                   Chart of Accounts

        Account
        Number          Account Name

        110             Cash
        130             Accounts Receivable
        170             Supplies
        180             Prepaid Insurance
        210             Office Furniture
        220             Computer System
        310             Accounts Payable
        410             Notes Payable
        510             Common Stock
        530             Dividends
        610             Service Revenue
        710             Wage Expense
        730             Delivery Expense
```

Notice that the accounts are designated by a three-digit account number. Keep in mind that the company is free to use any numbering scheme it likes. In this numbering scheme, the first digit in the account number for all current asset accounts is 1; 2 is used for non-current assets; 3 for current liabilities; 4 for all long-term liabilities, and so forth. The account numbers are not strictly sequential, allowing the company to add accounts in each category if the information needs of the business change.

This chart of accounts will be useful when we begin to record the effects of business transactions in the accounting records of Amanda's Typing Service. In later modules, additional accounts will be added as they are needed.

THE T-ACCOUNT

We've described an account as an information storage unit, but what does an account look like? It depends... Accounting systems can vary quite a bit. Some are manual (paper) systems, and others are electronic (computer-based). Accounting systems can be relatively simple or amazingly complex. Because of these variations, actual accounts can look very different. However, the representation of an account universally used to illustrate the effects of transactions is the **T-account**. A T-account for cash is presented below:

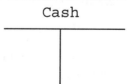

Basically, a T-account is simply a large "T" drawn under an account name. Results of transactions are recorded by placing the dollar amount on one side of the "T" or the other. As we will see, the placement of the dollar amount on either the left side or right side of the "T" is very significant.

DEBITS AND CREDITS

The T-account has a debit side and a credit side. The debit side is the left side and the credit side is the right side. Therefore, debits are always on the left, while credits are always on the right. The illustration below indicates the debit and credit sides of all T-accounts.

```
  ┌────────┬────────
  Debits │ Credits
  go on  │ go on
  this   │ this
  side   │ side
```

To debit an account, the dollar amount is simply placed on the left side of the "T". This action can be described as a debit to the account, as a debit entry, or it can be said that the account has been debited. A request to debit the Supplies account for $100 simply means to place $100 on the left side of the Supplies T-account. Likewise, an account is credited simply by placing a dollar amount on the right side of the T-account. A request to credit the Cash account for $100 simply means to place $100 on the right side of the Cash T-account. Debits and credits are used to add and subtract dollar amounts from accounts.

The T-accounts below show a $100 debit to Supplies and a $100 credit to Cash:

```
           Supplies
      ─────────────────
        100 │
            │

             Cash
      ─────────────────
            │ 100
            │
```

The example above illustrates several points: (1) the physical placement of the amounts is enough to indicate which account is being affected and whether the entry is a debit or credit; (2) there is no need to use a "+" or "—" sign to indicate the mathematical change in the account balance; (3) it is customary not to use the dollar sign ($) when making debit or credit entries. These basic guidelines will come in handy as we begin to record results of transactions in T-accounts.

There are basic rules about debits and credits which are always true. The first rule is that debits go on the left and credits go on the right. The second rule is that the total dollar amount of the debits must exactly equal the total dollar amount of the credits. Other universal statements like "debits always increase account balances and credits always decrease account balances", or "debits are good and credits are bad", are not true. Just remember the basic rules: (1) debits on the left, credits on the right; and (2) total debits must equal total credits.

Debits and credits are used to change the balances in accounts. That is, instead of using pluses and minuses, debits and credits are used to add and subtract dollar amounts in account totals. The total dollar amount of an account is called the **account balance**.

DETERMINING ACCOUNT BALANCES

Results of transactions will be recorded as debits and credits to accounts. At any point in time, you may need to determine the account balance. Regardless of the type of account involved, some basic rules apply:

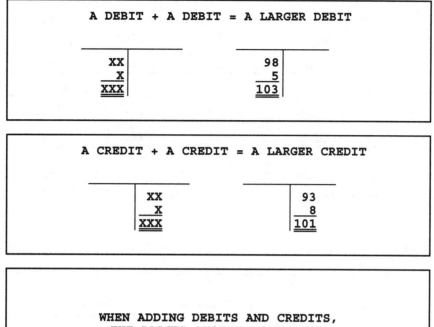

Now that you have seen the basic operation of the T-account, you need to know when to debit and when to credit an account. As you record the results of transactions in the accounts, it will be important that you be able to identify the types of accounts involved. In other words, not only must you be able to determine that the Cash account needs to be increased, but you must be able to identify Cash as an asset account. This is crucial because the basic rules guiding how to increase or decrease an account using debits and credits hinge on what type of account you are dealing with. In other words, you must know to which accounting element each account refers. The first accounting elements you learned about were the ones comprising the balance sheet. The chart below shows the effects of debits and credits on these accounting elements.

Effects of Debits and Credits on Assets, Liabilities, and Equity	
Assets	Increased by Debits *** Decreased by Credits
Liabilities	Decreased by Debits *** Increased by Credits
Equity	Decreased by Debits *** Increased by Credits

If you can remember the information in the chart above, you have mastered a very challenging aspect of the debit/credit system. Working with these rules will help you to remember them.

A different visual presentation of the debit/credit rules is based on the accounting equation:

```
        ASSETS     =   LIABILITIES  +     EQUITY
       +  |  −           −  |  +           −  |  +
```

We offer this alternative presentation of the debit/credit rules to show you how the rules relate to the accounting equation. The +'s and —'s indicate how to make asset, liability, and equity accounts increase and decrease. For instance, if an account is an asset, and we want the account balance to increase, we make an entry on the left (debit) side of the account. Credits reduce assets — thus, the "—" on the right (credit) side of the account. Notice accounts that are parts of the accounting elements on the other side of the equation (liabilities and equity) work just the opposite. For example, if you wish to increase the balance in a liability account, you must credit the account. Entries on the left (debit) side of liability accounts decrease these account balances.

Another illustration of the basic debit/credit rules applied to assets, liabilities and equity may be helpful. In the exhibit below, the accounting elements of assets, liabilities, and equity are organized in a format similar to that of an account form balance sheet. The asset side is separated from the liability and equity side by a shaded line. The significance of this shaded line is that items on the left side of the line are increased by debits, and items on the right side of the line are increased by credits. As shown below, these basic debit/credit rules apply to the T-accounts that represent asset, liability and equity accounts. The line is just an aid to help you remember debit and credit rules. However, even after you have practiced recording transactions applying these rules, you may find it helpful to rely on an imaginary line in place of the shaded one in the exhibit below.

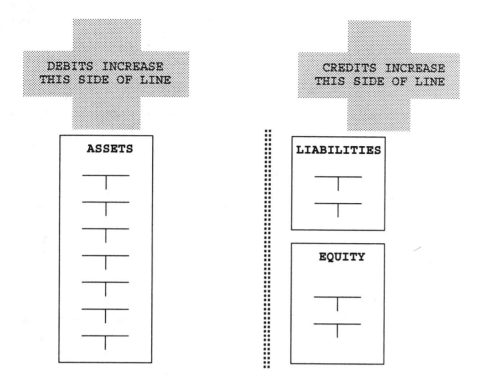

We will use the format above to illustrate T-accounts in this module. Placing T-accounts in this format offers two distinct advantages: (1) the shaded line makes the debit/credit rules easier to remember, and (2) the T-accounts are organized in an orderly fashion that helps when determining total assets, total liabilities, or equity.

It doesn't matter which of the three illustrations you use to help you remember the debit/credit rules. What IS important is that you know what action (a debit or a credit) makes each of these types of accounts (assets, liabilities, and equity) increase and decrease.

One more thing... not only must you know which action (a debit or a credit) will make an account balance go up or down, but you will also need to know the **normal balance** of assets, liabilities, and equity accounts. If you are told the dollar amount of an account's balance, but not whether that balance is a debit or a credit, you can assume the account has a normal balance. The normal balance of each account (debit or credit) is whatever makes the account balance increase. Based on what you've seen of the debit/credit rules so far, that means asset accounts have normal debit balances (because debits make assets go up) and liability and equity accounts have normal credit balances (because credits make these types of accounts go up).

NOTE: Often times previous experience with the words "debit" and "credit" make the basic debit/credit rules seem exactly *opposite* of what you might expect. *IF* your prior use of these words results in confusion, information in the box below may help.

DEBITS AND CREDITS IN BANKING

According to the basic debit/credit rules, debits increase assets. Since cash is an asset, an increase in cash is reflected as a debit to Cash. However, on your bank statement, an increase in your account balance is described as a credit to your account. How can that be? Very simple. Your bank statement is not a record of your Cash account; it is a record of the bank's liability to you, its depositor. When you deposit $100 in the bank, the bank debits its Cash account and the bank credits a liability account to indicate that it owes you $100. This liability is the part you see on your bank statement. So the entry does conform to the debit/credit rules.

DEBITS AND CREDITS ON CHARGE CARDS

Your account balance with a credit card company is the amount you owe. If you return a purchased item, your account is credited, and your account balance goes down — you owe less. But the basic debit/credit rules say liabilities go down with debits, not credits. How can this be? Your credit card statement reflects entries that the credit card company is making on their own accounting records. When your account is credited, you owe less. From the credit card company's point of view, accounts receivable has gone down. (Less is expected to be received from you.) The credit you see on your credit card statement is a credit to the card company's Accounts Receivable account.

Now it's time to dig in and record the business activity of Amanda's Typing Service in T-accounts. We will be returning to the same transactions used in Module 1, so you should be familiar with each transaction's effects on the financial statements. What is new is the recording of the transactions, applying what you've learned about the debit/credit system.

RECORDING TRANSACTIONS

As we prepare to record each transaction, we must answer four important questions:

1. Which accounts were affected?

2. Should the account balance be increased or decreased, and by how much?

3. Should the account be debited or credited?

4. Do debits equal credits?

As we analyze each transaction, Question 1 will focus our attention on the accounts involved. Then, Questions 2 and 3 will refer specifically to each of those accounts. Question 4 serves as a check to see that we have not violated a basic rule of the debit/credit system.

As we present the transactions and entries in this module we will address each of the above questions in a fairly formal fashion. Our hope is to foster an understanding of the process of making debit and credit entries. In later modules, as you gain experience making debit and credit entries, you may still go through a mental checklist of these four questions, but you will likely find it easier to answer them in a less formal fashion.

NOTE: As we identify which accounts were affected, you might find it helpful to refer to the company's chart of accounts presented earlier and repeated below:

```
            Amanda's Typing Service
              Chart of Accounts

      Account
      Number   Account Name

       110          Cash
       130          Accounts Receivable
       170          Supplies
       180          Prepaid Insurance
       210          Office Furniture
       220          Computer System
       310          Accounts Payable
       410          Notes Payable
       510          Common Stock
       530          Dividends
       610          Service Revenue
       710          Wage Expense
       730          Delivery Expense
```

TRANSACTION A: On January 1, 1996, the business was begun by an initial investment of $3,000 from the owners. As you recall from Module 1, the corporation issued 1,000 shares of no-par stock for $3 each.

Question 1: Which accounts were affected? The business received cash in exchange for ownership interest represented by shares of no-par common stock. Because cash was received, the *Cash account* will be affected. In addition, because the corporation sold no-par common stock, the *Common Stock account* will also be affected.

Question 2: Should the account balance be increased or decreased, and by how much? The company received $3,000 in cash, so the Cash account should be *increased by $3,000*. Further, the corporation issued $3,000 of no-par common stock. Therefore, the Common Stock account should also be *increased by $3,000*.

Question 3: Should the account be debited or credited? We want to increase the Cash account. Do we debit or credit it? Let's see... cash is an asset. What makes an asset account increase? A debit, so we should *debit Cash*. We also want to increase the Common Stock account. Do we debit or credit it? Let's see... Common Stock is an equity account. What makes an equity account increase? A credit, so we should *credit Common Stock*.

Question 4: Do debits equal credits? From our answers to Questions 2 and 3, we conclude that we should debit Cash for $3,000 and credit Common Stock for $3,000. Are debits and credits equal? Yes.

Now all that remains is to record the entry. This is done simply by placing 3,000 on the debit side of the Cash account and 3,000 on the credit of the Common Stock account. The amount for the debit to Cash is placed on the next available line on the debit side of the T-account while the amount for Common Stock is placed on the next available line on the credit side of the T-account. The exhibit below shows the recording of Transaction A in T-accounts.

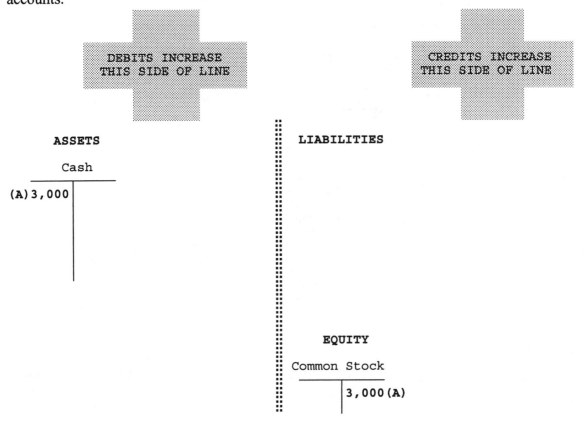

As we progress through this module, we will record quite a few transactions. We will accumulate the results of these transactions on the company's T-accounts. Accordingly, we have left room to add additional T-accounts. Some accounts will be affected by several entries. To make the results of each transaction easier to see, the letter of the transaction will be shown next to each part of the T-account entry.

Because you saw the results of each new entry on Amanda's financial statements as we worked through these transactions in Module 1, we will not present financial statements after each transaction. However, it may be helpful to show a balance sheet reflecting the first transaction so you can see how the accounts relate to the financial statements. Transaction A affects only the balance sheet. The company's first transaction, the sale of stock is reflected in the balance sheet shown below.

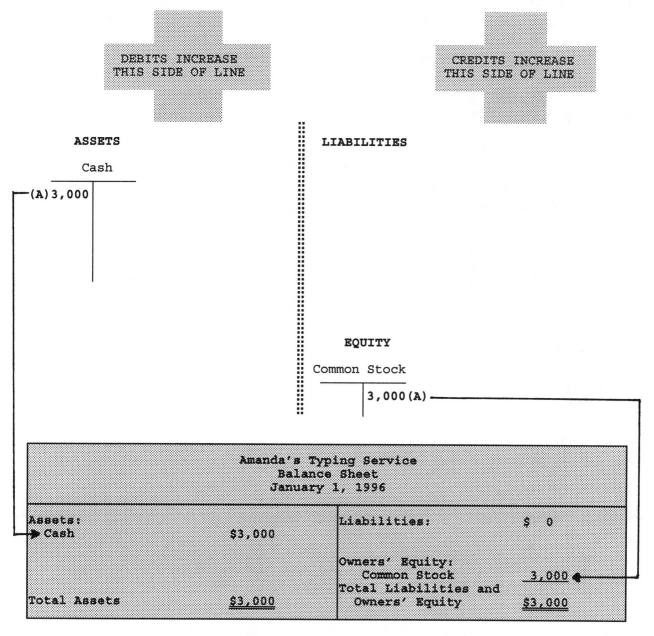

TRANSACTION B: On January 3, 1996 Amanda's Typing Service borrowed $5,000 from First Friendly Bank. Amanda signed a promissory note on behalf of the company, agreeing to repay the $5,000 principal plus interest in 18 months.

Again, we should answer the 4 questions as we prepare to make this entry.

Question 1: Which accounts were affected? Because Amanda's Typing Service received cash from the bank, the *Cash account* will be affected. Because the company now owes the bank, *Notes Payable*, a liability, will be affected.

Question 2: Should the account balance be increased or decreased, and by how much?
The company received $5,000 in cash, so the Cash account should be *increased by $5,000*. The company now owes $5,000 more, so Notes Payable should be *increased by $5,000*.

Question 3: Should the account be debited or credited? Again, we want to make Cash go up. Since Cash is an asset, to make it increase, we must *debit Cash*. We also want Notes Payable to increase. Do we debit or credit it? Let's see... Notes Payable is a liability. What makes a liability account increase? A credit, so we should *credit Notes Payable*.

Question 4: Do debits equal credits? For transaction B, the debit to Cash of $5,000 exactly equals the $5,000 credit to Notes Payable.

To make the entry for transaction B, we simply follow the same procedure used for transaction A. As we record transaction B in the T-accounts, we will see that transaction A is already there because it was recorded earlier. We will simply record transaction B on the next available line. Transaction B is shown in bold type on the T-accounts below.

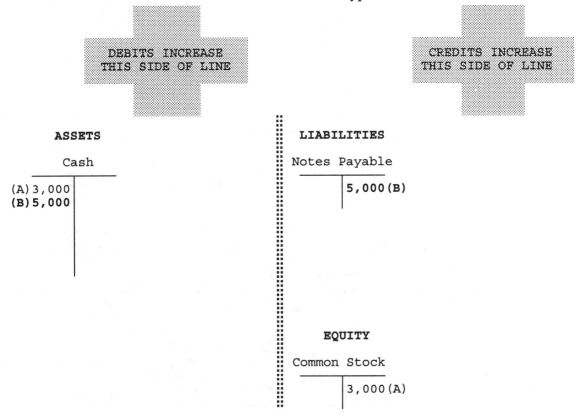

TRANSACTION C: On January 5, 1996, Amanda's Typing Service purchased supplies from Rebecca's Office Supplies. Amanda's Typing Service opened an account with Rebecca's and charged $300 worth of supplies. In other words, Amanda's Typing Service purchased $300 of supplies on account.

Question 1: Which accounts were affected? Amanda's Typing Service received supplies, so the *Supplies account* will be affected. Also, Amanda's Typing Service now owes $300 on account to Rebecca's Office Supplies so *Accounts Payable*, a liability, will also be affected.

Question 2: Should the account balance be increased or decreased, and by how much? Because Amanda's Typing Service purchased supplies costing $300, the Supplies account should be *increased by $300*. Also, because the purchase was charged on a charge account, an obligation to pay Rebecca's Office Supplies was created. Accounts Payable should be *increased by $300.*

Question 3: Should the account be debited or credited? Supplies is an asset account. In order to increase the account balance, we should *debit Supplies.* Like Notes Payable, Accounts Payable is a liability account and will be increased by credits. Therefore, to increase the account, we must *credit Accounts Payable.*

Question 4: Do debits equal credits? For transaction C, the $300 debit to Supplies exactly equals the $300 credit to Accounts Payable.

The entry to record Transaction C is done the same way as previous entries and is shown in bold type below.

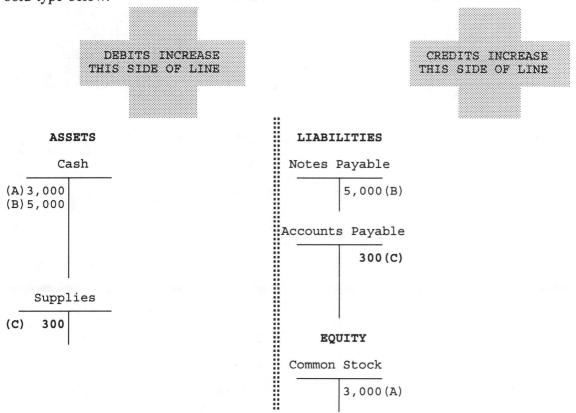

TRANSACTION D: On January 7, Amanda's Typing Service purchased a one-year liability insurance policy, paying cash of $1,200.

Question 1: Which accounts were affected? The company received a one-year insurance policy. The policy is paid in advance and provides insurance coverage for the company for an entire year. The insurance coverage has future value to the company and, therefore, should be considered an asset. Expenses paid for in advance, as was this insurance coverage, are assets to the company and are often called prepaid expenses. To be more specific, we will use a specific account: *Prepaid Insurance.* This insurance was paid for in cash and therefore the *Cash account* should also be affected.

Question 2: Should the account balance be increased or decreased, and by how much?

The entire cost of the policy will be shown in the Prepaid Insurance account, so it should be *increased by $1,200*. The company used up cash to pay for the policy, so the Cash account should be *decreased by $1,200*.

Question 3: Should the account be debited or credited? Because Prepaid Insurance is an asset account, a debit is required to increase it. We must *debit Prepaid Insurance*. In this transaction, Cash, which is also an asset, should be decreased. To decrease an asset, a credit is required. Accordingly, we must *credit Cash*.

Question 4: Do debits equal credits? For transaction D, the $1,200 debit to Prepaid Insurance exactly equals the $1,200 credit to Cash.

The entry to record Transaction D is shown in bold type below.

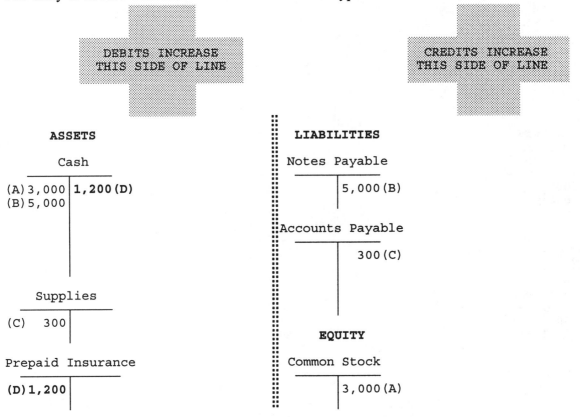

DEBITS INCREASE THIS SIDE OF LINE

CREDITS INCREASE THIS SIDE OF LINE

ASSETS

Cash

| (A) 3,000 | **1,200 (D)** |
| (B) 5,000 | |

Supplies

| (C) 300 | |

Prepaid Insurance

| **(D) 1,200** | |

LIABILITIES

Notes Payable

| | 5,000 (B) |

Accounts Payable

| | 300 (C) |

EQUITY

Common Stock

| | 3,000 (A) |

TRANSACTION E: On January 9, 1996 Amanda's Typing Service paid $2,500 in cash for a desk, three chairs, a small table and a file cabinet.

Question 1: Which accounts were affected? Amanda's Typing Service received office furniture in exchange for cash. Therefore, the *Office Furniture account* and the *Cash account* were affected.

Question 2: Should the account balance be increased or decreased, and by how much? Office furniture costing $2,500 was received by Amanda's Typing, Inc. in exchange for $2,500 in cash. Therefore, the Office Furniture account should be *increased by $2,500* and the Cash account should be *decreased by $2,500*.

Question 3: Should the account be debited or credited? To record the purchase of office furniture, an asset account should be increased, so we must *debit Office Furniture*. Cash, another asset account, should be decreased. Therefore, we must *credit Cash*.

Question 4: Do debits equal credits? For transaction E, the $2,500 debit to Office Furniture exactly equals the $2,500 credit to Cash.

The entry to record Transaction E is shown in bold type below.

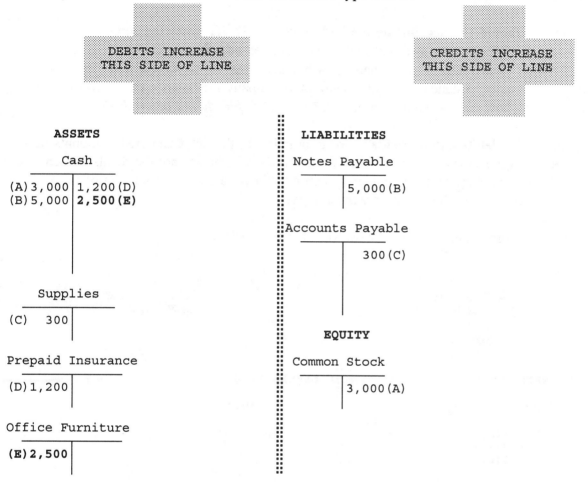

TRANSACTION F: On January 11, 1996, Amanda's Typing Service purchased a complete computer system from Carl's Computers for $7,000. A down payment of $2,000 was made, and Carl's Computers allowed Amanda's Typing Service to open a charge account with the store and charge the balance.

Question 1: Which accounts were affected? In this transaction, Amanda's Typing Service received a computer, so the *Computer System account* should be affected. Amanda's Typing Service paid $2,000 toward the purchase, so the *Cash account* is also affected. Since Carl's Computers allowed Amanda's Typing Service to charge the $5,000 balance, the *Accounts Payable account* should also be affected.

When more than two accounts are affected by a single transaction, the resulting entry is called a **compound entry**. The entry to record Transaction F is a compound entry because three accounts were affected.

Question 2: Should the account balance be increased or decreased, and by how much? In this transaction, the company received a computer system which cost $7,000 so the Computer System account should be *increased by $7,000*. Remember, assets should be recorded at their cost, whether or not that amount has been fully paid when the asset is purchased. Next, because Amanda's Typing Service paid $2,000 in cash to the computer company, the Cash account should be *decreased by $2,000*. And finally, Amanda's Typing Service charged $5,000 of the computer's cost on account, so the Accounts Payable account should be *increased by $5,000*.

Question 3: Should the account be debited or credited? To show the computer system coming into the business, an asset account must be increased. So, *the Computer System account should be debited*. The company's cash was decreased, so *the Cash account should be credited*. Finally, Amanda's owes the computer company the balance of the cost of the computer. To show the increased liability, *Accounts Payable should be credited*.

Question 4: Do debits equal credits? For transaction F, the debit and credit amounts of all three affected accounts must be considered to determine whether or not the debits and credits equal. The $7,000 debit to the computer system exactly equals the combination of the $2,000 credit to cash and the $5,000 credit to accounts payable.

The entry to record Transaction F is shown in bold type below.

```
       DEBITS INCREASE                      CREDITS INCREASE
       THIS SIDE OF LINE                    THIS SIDE OF LINE
```

ASSETS	LIABILITIES
Cash	**Notes Payable**
(A) 3,000 | 1,200 (D)	| 5,000 (B)
(B) 5,000 | 2,500 (E)	
| **2,000 (F)**	**Accounts Payable**
	| 300 (C)
	| **5,000 (F)**
Supplies	
(C) 300 |	**EQUITY**
Prepaid Insurance	**Common Stock**
(D) 1,200 |	| 3,000 (A)
Office Furniture	
(E) 2,500 |	
Computer System	
(F) 7,000 |	

TRANSACTION G: On January 13, Amanda's Typing Service paid a portion of the amount it owed to Rebecca's Office Supplies. The company paid $200 of the $300 it owed.

Question 1: Which accounts were affected? In transaction G, cash is used to make a partial payment on account. Therefore, the *Cash account* is affected as is the amount the company owes, *Accounts Payable*.

Question 2: Should the account balance be increased or decreased, and by how much? In this transaction, Amanda's Typing Service sent $200 in cash to Rebecca's Office Supplies so Amanda's Cash account should be *decreased by $200*. The $200 cash payment made by Amanda's Typing Service reduces the amount owed to Rebecca's so Amanda's Accounts Payable should be *decreased by $200*.

Question 3: Should the account be debited or credited? To show the decrease in the company's cash, *the Cash account should be credited*. To decrease the liability account, *Accounts Payable should be debited*.

Question 4: Do debits equal credits? For transaction G, the $200 debit to Accounts Payable exactly equals the $200 credit to Cash.

The entry to record Transaction G is shown in bold type below.

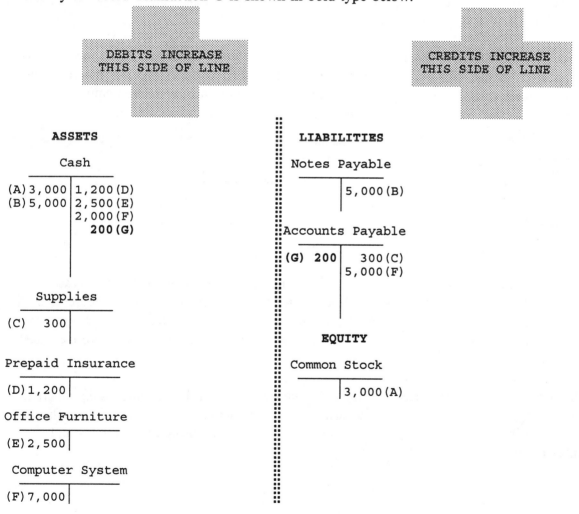

REVENUE AND EXPENSE ENTRIES

All transactions recorded thus far for Amanda's Typing Service have affected only three accounting elements: assets, liabilities, and equity. Now, we need to see how transactions affecting other accounting elements are recorded. As we anticipate recording transactions involving revenues and expenses, we must learn the debit/credit rules for those types of accounts. The chart below offers a summary of the debit/credit rules for assets, liabilities, equity, revenues, and expenses.

Effects of Debits and Credits on Assets, Liabilities, Equity, Revenues, and Expenses	
Assets	Increased by Debits *** Decreased by Credits
Liabilities	Decreased by Debits *** Increased by Credits
Equity	Decreased by Debits *** Increased by Credits
Revenues	Decreased by Debits *** Increased by Credits
Expenses	Increased by Debits *** Decreased by Credits

Information in the chart above may be difficult to memorize, but insight into how revenues and expenses relate to owners' equity will provide a basis for understanding how debits and credits affect these accounting elements.

By now, you should know that revenues increase income while expenses reduce income. You should also know that income increases owners' equity. So, revenues increase income which in turn increases equity, while expenses reduce income which in turn reduces equity. Ultimately, revenues and expenses feed into equity as shown in the exhibit below:

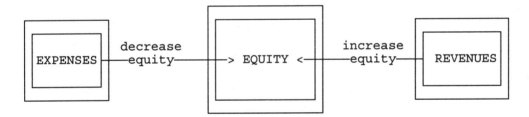

Now, let's look at how all this relates to debits and credits. Revenues work to increase equity, and therefore it makes sense that both equity and revenue follow the same debit/credit rules. As you have learned in this module, equity is increased by credits. Because revenues increase equity and equity is increased by credits, it follows that revenues, too, are increased by credits.

On the other hand, expenses decrease equity so the debit/credit rules for increasing expenses are exactly opposite of the rules for increasing equity. Expenses are increased by debits and these debits ultimately reduce equity. The debit and credit relationship of revenues and expenses to equity is illustrated below:

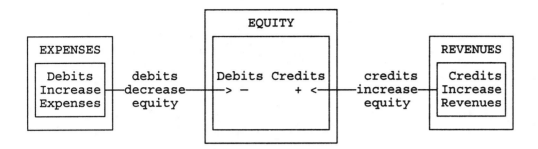

Do not worry if you fail to follow the explanation above when you read it for the first time. Visual representations of the debit/credit rules for expenses and revenues will help to make this clear.

The illustration presented earlier to show how debit/credit rules relate to the accounting equation can be expanded to show how the rules are applied to revenues and expenses:

```
┌──────────────────────────────────────────────────────────┐
│                                                          │
│      ASSETS    =   LIABILITIES   +     EQUITY            │
│     ─────────     ─────────────      ─────────          │
│      +  │  −       −  │  +           −  │  +             │
│         │             │                 │                │
│                                                          │
│                              Expenses      Revenues     │
│                             ──────────    ──────────    │
│                              +  │  −       −  │  +       │
│                                 │             │          │
└──────────────────────────────────────────────────────────┘
```

Again, revenues and expenses ultimately impact owners' equity. As you can see, because revenues *help* owners' equity, the debit/credit rules for revenues are the same as those for owners' equity. Since expenses *work against* owners' equity, the debit/credit rules for expenses are just the opposite of those for owners' equity.

Now let's see how revenues and expenses fit into our illustrations using the shaded line. Because of the relationship that revenues and expenses have to equity, we will flank equity with expenses on the left and revenue on the right. Note that in the exhibit below, expenses are appropriately on the left side of the debit/credit line. You should think of expenses as being grouped with equity, even though the shaded debit/credit line seems to separate the two.

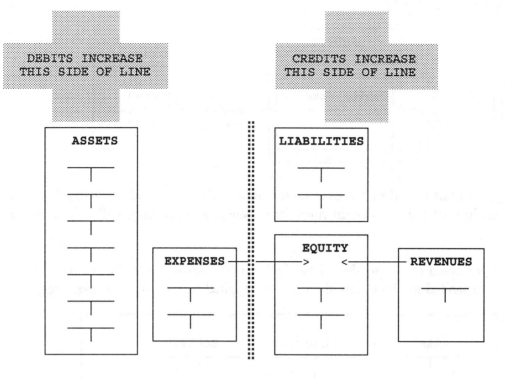

The exhibit above highlights the fact that assets and expenses follow the same debit/credit rules. Because the two types of accounts seem so different from one another, it may seem odd that they operate the same way. But consider this: both assets and expenses are acquired at some cost to the company. That is, they are not free. In general, an item that has been acquired at a cost will be an asset or an expense depending on whether the cost has a future value or not.

A cost that has no future value is called an expired cost. That is, the value of the cost has expired. As you may have already guessed, another name for an expired cost is an expense. An expense is a cost that has no future value to the company.

A cost that has a future value is called an unexpired cost. That is, the value of the cost has *not* expired. Again, you may have guessed that another name for an unexpired cost is an asset.

The main distinction between an asset and an expense lies in whether or not the cost has future value. Otherwise, assets and expenses are quite similar. This similarity may help explain why both assets and expenses are increased by debits and decreased by credits.

With that introduction to how debits and credits affect expense and revenue accounts, we will continue to record transactions for Amanda's Typing Service.

TRANSACTION H: During the month, Amanda's Typing Service performed services for customers and received $800 cash.

Question 1: Which accounts were affected? In this transaction, Amanda's Typing Service received cash for services provided to customers. Accordingly the *Cash account* should be affected, and because the company earned revenue by providing services, the *Service Revenue* *account* should also be affected.

Question 2: Should the account balance be increased or decreased, and by how much?
Amanda's Typing Service received cash for the services, so the Cash account must be
increased by $800. The company must show that revenue has been earned, so the Service
Revenue account is also *increased by $800*.

Question 3: Should the account be debited or credited? To show the company's increase
in cash, *the Cash account must be debited*. Credits increase revenue accounts. Therefore, *the
Service Revenue account must be credited*.

Question 4: Do debits equal credits? For transaction H, the $800 debit to the Cash account
exactly equals the $800 credit to Service Revenue.

The entry to record Transaction H is shown in bold type below.

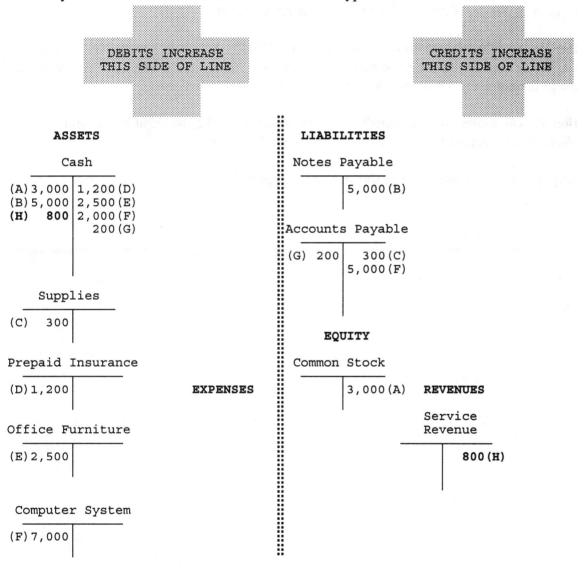

TRANSACTION I: Amanda's Typing Service billed customers $2,100 for services performed during January. These customers have charge accounts with Amanda's Typing Service and are expected to pay for the typing services next month.

Question 1: Which accounts were affected? Customers were billed for work performed. $2,100 has been earned and is expected to be received next month. It is *receivable* from customers who have *accounts* with Amanda's Typing Service. Although this transaction does not affect Cash, in order to present the company's true position, it must be recorded. Amanda's Typing Service has an accounts receivable from these customers; therefore, the *Accounts Receivable account* is affected. The company earned revenue by providing services, so the *Service Revenue account* should also be affected.

Question 2: Should the account balance be increased or decreased, and by how much? The amount Amanda's Typing Service expects to receive from its customers has increased. Therefore, *Accounts Receivable should be increased by $2,100.* To reflect the additional amount earned, *Service Revenue should be increased by $2,100.*

Question 3: Should the account be debited or credited? Accounts Receivable is an asset account. To reflect the increase, we must *debit Accounts Receivable.* As in transaction H, an increase in the company's revenues requires *a credit to Service Revenue.*

Question 4: Do debits equal credits? For transaction I, the $2,100 debit to Accounts Receivable exactly equals the $2,100 credit to Service Revenue.

The entry to record Transaction I is shown in bold type below.

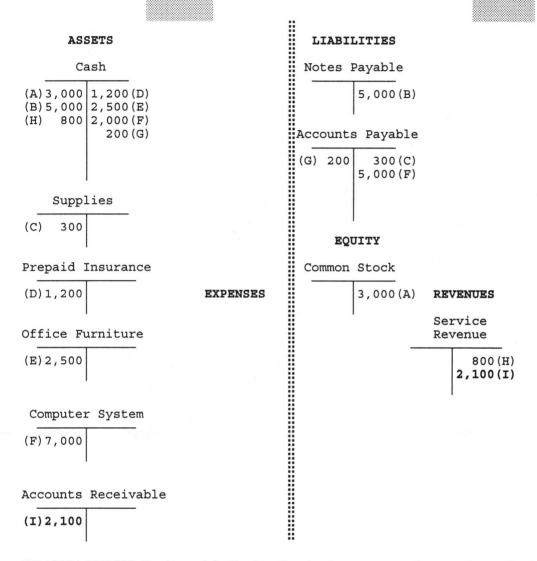

ASSETS

Cash

(A)	3,000	1,200	(D)
(B)	5,000	2,500	(E)
(H)	800	2,000	(F)
		200	(G)

Supplies

(C) 300

Prepaid Insurance

(D) 1,200   **EXPENSES**

Office Furniture

(E) 2,500

Computer System

(F) 7,000

Accounts Receivable

(I) 2,100

LIABILITIES

Notes Payable

5,000 (B)

Accounts Payable

(G)	200	300	(C)
		5,000	(F)

EQUITY

Common Stock

3,000 (A)   **REVENUES**

Service
Revenue

800 (H)
2,100 (I)

TRANSACTION J: Amanda's Typing Service has two part-time workers who key documents into the computer system and help in the office. During the month, the company paid these employees a total of $1,100.

Question 1: Which accounts were affected? Cash of $1,100 was paid to employees for the wages they earned. Therefore, *Wage Expense* and *Cash* are the two affected accounts.

Question 2: Should the account balance be increased or decreased, and by how much? The payment to employees for the wages they earned *increased Wage Expense by $1,100*. The payment also *decreased Cash by $1,100*.

Question 3: Should the account be debited or credited? Like all other expenses, *Wage Expense requires a debit to increase the account. Cash is decreased by a credit.*

Question 4: Do debits equal credits? For transaction J, the $1,100 debit to Wage Expense exactly equals the $1,100 credit to Cash.

The entry to record Transaction J is shown in bold type below.

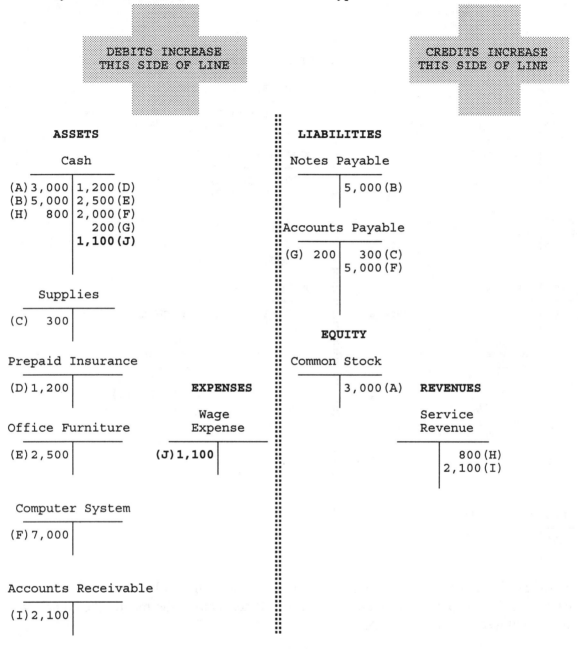

TRANSACTION K: Speedy Delivery Service picks up completed jobs from Amanda's Typing Service and delivers them to customers. On January 30, Amanda's Typing Service received a bill from Speedy for $100, for the deliveries made during January. The company expects to pay the bill early next month.

Question 1: Which accounts were affected? Although Amanda's Typing Service is not spending cash now, the company owes Speedy for the $100 worth of delivery service provided. The expense must be recorded in the *Delivery Expense account*, and to reflect the increased debt, *Accounts Payable* should be affected.

Question 2: Should the account balance be increased or decreased, and by how much? Both Delivery Expense and Accounts Payable should be *increased by $100*.

Question 3: Should the account be debited or credited? Expenses are increased by debits, so *Delivery Expense should be debited*. Liabilities are increased by credits, so *Accounts Payable should be credited*.

Question 4: Do debits equal credits? For transaction K, the $100 debit to Delivery Expense exactly equals the $100 credit to Accounts Payable.

The entry to record Transaction K is shown in bold type below.

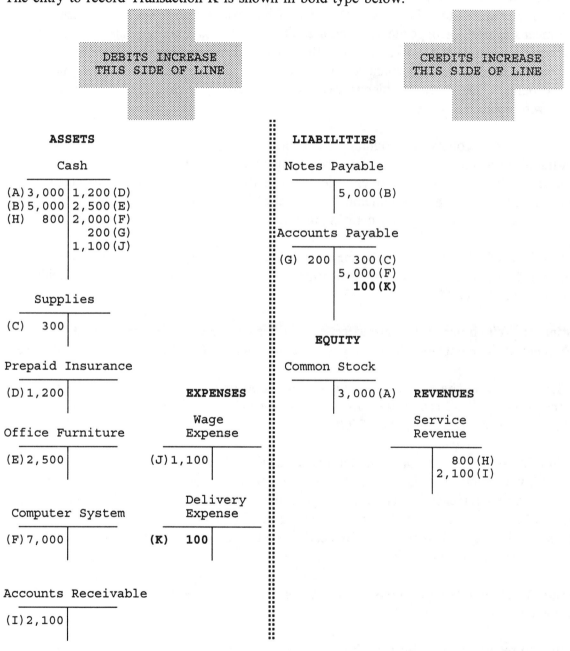

DISTRIBUTIONS TO OWNERS

Thus far, we have recorded transactions involving investments by owners, assets, liabilities, equity, revenues, and expenses. Now, we're ready to examine a transaction involving one other accounting element — distributions to owners. These distributions are NOT expenses to the company — they do not affect net income. Rather, distributions to owners are reductions of equity.

In a corporation, distributions to owners are called dividends. As we saw in Module 1, dividends reduce the portion of owners' equity known as Retained Earnings. The interesting thing about the Dividends account is that, even though it is classified as an equity account, its balance actually works to reduce owners' equity. Dividends is a contra-equity account. Contra means against, or opposite. A contra-equity account has a normal balance opposite that of equity accounts and works to reduce the amount of owners' equity. Because dividends reduce equity, the Dividends account follows debit/credit rules opposite those for regular equity accounts. That is, the Dividends account is increased by debits, even though it is grouped with equity accounts.

The use of contra accounts in accounting is not limited to equity. There are contra-asset and contra-liability accounts as well. Whenever you encounter a contra account, just remember that the it will follow debit/credit rules which are exactly opposite those of the associated account. Accordingly, we must remember that contra accounts require an opposite entry to the one indicated by our imaginary debit/credit line.

TRANSACTION L: On January 31, the owners of Amanda's Typing Service determined the company had sufficient cash and retained earnings to pay a dividend. A $500 cash dividend was paid to the stockholders.

Question 1: Which accounts were affected? In this case, a cash dividend is paid to shareholders of the company. Both the *Cash account* and the *Dividends account* are affected.

Question 2: Should the account balance be increased or decreased, and by how much? Payment of the dividend caused the *Cash account to be decreased by $500* while the *Dividends account was increased by $500*.

Question 3: Should the account be debited or credited? The Dividend account is a contra-equity account. That is, it is in the equity classification but actually reduces owners' equity. Because Dividends is a contra-equity account, it is increased by a debit which is the opposite of how regular equity accounts are increased. The Dividends account is increased by debits, so to show the payment of the dividend, we must *debit the Dividends account. Cash should be decreased with a credit.*

Question 4: Do debits equal credits? For transaction L, the $500 debit to Dividends exactly equals the $500 credit to Cash.

The entry to record Transaction L is shown in bold type below. Because this is the last transaction to record, we have also presented account balances in this exhibit. If an account has only one entry in it, the amount of that entry is the account balance.

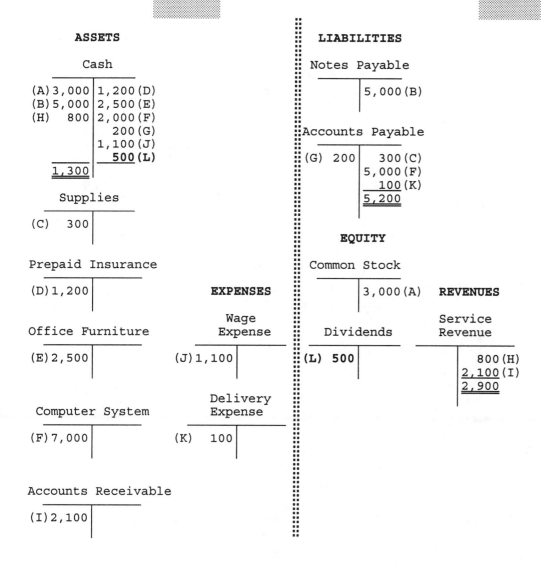

ASSETS

Cash

(A) 3,000	1,200 (D)
(B) 5,000	2,500 (E)
(H) 800	2,000 (F)
	200 (G)
	1,100 (J)
	500 (L)
1,300	

Supplies

(C) 300	

Prepaid Insurance

(D) 1,200	

Office Furniture

(E) 2,500	

Computer System

(F) 7,000	

Accounts Receivable

(I) 2,100	

EXPENSES

Wage
Expense

(J) 1,100	

Delivery
Expense

(K) 100	

LIABILITIES

Notes Payable

	5,000 (B)

Accounts Payable

(G) 200	300 (C)
	5,000 (F)
	100 (K)
	5,200

EQUITY

Common Stock

	3,000 (A)

Dividends

(L) 500	

REVENUES

Service
Revenue

	800 (H)
	2,100 (I)
	2,900

PREPARING FINANCIAL STATEMENTS

Now that all the transactions have been recorded, we can use the balances in the T-accounts to prepare financial statements. Because of the format we used for the T-accounts, related accounts are grouped together. This makes preparation of financial statements from the balances in the T-accounts much easier. Financial statements for Amanda's Typing Service are presented below:

```
                    Amanda's Typing Service
                        Income Statement
                  For the Month of January, 1996

        Service Revenue                              $2,900
        Less:
          Wages Expense                  $1,100
          Delivery Expense                  100
            Total Expenses                            1,200
          Net Income                                 $1,700
```

```
                    Amanda's Typing Service
                  Statement of Retained Earnings
                  For the Month of January, 1996

        Retained Earnings  January 1, 1996      $     0
        Add Net Income                            1,700
                                                 $1,700
        Less Dividends                              500
        Retained Earnings January 31, 1996       $1,200
```

```
                    Amanda's Typing Service
                         Balance Sheet
                       January 31, 1996

Assets:                          Liabilities:
 Current Assets:                  Current Liabilities:
  Cash              $1,300         Accounts Payable      $ 5,200
  Accounts Receivable 2,100       Long-term Liabilities:
  Supplies             300         Notes Payable           5,000
  Prepaid Insurance  1,200          Total Liabilities    $10,200
    Total Current Assets  $ 4,900
                                 Owners' Equity:
 Long-term Assets:                Common Stock      $3,000
  Office Furniture $2,500          Retained Earnings  1,200
  Computer System   7,000        Total Owners' Equity    4,200
    Total Long Term Assets 9,500
                                 Total Liabilities and
Total Assets        $14,400        Owners' Equity       $14,400
```

RECORDING TRANSACTIONS FOR PROPRIETORSHIPS AND PARTNERSHIPS

In Module 1, we saw that the differences between the financial statements of corporations and those of proprietorships and partnerships are related to how the businesses present owners' equity. The differences in how these types of businesses record transactions also center on equity.

Proprietorships and partnerships will not have Common Stock or Additional Paid-in Capital accounts. When cash is invested in a proprietorship, the owner's Capital account is increased. In a partnership, each partner's investment is recorded as an increase to his or her Capital account. Capital accounts are equity accounts and follow the debit/credit rules for equity accounts described earlier in this module. That is, Capital accounts are increased with credits and decreased with debits.

Proprietorships and partnerships do not have Dividends accounts. These types of businesses, however, can make distributions to owners. As we saw in the financial statements presented in Module 1, distributions to owners for proprietorships and partnerships are called drawings or withdrawals. Recording a withdrawal by an owner requires an increase in the Drawings (or Withdrawals) account. In a partnership, a separate Drawings account is maintained for each partner. Drawings is a contra-equity account similar in nature to Dividends. Thus, Drawings follows debit/credit rules just the opposite of the equity account, Capital. A Drawings account is increased with debits and decreased with credits.

When recording transactions for proprietorships and partnerships, the basic debit/credit rules described throughout this module apply. No differences exist in the recording of revenues, expenses, assets or liabilities for a corporation, proprietorship, or partnership.

LOOKING AHEAD

In this module we explored the system used in accounting to record increases and decreases in accounts. The debit/credit system provides a foundation for the formal procedures used in accounting to record transactions. These procedures involve the use of journals, ledgers, and other accounting documents — the focus of Module 3.

APPLY WHAT YOU HAVE LEARNED

2-1. (Effect of Debits and Credits on Accounting Elements)

Required: In the space provided in the table below, indicate the effect that debits and credits have on the accounting elements shown.
Use a "+" to indicate increases. Use a "—" to indicate decreases.

EFFECTS OF DEBITS AND CREDITS		
	DEBIT	CREDIT
Assets		
Liabilities		
Equity		
Revenues		
Expenses		

2-2. (Classification of Accounts by Accounting Element)

Required: Classify each of the following accounts as either an asset, a liability, an equity, a revenue, or an expense. Indicate your selection by placing an "X" in the appropriate box.

ACCOUNT	ASSET	LIABILITY	EQUITY	REVENUE	EXPENSE
Supplies Expense					
Supplies					
Inventory					
Common Stock					
Store Rent					
Rent Revenue					
Interest Income					
Interest Expense					
Prepaid Rent					
Accounts Payable					
Additional Paid-in Capital					
Cash					
Accounts Receivable					
Notes Payable					
Expired Insurance					
Prepaid Insurance					
Equipment					
John Doe, Capital					
Buildings					
Wage Expense					
Sales					

2-3. (Effect of Debits and Credits on Accounts)

Required:

In the space provided in the table below, indicate the effect that debits and credits have on the accounts shown.

ACCOUNT	+ = INCREASE - = DECREASE	
	DEBIT	CREDIT
Supplies Expense		
Supplies		
Inventory		
Common Stock		
Store Rent		
Rent Revenue		
Interest Income		
Interest Expense		
Prepaid Rent		
Accounts Payable		
Additional Paid-in Capital		
Cash		
Accounts Receivable		
Notes Payable		
Expired Insurance		
Prepaid Insurance		
Equipment		
John Doe, Capital		
Buildings		
Wage Expense		
Sales		

2-4. (Determining Account Balances)

Required:

    Enter the account balance in each of the T-accounts below.

Cash			Notes Payable	
1,000	500		2,000	12,000
300	400		2,000	
	200			

Supplies			Accounts Payable	
500			4,000	3,000
300			3,000	5,000
100				4,000

Prepaid Insurance			Bonds Payable	
1,200	600			100,000
	600			200,000

2-5. (Normal Balances)

Required: In the table below, indicate the normal balance of each accounting element.

Normal Balance	
Accounting Element	**Normal Balance (Debit or Credit)**
Assets	
Liabilities	
Equity	
Revenues	
Expenses	

2-6. (Entries in Provided T-accounts with Debit/Credit Line)

Anderson Engineering began operations in January 1995. During its first month of operations the following transactions occurred:

a.   Sold 1,000 shares of no-par common stock for cash of $10,000.

b.   Borrowed $12,000 from Money-To-Go Bank. A promissory note was signed stating that the loan plus 12% interest would be repaid in 18 months.

c.   Purchased $500 worth of office supplies for cash.

d.   Purchased equipment costing $11,000, paying $2,000 down with the balance on account.

e.   Received cash of $7,500 for services performed during January.

f.   Billed customers $9,000 for services performed during January.

g.   Paid $2,500 rent for January 1995.

h.   Paid $500 for utilities for January 1995.

i.   Paid $900 to part-time employees for wages.

j.   Paid a cash dividend to shareholders in the amount of $500.

Required:

1.   Record the above transactions in the provided T-accounts.

2.   Calculate ending account balances.

DEBITS INCREASE
THIS SIDE OF LINE

CREDITS INCREASE
THIS SIDE OF LINE

ASSETS

Cash

LIABILITIES

Notes Payable

Accounts Payable

Supplies

Equipment

EQUITY

Common Stock

Accounts Receivable

Dividends

EXPENSES

Rent
Expense

REVENUES

Service
Revenue

Utilities
Expense

Wages
Expense

T-ACCOUNTS & THE DEBIT/CREDIT SYSTEM **2-35**

2-7. (Entries in Provided T-accounts with Debit/Credit Line)

Florence's Swimming School began operations in March 1995.
During its first month of operations the following transactions
occurred:

a. Sold 100 shares of $3 par common stock for cash of $1,000.

b. Purchased equipment costing $900, paying $200 down with the
balance on account.

c. Received cash of $800 for swimming instruction provided
during March.

d. Billed customers $400 for swimming instruction provided
during March.

e. Paid $250 rent for pool facility for the month of March.

f. Paid a cash dividend to shareholders in the amount of $100.

Required:

Record the above transactions in the provided T-accounts, and
determine each account balance.

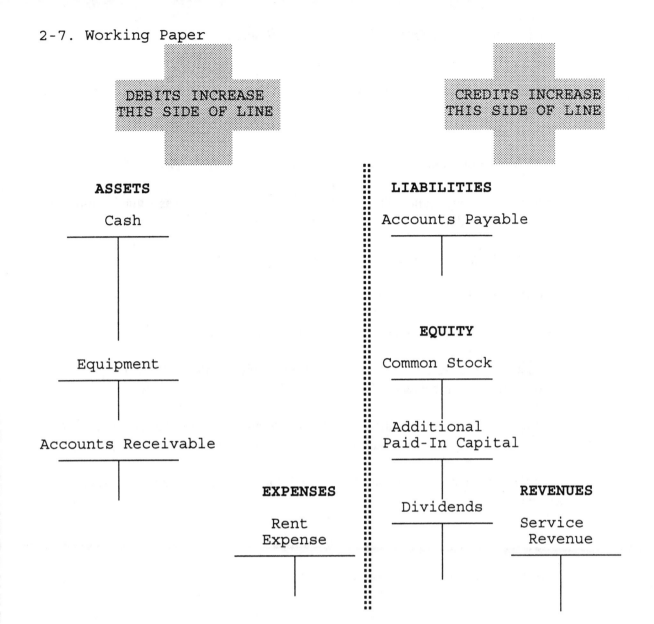

2-8. (Recording Entries in T-accounts — Unlabeled T-accounts Provided)

Quick Cut Lawn Service began operations in June 1995. During its first month of operations the following transactions occurred.

a.   Sold 2,000 shares of common stock ($1 par value per share) for cash of $8,000.

b.   Borrowed $4,000 from Money-To-Go Bank. A promissory note was signed stating that the loan plus 10% interest would be repaid in 2 years.

c.   Purchased $200 worth of trash bags and other supplies on account.

d.   Paid $80 for liability insurance for June.

e.   Purchased lawn cutting equipment costing $3,000 on account.

f.   Purchased a trailer to haul equipment for $2,000 paying cash of $500 and signing a promissory note for the balance. The note plus 10% interest is to be paid in 90 days.

g.   Provided lawn services to customers during June totaling $2,300. Received cash of $1,400 for these lawn services and billed customers for the remaining $900.

h.   Received a bill for gasoline purchased and used during June 1995 totaling $120. The bill will be paid next month.

i.   Paid $400 to part-time employees for wages.

j.   Paid a cash dividend to shareholders in the amount of $200.

Required:

1.   In the space provided, label the Assets, Liabilities, Equity, Revenues, and Expenses classifications.

2.   Draw the line that separates the accounts that are increased by debits from the accounts that are increased by credits.

3.   In the space provided at the top of the page, indicate whether a debit or a credit is required to increase the accounts on the corresponding side of the line drawn for part 2. of this problem.

4.   Record the above transactions in the provided T-accounts. Label each T-account with the account name as it is used.

INCREASE
THIS SIDE OF LINE

INCREASE
THIS SIDE OF LINE

2-9. (Entries in T-accounts — No Work Papers Provided)

Smith's Income Tax Service began operations in July 1995. During its first month of operations the following transactions occurred:

a.   Smith invested $7,000 cash in the company. Smith opened a checking account with the $7,000 in the name of Smith's Income Tax Service, a sole proprietorship.

b.   Purchased $800 worth of office supplies on account.

c.   Paid $1,200 for a one-year liability insurance policy.

d.   Purchased office equipment for $1,500 on account.

e.   Purchased a small computer system for $2,200, paying cash.

f.   Provided tax services to customers during July totaling $5,500. Received cash of $3,500 for these services and billed customers for the remaining $2,000.

g.   Received a $150 electric bill for electricity used during July 1995. The bill will be paid in August.

h.   Paid $1,800 to employees for wages.

i.   Received the $80 telephone bill for July. The bill will be paid in August.

j.   Paid $1,000 for July's office rent.

k.   Paid for the office supplies purchased in transaction b.

l.   The company issued a check for $2,500 to Smith, the owner.

Required:

1.   Record the above transactions in T-accounts. Try to organize your T-accounts in an orderly fashion. Also, as you add T-accounts, scan the transactions to see if the account is used again. This will help you estimate how tall the T-account needs to be to accommodate all the entries. Remember, cash usually has many entries so leave plenty of room. When in doubt, leave extra space for entries. It is better to have too much space than not enough.

2.   Calculate the ending account balances for July 1995.

2-10. (Debit and Credit Rules)

Required: In the table below, indicate how each of the accounting elements is increased and decreased.

Debit and Credit Rules		
Accounting Element	To Increase (Debit or Credit)	To Decrease (Debit or Credit)
Assets		
Liabilities		
Equity		
Revenues		
Expenses		

2-11. (Debit and Credit Rules)

Required: In the table below, indicate how each of the accounts is increased and decreased.

Debit and Credit Rules		
Accounts	To Increase (Debit or Credit)	To Decrease (Debit or Credit)
Accounts Receivable		
Accounts Payable		
Additional Paid-in Capital		
Buildings		
Cash		
Common Stock		
Equipment		
Expired Insurance		
Interest Income		
Interest Expense		
Inventory		
Len Dawson, Capital		
Notes Payable		
Prepaid Insurance		
Prepaid Rent		
Rent Expense		
Rent Revenue		
Supplies		
Supplies Expense		
Sales		

2-12. (Account Classifications and Normal Balances)

Required: In the table below, indicate the classification and the normal balance of each of the accounts. Use the following abbreviations for classifications:
A = ASSET, **L** = LIABILITY, **O** = OWNERS' EQUITY, **R** = REVENUE, and **E** = EXPENSE.

Accounts	Classification	Normal Balance (Debit or Credit)
Accounts Receivable		
Accounts Payable		
Additional Paid-in Capital		
Buildings		
Cash		
Common Stock		
Equipment		
Expired Insurance		
Interest Income		
Interest Expense		
Inventory		
Len Dawson, Capital		
Notes Payable		
Prepaid Insurance		
Prepaid Rent		
Rent Expense		
Rent Revenue		
Supplies		
Supplies Expense		
Sales		

2-13. (Recording Transactions — Proprietorship)

Annie Bryan began Annie's Rainbow in October 1995 and completed the following transactions during the first month of operations.

a.   Invested $40,000 cash to start the business, which is to be organized as a sole proprietorship.

b.   Purchased $875 of office supplies on account.

c.   Purchased equipment of $25,000 with a down payment of $15,000, and signed a 3-year note for the balance, with interest at 12%.

d.   Performed services for customers for $5,800 cash.

e.   Paid $500 of the amount owed from transaction b.

f.   Performed services of $7,000 for customers on account.

g.   Collected $3,250 from customers on account.

h.   Paid the following expenses for October: rent $2,400, wages $3,300, and utilities $1,375.

i.   Annie withdrew $1,100 from the business for personal expenses.

Required:

Record the above transactions in T-accounts and determine the ending balance in each account.

2-14. (Equality of Debits and Credits)

Required:

Using the information from Problem 2-13, list the T-account balances in the table below. Then, total the debit and credit columns to see if debits equal credits.

Do Debits = Credits?		
Accounts	DEBIT Balances	CREDIT Balances
Accounts Payable		
Accounts Receivable		
Annie, Withdrawals		
Annie, Capital		
Cash		
Equipment		
Notes Payable		
Office Supplies		
Rent Expense		
Service Revenue		
Utilities Expense		
Wages Expense		
TOTALS		

2-15. (Preparing Financial Statements — Proprietorship)

Required:

Using the information from Problem 2-14, prepare an income statement, a statement of capital, and a balance sheet for Annie's Rainbow as of October 31, 1995.

2-16. (Recording Transactions — Corporation)

Debbie's Computer Surf completed the following transactions during the month of December 1995.

a.   Sold 10,000 shares of $1 par value common stock for $3 per share.

b.   Purchased $1,650 of computer supplies on account.

c.   Purchased equipment of $18,000 with a down payment of $12,000, and signed a 2-year promissory note for the balance, with interest at 10%.

d.   Performed services for customers for $7,200 cash.

e.   Paid $700 of the amount owed from transaction b.

f.   Performed $9,500 of services for customers on account.

g.   Collected $4,675 from customers on account.

h.   Paid the following expenses for December: rent $2,800, wages $4,500, and utilities $2,475.

i.   Paid cash dividends of $4,000.

j.   Purchased a two-year insurance policy for $4,800.

Required:

Record the above transactions in T-accounts and determine the ending balance in each account.

2-17. (Equality of Debits and Credits)

Using the information from Problem 2-16, list the T-account balances in the table below. Then, total the debit and credit columns to see if debits equal credits.

Do Debits = Credits?		
Accounts	DEBIT Balances	CREDIT Balances
Accounts Receivable		
Accounts Payable		
Additional Paid-in Capital		
Cash		
Common Stock		
Computer Supplies		
Dividends		
Equipment		
Notes Payable		
Prepaid Insurance		
Rent Expense		
Service Revenue		
Utilities Expense		
Wages Expense		
TOTALS		

2-18. (Preparation of Financial Statements — Corporation)

Required:

Using the information from Problem 2-17, prepare an income statement, a statement of retained earnings, and a balance sheet for Debbie's Computer Surf as of December 31, 1995.

MODULE 3

JOURNALIZING AND POSTING BUSINESS TRANSACTIONS

In Module 2, you learned how to make debit and credit entries in T-accounts. As we said in Module 2, the use of T-accounts is limited to illustrations of accounting procedures for educational purposes and in business to work through complicated accounting entries before they are entered in formal accounting records. In this module, we will explore how debit and credit entries are recorded in an accounting system.

Entries are initially recorded in a **journal**. Journals are often called the books of original entry because they are where the results of business transactions are *originally* recorded. However, entering transactions in a journal is just the beginning of the accounting process. As you will see in later sections of this module, information initially recorded in journals is used in subsequent steps of the recording process.

Journals come in various forms, depending on the type of accounting system being used. For instance, in a computerized system, the actual journal may be an area on the hard drive of a computer. In a manual system, journals may be actual pages of paper. Regardless of the form, a journal is a place where results of business transactions are originally recorded. In other words, if we wanted to see a record of these results, we would look at a journal; we may examine information stored in a specific location in a computer's memory or in the pages of a book, but in any case, we would explore a journal.

As we examine the use of journals, our illustrations will assume the use of a manual system. Documents used in manual systems provide more tangible examples of the various aspects of the recording process. In addition, formats of journals and other components of the recording process used in manual systems are fairly standard, whereas computerized systems use a wide variety of formats for these items. Even though the illustrations presented and the practice you will experience with this text are based on a manual system, the basic principles you learn will apply to computerized systems as well.

Entries recorded in journals follow the same debit/credit rules that we practiced in Module 2. In fact, the thought process behind the recording of entries in a journal is identical to that used when recording transactions in T-accounts. The only difference is the format of the document in which the entry is recorded.

As an example, let's assume that on March 2, 1995, a company bought supplies for $100 and paid cash. Recall the four questions offered in Module 2 as a guide for your thought process to determine how to record the results of a business transaction:

1. Which accounts were affected?

2. Should the account balance be increased or decreased, and by how much?

3. Should the account be debited or credited?

4. Do debits equal credits?

These questions, and the thought process practiced in Module 2 will be the same whether you are recording transactions in T-accounts or in a journal. If you were recording the results of the transaction described above, using T-accounts, the entry would be:

Supplies	Cash
100			100

To record the transaction, the Supplies account should be debited $100 and the Cash account should be credited $100. The same holds true when the entry is recorded in a journal. Whether making an entry in T-accounts or a journal, the debits and credits, and the dollar amounts are the same. It's just the format that is different. Recording transactions in a journal is called **journalizing**. The **journal entry** to record the transaction from our example would be:

General Journal				Page 36	
Date 1995		Description	Post Ref	Debit	Credit
March	2	Supplies		100	
		Cash			100
		Bought supplies from			
		Kramer's Office Warehouse			

When entries are recorded in T-accounts, only the dollar amount of the debit or credit is depicted. In the general journal however, the entry includes additional detail. The general journal provides space for information which is not recorded when only T-accounts are used. The general journal has the following columns:

Columns of the General Journal

The **date column**. This column provides information about *when* the transaction occurred.

The **description column**. This column provides space for the names of the accounts being affected and for a brief description of the transaction.

The **posting reference column**. This column is not used when transactions are initially recorded in the journal, but rather provides space to indicate that transaction information was transcribed to other accounting documents. (More about this column later.)

The **debit column**. This column is used to record the dollar amount of the debit entries.

And finally, the **credit column**. As you might have guessed, this column is used to record the dollar amount of the credit entries.

As with T-accounts, the space for the debit amount is to the left, and the space for the credit amount is to the right in the general journal.

Notice in the exhibit above, the journal is referred to as the general journal. The fact is, there are several types of journals used in accounting. However, in this module we will focus our attention on only one, the general journal. The **general journal** is an all-purpose journal which can be used to record *any* business transaction.

Shortly, you will be required to journalize transactions in the general journal *in good form.* In order to help you perfect the proper form of general journal entries, we will examine the step-by-step process performed to make the entry shown above.

1. **The date:** First, each entry is dated. The year is placed at the top of the date column. It is unnecessary to repeat the year for each entry on the page because if the year changes, a new page of the journal will be started. If 1995 is indicated at the top of the page, only 1995 entries should be made on that page. Next, the month and day are entered on the first line of the first entry. For subsequent entries on the page, as long as the entry is for the same month, only the day needs to be entered. However, even if there are several entries on the same day, the day is entered for each entry.

2. **The account(s) to be debited:** After the date is entered, the name of the account being debited is entered. The account name is entered flush left; that is, the first word begins all the way to the left in the description column. Entering the debit side of the entry first is a well-recognized accounting custom that *must* be followed. If an individual transaction requires that more than one account be debited, all debited accounts must be entered before any credit entries are made. Remember, for each transaction, record all the debits first!

3. **The dollar amount(s) to be debited:** The dollar amount of each debit is recorded in the debit column. As with T-accounts, it is customary not to use a dollar sign when making journal entries. Some forms of journal paper divide the debit and credit columns into spaces for each digit of the dollar amount. For clarity, we use a simplified format that provides sufficient room for the dollar amount, but does not indicate space for each digit. Also, in this module, for simplicity, our examples deal only with whole dollars, so we will not indicate "cents".

4. **The account(s) to be credited:** After all the debits have been entered, the credit side of the entry is made. Note that the account name in the credit part of the entry is indented. This, too, is an important accounting custom that must not be overlooked. In fact, when an entry is made in proper form, even if one does not look at the debit or credit *amounts*, a glance at just the account names reveals which accounts have been debited and which have been credited.

5. **The dollar amount(s) to be credited:** The dollar amount of each credit is recorded in the credit column.

NOTE: After these steps have been completed, it is important to review the journal entry to make certain that the total dollar amount of debits is equal to the total dollar amount of credits recorded in the entry.

6. **The description:** Recall that the general journal can be used to record any type of business transaction. Because of the variety of entries, it is often helpful to provide a brief description of the facts pertaining to the transaction. Although descriptions are not required, information recorded in this area is often useful later when details of the transaction may have been forgotten. In our example, if the company buys supplies from several different vendors, the information in the description may be helpful.

7. **The next entry:** It is customary to leave a blank line between each general journal entry.

Now that you have been introduced to the basics of journalizing, it's time to dig in and see how various transactions are recorded in the general journal. As our examples, we will use the transactions from Amanda's Typing Service which you saw in Module 2. Again, the four-question thought process remains exactly the same, so we will not repeat it here. However, for each transaction, be sure you understand how we determined which accounts to debit and credit and for how much. If that part of the recording process is still unclear to you, review the debit and credit presentation in Module 2. Here in Module 3, it is assumed that you already understand how debits and credits work. Accordingly, we will simply provide a brief description of each transaction on the left page, and show the journal entries on the right page.

TRANSACTION A: On January 1, 1996, Amanda's Typing Service was begun by an initial investment of $3,000 from the owners. The corporation issued 1,000 shares of no-par stock for $3 each.

TRANSACTION B: On January 3, 1996 Amanda's Typing Service borrowed $5,000 from First Friendly Bank. Amanda signed a promissory note on behalf of the company, agreeing to repay the loan plus interest in 18 months.

TRANSACTION C: On January 5, 1996, Amanda's Typing Service purchased $300 worth of supplies on account from Rebecca's Office Supplies.

TRANSACTION D: On January 7, Amanda's Typing Service purchased a one-year liability insurance policy paying cash of $1,200.

TRANSACTION E: On January 9, 1996 Amanda's Typing Service paid $2,500 in cash for a desk, three chairs, a small table and a file cabinet.

TRANSACTION F: On January 11, 1996, Amanda's Typing Service purchased a complete computer system from Carl's Computers for $7,000. Amanda's Typing Service paid $2,000 cash. Carl's Computers allowed Amanda's to charge the $5,000 balance.

Date 1996		Description	Post Ref	Debit	Credit
Jan.	1	Cash		3,000	
		Common Stock			3,000
		Issued no-par stock; 600 shares			
		to Amanda Wells, 400 shares to J. Wells			
	3	Cash		5,000	
		Notes Payable			5,000
		Due in 18 months to First Friendly Bank			
	5	Supplies		300	
		Accounts Payable			300
		Owe Rebecca's Office Supplies			
	7	Prepaid Insurance		1,200	
		Cash			1,200
		Liability coverage for one year			
	9	Office Furniture		2,500	
		Cash			2,500
		1 desk, 3 chairs, 1 table, 1 file cabinet			
	11	Computer System		7,000	
		Cash			2,000
		Accounts Payable			5,000
		Owe Carl's Computers			

NOTE: Transactions H, I, and J describe activity that took place throughout the month. In actuality, the company would make several repetitive entries, recording these activities as they occurred. For illustration purposes, we offer Transactions H, I, and J as "summary transactions" and assign each a transaction date of January 25.

TRANSACTION G: On January 13, Amanda's Typing Service made a partial payment of $200 on the balance it owed Rebecca's Office Supplies.

TRANSACTION H: During the month, Amanda's Typing Service performed services for customers and received $800 cash.

TRANSACTION I: Amanda's Typing Service billed customers $2,100 for services performed. These customers are expected to pay for the typing services next month.

TRANSACTION J: During the month Amanda's Typing Service paid part-time employees $1,100 for the wages they earned.

TRANSACTION K: On January 30, Amanda's Typing Service received a bill from Speedy Delivery Service for $100, for the deliveries made during January. Because the delivery services were performed in January, Amanda's should record the bill in January even though it expects to pay it early next month.

TRANSACTION L: On January 31, the owners of Amanda's Typing Service determined the company had sufficient cash and retained earnings to pay a dividend. A $500 cash dividend was paid to the stockholders.

Date 1996		Description	Post Ref	Debit	Credit
Jan.	13	Accounts Payable		200	
		Cash			200
		Payment to Rebecca's Office Supplies			
	25	Cash		800	
		Service Revenue			800
		Cash received at time of service			
	25	Accounts Receivable		2,100	
		Service Revenue			2,100
	25	Wage Expense		1,100	
		Cash			1,100
		Last payday - Jan. 24 for			
		work through Jan. 20			
	30	Delivery Expense		100	
		Accounts Payable			100
		Owe Speedy Delivery Service			
		Due by Feb. 10.			
	31	Dividends		500	
		Cash			500

Now we have the January business activity of Amanda's Typing Service recorded in the company's general journal. The information contained in journals is very valuable. Journals are *chronological* lists of business transactions, so from the journal we can learn *what* happened *when*. Also, if descriptions are provided, the journal provides information regarding other details about the transactions. Indeed, for a variety of settings, the journal will tell us just what we want to know.

Now that results of all the month's business activity for Amanda's Typing Service has been recorded, we might want to know how much cash the company has or how much the business owes its suppliers. Look back at the pages of the company's general journal and think about how you would use the information from the journal to determine how much cash the company has or how much it owes its suppliers...

As you pondered how to determine the company's cash balance or balance in accounts payable, you may have concluded that if the general journal is the only document available, determining the ending balance in an account would require sorting through every entry to gather data affecting that account. Indeed, the general journal does a poor job of providing information about how an individual account was affected by the transactions recorded during the accounting period. That's because even though all the transactions are included in the general journal, they are listed chronologically and grouped by transaction, not by the accounts affected.

So, back to the question: What if we want to know how much cash Amanda's Typing Service has or how much the business owes its suppliers after the impact of all the January transactions? Journals are not the best source of that information — we have figured that out. In fact, when the entries were originally recorded in T-accounts, the current amount of cash and accounts payable was more easily determined. The journal's strength is not in determining account balances, but rather in presenting the data relating to each specific transaction in one place. So, to provide the most information possible, results of business transactions are first recorded in journals and then the information is transcribed to an account-by-account summary similar to a set of T-accounts.

THE GENERAL LEDGER

Information about the effects of the transactions on each account and current account balances is gathered in an account-by-account summary of debit and credit information known as the general ledger. After the results of transactions are recorded in journals, the information is gathered and transformed to show the impact of the transactions on each account, and the current balance in each account. The **general ledger** is the place where the information from the journals is reorganized to provide this additional information.

As was the case with journals, ledgers take various forms depending on the type of accounting system in place. Again, in a computerized environment, the ledger may be a sector of memory within a computer. For our illustrations, we will assume a manual system in which the general ledger is maintained on paper. As we suggested earlier, the general ledger functions in a way similar to a set of T-accounts. The general ledger as a whole is a collection of general ledger accounts — one for each account used by the company. An illustration of a ledger account for Rent Expense is shown below.

| Name of Account: Rent Expense | | | | | | | |
| Account No.: 728 | | | | | | | |

Date 1995	Description	Post Ref	Debit	Credit	Balance Debit	Balance Credit
Oct. 12	Rent through Oct. 31	GJ3	500		500	

Each account has a separate ledger page. Even if the account has only a single entry during the entire accounting period, the account occupies a page of its own. That is, each account is important enough to warrant a ledger page by itself, so no more than one account is allowed per page. Think of each ledger account as a piece of paper in a binder. The entire binder would be referred to as the general ledger.

Now, let's take a closer look at the general ledger page shown above. The account name and account number appear at the top of page and the transaction date is entered in the date column. Next, a column is provided for a description of the entry. Often the nature of the entry is evident even without a narrative description. In such cases, the space provided for the description is left blank.

The posting reference column is used to enter the journal name and page number from which the entry is taken. In the example above, the entry came from GJ 3 which means the general journal (GJ 3) page 3 (GJ 3). In our basic illustrations, the posting reference may not seem as important as it really is. Recall that we are working with only one journal, but in many cases, a company may have four or five journals and may be dealing with dozens of transactions. In case of an error, or when tracing specific details of a transaction, the posting reference provides crucial information.

The debit and credit columns appear next. As with T-accounts, the debit column is on the left and the credit column is on the right. Finally, the ledger has an area to show the account balance, which may be recalculated after each entry. In our illustrations, we will use ledgers that have both debit and credit columns in the balance section. However, in some formats, the space provided to show the account balance may have only one column. If only a single column is used to indicate account balances, the user of the system must know the normal balance (debit or credit) of each type of account. Amounts shown in a single column balance are assumed to be the normal balance of the account. If an account has an abnormal balance (e.g., a debit balance in a liability account), the situation is indicated with parentheses around the balance amount or a written notation of debit or credit.

O.K., now you have been introduced to the general ledger and the construction of a ledger account. The purpose of the general ledger is to summarize (by account) the information already recorded in the journal. Next, we will show how the information from journals gets into the general ledger accounts. The process is known as posting.

POSTING

Posting is the process of transcribing entries from a journal to the ledger. Posting is not a difficult part of the recording process, but it is one which requires precision and care. Recall that as each entry was recorded in the journal, we were careful that the total dollar amount of debits equaled the total dollar amount of credits. When completed properly, the posting process will maintain the equality of debits and credits.

Now let's see how the posting process really works. Remember, the goal is to move information *from* the journal *to* the ledger accounts. A systematic approach to the important process of posting helps to reduce the likelihood of posting errors. There are 6 basic steps in the posting process:

1.   Identify and locate the correct ledger account.

2.   Enter the date in the ledger account.

3.   Enter the explanation in the ledger account if one is necessary.

4.   Enter the dollar amount of the entry in the appropriate debit or credit column in the ledger account.

5.   Enter an abbreviation for the journal name and the journal page number in the posting reference column of the ledger account.

6.   Lastly, enter the account number of the ledger account in the posting reference column back on the *journal*. NOTE: In the case of a company that does not use account numbers, a check mark is entered in the posting reference column of the journal.

Each debit and each credit is posted one-by-one, until all the general journal entries have been posted. When posting from the general journal, it is not permissible to summarize all the entries for a particular account in an attempt to make fewer postings. This is because summarization would introduce a high probability of error. Also, it is not wise to do the 6-step posting procedure out of sequence because this, too, increases the chance of error. For example, it may be quicker to enter the account numbers in the journal's posting reference column before the entry is posted to the ledger accounts. But, if the bookkeeper is called away or distracted during the posting process, when he or she returns to the task of posting, the completed posting reference column would make it appear as though the entry had already been posted. Thinking the entry was already posted, the bookkeeper might move on to the next entry even though the most crucial steps of the posting process were not accomplished for the prior entry.

To illustrate the 6-step posting process, we will post Transaction A for Amanda's Typing Service. The posting process begins with a look at the entry to be posted. Earlier, we recorded Transaction A in the company's general journal as:

General Journal					Page 1
Date 1996		Description	Post Ref	Debit	Credit
Jan.	1	Cash		3,000	
		Common Stock			3,000
		Issued no-par stock; 600 shares			
		to Amanda Wells, 400 shares to J. Wells			

Recall that posting from the general journal is done line-by-line, so we begin with the first line of the entry, and apply the 6-step process:

1. Identify and locate the correct ledger account. The chart of accounts for Amanda's Typing Service lists 13 accounts, which means the company's general ledger includes 13 separate ledger accounts. Since our first posting relates to the Cash account, we must locate the ledger account for Cash. We have shown the Cash ledger account below. As we describe the remaining steps in the posting process, you can see the results of each step indicated by number in the exhibit.

2. Enter the date in the ledger account. A review of the transaction as it appears in the journal suggests the transaction date is January 1, 1996. This date is recorded in the Cash ledger account.

3. Enter the explanation in the ledger account if one is necessary. Since we are posting results of a transaction which is not a recurring part of the company's business activity, we have indicated the nature of the activity in the description column. When posting results of routine transactions, the description is often omitted.

4. Enter the dollar amount of the entry in the appropriate debit or credit column in the ledger account. The line we are posting indicates a $3,000 debit to Cash, so we enter that amount in the debit column.

5. Enter an abbreviation for the journal name and the journal page number in the posting reference column of the ledger account. A look back at the journal indicates the entry we are posting was initially recorded on Page 1 of the company's general journal. The notation GJ1 indicates where the information now recorded in the Cash ledger account was originally recorded.

6. Lastly, enter the account number of the ledger account in the posting reference column back on the *journal*. This final step of the posting process requires us to return to the company's general journal. Below the Cash ledger account, we have repeated the illustration of the entry from the general journal. Note that this illustration shows the result of step 6 — we recorded the account number for Cash to indicate that this line of the journal has now been posted.

Name of Account: Cash

Account No. 110

Date 1996		Description	Post Ref	Debit	Credit	Balance Debit	Balance Credit
						Debit	Credit
Jan.	1	issued stock (1000 shares)	GJ1	3,000			

General Journal					Page 1	
Date 1996		Description	Post Ref	Debit	Credit
Jan.	1	Cash	110	3,000	
		Common Stock			3,000
		Issued no-par stock; 600 shares			
		to Amanda Wells, 400 shares to J. Wells			

As the posting reference column in the illustration above indicates, only half of Transaction A has been posted. It is necessary to repeat the 6-step process to post the credit part of the entry. When that process is complete, the Common Stock ledger account and Transaction A in the company's general journal would appear as follows:

Name of Account: **Common Stock**

Account No.: **510**

Date 1996		Description	Post Ref	Debit	Credit	Balance Debit	Balance Credit
Jan.	1	1000 shares no-par	GJ1		3,000		

		General Journal			Page 1
Date 1996		Description	Post Ref	Debit	Credit
Jan.	1	Cash	110	3,000	
		Common Stock	510		3,000
		Issued no-par stock; 600 shares			
		to Amanda Wells, 400 shares to J. Wells			

Now you have seen the results of the posting process illustrated for one transaction. The same step-by-step posting process would be followed for the remaining entries of Amanda's Typing Service. On the following pages, we offer the company's general journal and general ledger after all the transactions have been posted. Notice that the posting reference column of the general journal now shows the ledger account numbers indicating that the transactions have been posted. After all the transactions were posted, the balance in each ledger account was determined and recorded.

Date 1996		Description	Post Ref	Debit	Credit
Jan.	1	Cash	110	3,000	
		Common Stock	510		3,000
		Issued no-par stock; 600 shares			
		to Amanda Wells, 400 shares to J. Wells			
	3	Cash	110	5,000	
		Notes Payable	410		5,000
		Due in 18 months to First Friendly Bank			
	5	Supplies	170	300	
		Accounts Payable	310		300
		Owe Rebecca's Office Supplies			
	7	Prepaid Insurance	180	1,200	
		Cash	110		1,200
		Liability coverage for one year			
	9	Office Furniture	210	2,500	
		Cash	110		2,500
		1 desk, 3 chairs, 1 table, 1 file cabinet			
	11	Computer System	220	7,000	
		Cash	110		2,000
		Accounts Payable	310		5,000
		Owe Carl's Computers			

Date 1996		Description	Post Ref	Debit	Credit
Jan.	13	Accounts Payable	310	200	
		Cash	110		200
		Payment to Rebecca's Office Supplies			
	25	Cash	110	800	
		Service Revenue	610		800
		Cash received at time of service			
	25	Accounts Receivable	130	2,100	
		Service Revenue	610		2,100
	25	Wage Expense	710	1,100	
		Cash	110		1,100
		Last payday – Jan. 24 for			
		work through Jan. 20			
	30	Delivery Expense	730	100	
		Accounts Payable	310		100
		Owe Speedy Delivery Service			
		Due by Feb. 10.			
	31	Dividends	530	500	
		Cash	110		500

Name of Account: Cash

Account No.: 110

Date 19 96		Description	Post Ref	Debit	Credit	Balance Debit	Balance Credit
Jan.	1	issued stock (1000 shs.)	GJ1	3,000			
	3	Note due in 18 months	GJ1	5,000		8,000	
	7		GJ1		1,200	6,800	
	9		GJ1		2,500	4,300	
	11	down payment on computer	GJ1		2,000		
	13		GJ2		200	2,100	
	25		GJ2	800		2,900	
	25		GJ2		1,100		
	31	dividend	GJ2		500	1,300	

Name of Account: Accounts Receivable

Account No.: 130

Date 19 96		Description	Post Ref	Debit	Credit	Balance Debit	Balance Credit
Jan.	25		GJ2	2,100		2,100	

Name of Account: Supplies

Account No.: 170

Date 19 96		Description	Post Ref	Debit	Credit	Balance Debit	Balance Credit
Jan.	5		GJ1	300		300	

Name of Account: Prepaid Insurance

Account No.: 180

Date 19 96		Description	Post Ref	Debit	Credit	Balance Debit	Balance Credit
Jan.	7	liability coverage – 1year	GJ1	1,200		1,200	

Name of Account: Office Furniture

Account No.: 210

Date 19 96		Description	Post Ref	Debit	Credit	Balance Debit	Balance Credit
Jan.	9	desk, table, file cabinet, 3 chairs	GJ1	2,500		2,500	

Name of Account: Computer System

Account No.: 220

Date 19 96		Description	Post Ref	Debit	Credit	Balance Debit	Balance Credit
Jan.	11	system from Carl's Computers	GJ1	7,000		7,000	

Name of Account: Accounts Payable

Account No.: 310

Date 19 96		Description	Post Ref	Debit	Credit	Balance Debit	Balance Credit
Jan.	5	Rebecca's Office Supplies	GJ1		300		
	11	Carl's Computers	GJ1		5,000		5,300
	13	Rebecca's Office Supplies	GJ2	200			5,100
	30	Speedy Delivery Service	GJ2		100		5,200

Name of Account: Notes Payable

Account No.: 410

Date 19 96		Description	Post Ref	Debit	Credit	Balance Debit	Balance Credit
Jan.	3	First Friendly Bank - 18 months	GJ1		5,000		5,000

Name of Account: Common Stock

Account No.: 510

Date 19 96		Description	Post Ref	Debit	Credit	Balance Debit	Balance Credit
Jan.	1	1000 shares no-par	GJ1		3,000		3,000

Name of Account: Dividends

Account No.: 530

Date 19 96		Description	Post Ref	Debit	Credit	Balance Debit	Balance Credit
Jan.	31		GJ2	500		500	

Name of Account: Service Revenue

Account No.: 610

Date 19 96		Description	Post Ref	Debit	Credit	Balance Debit	Balance Credit
Jan.	25	services for cash	GJ2		800		
	25	services on account	GJ2		2,100		2,900

Name of Account: Wage Expense

Account No.: 710

Date 1996		Description	Post Ref	Debit		Credit		Balance Debit	Balance Credit
Jan.	25	through Jan. 20	GJ2	1,100				1,100	

Name of Account: Delivery Expense

Account No.: 730

Date 1996		Description	Post Ref	Debit		Credit		Balance Debit	Balance Credit
Jan.	30		GJ2	100				100	

Now you have explored two major parts of the recording process: journalizing transactions in a journal and posting the information to a general ledger. Journals and ledgers serve distinct purposes, and both are crucial to the accumulation of useful accounting information. The general journal shows each entry, in its entirety, while the general ledger shows the effect of entries on each individual ledger account. Even though all the transactions are included in both the general journal and the general ledger, these two documents meet different informational needs. Both are necessary in order to properly keep track of the impacts of business transactions on the financial well-being of a business.

Earlier in this module, we recorded results of the business activity of Amanda's Typing Service for the month of January in the company's general journal. Then, we asked how to go about determining the amount of cash the company has or the amount the business owes its suppliers. The need for that type of information led us to the posting process and the general ledger. Now, we have posted all the information and determined the balance in each of the company's general ledger accounts. So, if we wanted to know the balance in Cash or Accounts Payable, we could flip through the pages of the general ledger and locate each account. With only 13 ledger accounts, the task would not be too difficult, but in a larger business, with many more accounts, scanning the pages of the general ledger would be very inefficient. To provide information about the balances in a company's accounts, a trial balance is created.

THE TRIAL BALANCE

The **trial balance** is an accounting schedule that lists all of the accounts and their balances. It is simple to prepare. All that is required is that the bookkeeper page through the general ledger and list each account and its balance. The balances are reported in two columns — the left column shows the account balances which are debits and the right column shows the account balances which are credits.

Based on the general ledger produced on the previous pages, we can list the accounts and their balances for Amanda's Typing Service as of the end of January. The resulting trial balance is shown below.

Amanda's Typing Service Trial Balance As of January 31, 1996		
Cash	$ 1,300	
Accounts Receivable	2,100	
Supplies	300	
Prepaid Insurance	1,200	
Office Furniture	2,500	
Computer System	7,000	
Accounts Payable		$ 5,200
Notes Payable		5,000
Common Stock		3,000
Dividends	500	
Service Revenue		2,900
Wage Expense	1,100	
Delivery Expense	100	
	$16,100	$16,100

As we said, the trial balance is really nothing more than a list of the company's accounts and their balances. The trial balance is *NOT* a financial statement. In fact, a trial balance is generally not made available to individuals outside the company. Rather, it is a tool used as part of the internal workings of the recording process. A trial balance can be created *whenever* the information it provides is needed.

In addition to offering a concise summary of the balance in each ledger account, the trial balance serves another very important purpose. Notice that in the illustration of the trial balance for Amanda's Typing Service, the account balances in the left (debit) column were totaled, and those in the right (credit) column were also totaled. Each column totaled to $16,100. The fact that these columns total is no coincidence. Herein lies the other benefit of trial balances — they serve as a check that the total debits and total credits recorded in the general ledger are equal. Recall that as we made each entry in the general journal, we were careful to keep the total dollar amount of debits equal to the total dollar amount of credits.

We said that the posting process, if completed properly, would maintain this equality between debits and credits. By preparing a trial balance, we can determine if, in fact, this basic rule of "debits = credits" was followed. The trial balance *CANNOT* assure us that the entries were posted to the proper accounts, or even that the original journal entries were correct, but it can provide evidence that we have kept an equality between debits and credits. In this way, a trial balance often uncovers careless mistakes made during the posting process.

A trial balance may also be a wonderful source of the information needed to prepare financial statements. This listing of accounts and their balances makes the preparation of the income statement, the statement of owners' equity and the balance sheet nearly as simple as copying information from one page to the next. However, before financial statements are prepared, care should be taken to assure that the account balances are correct and that they reflect all of the economic events that have occurred during the period. In most cases, ledger account balances must be adjusted to reflect last minute events and other items so that the information in financial statements is as accurate as possible. For this reason, we will not prepare financial statements for Amanda's Typing Service at this time, but instead wait until we have explored the adjustment process, which is the focus of the next module.

APPLY WHAT YOU HAVE LEARNED

3-1.   (Journalizing Transactions in the General Journal)

Florence Kundrat Swimming Instruction, Inc. had the following transactions during January 1995:

a.   January 1, 1995 — Paid cash of $150 for January pool rent.

b.   January 5, 1995 — Paid $50 for pool maintenance.

c.   January 31, 1995 — Paid $300 for wages to part-time instructors.

d.   January 31, 1995 — Received $950 from students for January swimming instruction.

Required: Journalize January's transactions for Florence Kundrat Swimming Instruction.

Date		Description	Post Ref	Debit	Credit
General Journal				Page _____	

3-2. (Journalizing Transactions in the General Journal)

Mauro Montoya Moving Company had the following transactions during July 1995:

a. July 1, 1995 — Paid cash of $300 for July's truck rental on a short-term lease.

b. July 15, 1995 — Purchased $200 worth of fuel for the truck on account.

c. July 31, 1995 — Paid $1,200 for wages to part-time laborers.

d. July 31, 1995 — Received $3,200 from customers for moving services rendered during July.

Required: Journalize July's transactions for Mauro Montoya Moving Company.

Date		Description	Post Ref	Debit	Credit

General Journal — Page _____

3-3. (Journalizing Transactions in the General Journal)

Bill Hudik established Hudik Engineering on May 1, 1995. The following transactions occurred during May:

a.   May 1, 1995 — Bill Hudik invested cash of $5,000 in exchange for 1,000 shares of Hudik Engineering's no-par common stock.

b.   May 1, 1995 — Hudik Engineering rented office space and paid $900 for May's rent.

c.   May 2, 1995 — The company purchased $200 worth of office supplies on account from Bowden Supply Company.

d.   May 12, 1995 — Received cash of $1,200 for engineering services provided to David Butterfield Construction Co.

e.   May 29, 1995 — Billed Maupin & Company $2,300 for engineering services completed.

f.   May 31, 1995 — Received a bill for $225 from Edison Power & Light Company for electricity consumed during May.

g.   May 31, 1995 — Received a bill for $112 from Regional Bell for telephone service for May.

Required: Journalize the transactions for Hudik Engineering in the general journal provided. Your entries should be made in good form.

General Journal				Page _____	
Date	Description	Post Ref	Debit	Credit	

3-4. (Posting to the General Ledger and Preparation of a Trial Balance)

Refer to the general journal entries prepared for Problem 3-3.

Required:

a. Post the general journal entries prepared for Problem 3-3 to the general ledger pages that follow.

b. Calculate account balances for each account and, in the space below, prepare a trial balance for Hudik Engineering as of May 31, 1995.

Name of Account:

Account No.:

Date 19__		Description	Post Ref	Debit	Credit	Balance	
						Debit	Credit

Name of Account:

Account No.:

Date 19__		Description	Post Ref	Debit	Credit	Balance	
						Debit	Credit

Name of Account:

Account No.:

Date 19__		Description	Post Ref	Debit	Credit	Balance	
						Debit	Credit

Name of Account:

Account No.:

Date 19__	Description	Post Ref	Debit	Credit	Balance Debit	Balance Credit

Name of Account:

Account No.:

Date 19__	Description	Post Ref	Debit	Credit	Balance Debit	Balance Credit

Name of Account:

Account No.:

Date 19__	Description	Post Ref	Debit	Credit	Balance Debit	Balance Credit

Name of Account:

Account No.:

Date 19__		Description	Post Ref	Debit	Credit	Balance	
						Debit	Credit

Name of Account:

Account No.:

Date 19__		Description	Post Ref	Debit	Credit	Balance	
						Debit	Credit

Name of Account:

Account No.:

Date 19__		Description	Post Ref	Debit	Credit	Balance	
						Debit	Credit

3-5. (Preparation of Financial Statements from a Trial Balance)

Refer to the trial balance prepared for Problem 3-4.

Required:

     a.   Prepare an income statement for Hudik Engineering for the month ended May 31, 1995.

     b.   Prepare a statement of retained earnings for Hudik Engineering for the month ended May 31, 1995.

     c.   Prepare a balance sheet for Hudik Engineering as of May 31, 1995.

3-6. (Journalizing Transactions in the General Journal)

Bob Jureit established Jureit Consulting on June 1, 1995. The following transactions occurred during June:

a.   June 1, 1995 — Bob Jureit invested cash of $3,000 in exchange for 300 shares of Jureit Consulting $2 par common stock.

b.   June 1, 1995 — Jureit Consulting rented office space and paid $500 for June's rent.

c.   June 3, 1995 — The company purchased $100 worth of office supplies on account from Carol's Office Supply Company.

d.   June 15, 1995 — Received cash of $2,200 for consulting services provided to Anderson Sales Company.

e.   June 25, 1995 — Billed Mathies Company $3,400 for consulting services completed.

f.   June 30, 1995 — Received a bill for $180 from Eastern Power & Light Company for electricity consumed during June.

g.   June 30, 1995 — Received a bill for $150 from Southern Bell for telephone service for June.

Required: Journalize the transactions for Jureit Consulting in the general journal provided. Your entries should be made in good form.

General Journal			Post Ref	Debit	Credit
Date		Description			

Page _____

3-7. (Posting to the General Ledger and Preparing a Trial Balance)

Refer to the general journal entries prepared for Problem 3-6.

Required:

a. Post the general journal entries prepared for Problem 3-6 to the general ledger pages that follow.

b. Calculate account balances for each account and, in the space provided below, prepare a trial balance for Jureit Consulting as of June 30, 1995.

Name of Account:

Account No.:

Date 19__	Description	Post Ref	Debit	Credit	Balance Debit	Credit

Name of Account:

Account No.:

Date 19__	Description	Post Ref	Debit	Credit	Balance Debit	Credit

Name of Account:

Account No.:

Date 19__	Description	Post Ref	Debit	Credit	Balance Debit	Credit

Name of Account:

Account No.:

Date 19__		Description	Post Ref	Debit	Credit	Balance	
						Debit	Credit

Name of Account:

Account No.:

Date 19__		Description	Post Ref	Debit	Credit	Balance	
						Debit	Credit

Name of Account:

Account No.:

Date 19__		Description	Post Ref	Debit	Credit	Balance	
						Debit	Credit

Name of Account:

Account No.:

Date 19__	Description	Post Ref	Debit	Credit	Balance	
					Debit	Credit

Name of Account:

Account No.:

Date 19__	Description	Post Ref	Debit	Credit	Balance	
					Debit	Credit

Name of Account:

Account No.:

Date 19__	Description	Post Ref	Debit	Credit	Balance	
					Debit	Credit

Name of Account:

Account No.:

Date 19__	Description	Post Ref	Debit	Credit	Balance	
					Debit	Credit

3-8. (Preparation of Financial Statements from a Trial Balance)

Refer to the trial balance prepared for Problem 3-7.

Required:

a. Prepare an income statement for Jureit Consulting for the month ended June 30, 1995.

b. Prepare a statement of retained earnings for Jureit Consulting for the month ended June 30, 1995.

c. Prepare a balance sheet for Jureit Consulting as of June 30, 1995.

3-9. (Posting to the General Ledger and Preparing a Trial Balance)

The following general journal entries were made for Alberto Pons and Company during August 1995:

General Journal				Page	1
Date 1995		Description	Post Ref	Debit	Credit
Aug	1	Cash		15,000	
		Common Stock			15,000
	2	Rent Expense		1,500	
		Cash			1,500
	2	Cleaning Supplies		100	
		Accounts Payable			100
	15	Cash		2,900	
		Service Revenue			2,900
	28	Accounts Receivable		3,800	
		Service Revenue			3,800
	29	Accounts Payable		100	
		Cash			100
	31	Utility Expense		320	
		Accounts Payable			320
	31	Telephone Expense		150	
		Accounts Payable			150

(REQUIREMENTS ARE ON THE NEXT PAGE.)

Required:

a. Post the entries for Alberto Pons and Company to the general ledger that follows.

b. In the space below, prepare a trial balance for Alberto Pons and Company as of August 31, 1995.

Name of Account:

   Account No.:

Date 19__		Description	Post Ref	Debit	Credit	Balance	
						Debit	Credit

Name of Account:

   Account No.:

Date 19__		Description	Post Ref	Debit	Credit	Balance	
						Debit	Credit

Name of Account:

   Account No.:

Date 19__		Description	Post Ref	Debit	Credit	Balance	
						Debit	Credit

Name of Account:

Account No.:

Date 19__		Description	Post Ref	Debit	Credit	Balance	
						Debit	Credit

Name of Account:

Account No.:

Date 19__		Description	Post Ref	Debit	Credit	Balance	
						Debit	Credit

Name of Account:

Account No.:

Date 19__		Description	Post Ref	Debit	Credit	Balance	
						Debit	Credit

Name of Account:

Account No.:

Date 19__		Description	Post Ref	Debit	Credit	Balance Debit	Credit

Name of Account:

Account No.:

Date 19__		Description	Post Ref	Debit	Credit	Balance Debit	Credit

Name of Account:

Account No.:

Date 19__		Description	Post Ref	Debit	Credit	Balance Debit	Credit

3-10. (Posting to the General Ledger and Preparation of a Trial Balance)

The following general journal entries were made for Val's Service Company during February 1995:

General Journal				Page	1
Date 1995		Description	Post Ref	Debit	Credit
Feb	1	Cash		2,000	
		Common Stock			2,000
	2	Rent Expense		500	
		Cash			500
	14	Office Supplies		50	
		Accounts Payable			100
	20	Cash		700	
		Service Revenue			700
	22	Accounts Receivable		800	
		Service Revenue			800
	24	Accounts Payable		50	
		Cash			50
	28	Utility Expense		90	
		Accounts Payable			320
	28	Wage Expense		450	
		Cash			450

(REQUIREMENTS ARE ON THE NEXT PAGE.)

Required:

    a.   Post the entries for Val's Service Company to the general ledger that follows.

    b.   In the space below, prepare a trial balance for Val's Service Company as of February 28, 1995.

Name of Account:

Account No.:

Date 19__		Description	Post Ref	Debit	Credit	Balance	
						Debit	Credit

Name of Account:

Account No.:

Date 19__		Description	Post Ref	Debit	Credit	Balance	
						Debit	Credit

Name of Account:

Account No.:

Date 19__		Description	Post Ref	Debit	Credit	Balance	
						Debit	Credit

Name of Account:

Account No.:

Date 19__		Description	Post Ref	Debit	Credit	Balance Debit	Credit

Name of Account:

Account No.:

Date 19__		Description	Post Ref	Debit	Credit	Balance Debit	Credit

Name of Account:

Account No.:

Date 19__		Description	Post Ref	Debit	Credit	Balance Debit	Credit

Name of Account:

Account No.:

Date 19__		Description	Post Ref	Debit	Credit	Balance	
						Debit	Credit

Name of Account:

Account No.:

Date 19__		Description	Post Ref	Debit	Credit	Balance	
						Debit	Credit

Name of Account:

Account No.:

Date 19__		Description	Post Ref	Debit	Credit	Balance	
						Debit	Credit

3-11. (Journalizing Transactions)

Anderson Engineering began operations in January 1995. During its first month of operations the following transactions occurred:

a. Sold 1,000 shares of no-par common stock for cash of $10,000.

b. Borrowed $12,000 from Money-To-Go Bank. A promissory note was signed stating that the loan plus 12% interest would be repaid in 18 months.

c. Purchased $500 worth of office supplies for cash.

d. Purchased equipment costing $11,000, paying $2,000 down with the balance on account.

e. Received cash of $7,500 for services performed during January.

f. Billed customers $9,000 for services performed during January.

g. Paid $2,500 rent for January 1995.

h. Paid $500 for utilities for January 1995.

i. Paid $900 to part-time employees for wages.

j. Paid a cash dividend to shareholders in the amount of $500.

Required:

Prepare journal entries for the above transactions.

3-12. (Journal Entries from T-accounts)

Some transactions of Players Sport have been entered in T- accounts as follows:

Cash		Accounts Receivable		Service Revenue	
(a) 10,000	4,000 (b)	(c) 6,300	3,500 (d)		6,300 (c)
(d) 3,500	2,800 (f)				3,250 (e)
(e) 3,250					

Equipment		Notes Payable		Common Stock	
(b) 12,000		(f) 2,800	8,000 (b)		10,000 (a)

Required: Prepare general journal entries for each of the transactions that were entered in the T-accounts above.

3-12. Working Papers

Date		Description	Post Ref	Debit	Credit
		General Journal		Page ____	

3-13. (Journal Entries from T-accounts)

Some transactions for Jens Hits have been entered in T-accounts as follows:

Cash		Accounts Receivable		Service Revenue	
(a) 15,000	2,000 (b)	(c) 4,700	3,200 (d)		4,700 (c)
(d) 3,200	2,800 (g)				5,250 (e)
(e) 5,250					

Supplies		Accounts Payable		Capital	
(b) 2,000		(g) 2,800	(f) 3,800		15,000 (a)
(f) 3,800					

Required:

Prepare general journal entries for each of the transactions that were entered in the T-accounts above.

	General Journal		Page _____	

Date		Description	Post Ref	Debit	Credit

3-14. (Preparation of a Trial Balance)

Account balances for The Bartlett Corporation at June 30, 1995, the end of its first month of operations, are listed below in alphabetical order:

```
Accounts Receivable       $ 4,000
Accounts Payable            3,500
Cash                        3,000
Common Stock               10,000
Dividends                   5,000
Equipment                   9,900
Notes Payable (3 years)     8,500
Office Furniture           10,500
Prepaid Insurance           1,600
Rent Expense               15,000
Service Revenue            40,000
Supplies                    1,000
Wages Expense              12,000
```

Required:

Prepare a trial balance for The Bartlett Corporation at June 30, 1995, listing the accounts in proper sequence.

_____

_____

_____

_____

_____

_____

_____

_____

_____

_____

_____

_____

_____

3-15. (Preparation of a Trial Balance)

Account balances for Kippler Associates at November 30, 1995, the end of her first month of operations, are listed below in alphabetical order:

```
Accounts Receivable          $ 8,000
Accounts Payable               7,000
Cash                           6,000
Equipment                     19,800
Notes Payable (4 years)       17,000
Office Furniture              21,000
Prepaid Insurance              3,200
Rent Expense                  30,000
Service Revenue               80,000
Supplies                       2,000
Tammy, Withdrawals            10,000
Tammy, Capital                20,000
Wages Expense                 24,000
```

Required:

Prepare a trial balance for Kippler Associates at November 30, 1995, listing the accounts in proper sequence.

3-16. (Journalizing Transactions)

Robert Zelin began his business on October 1, 1995. The following transactions occurred during the month of October.

a.   Invested $40,000 cash to start the business, which is to be organized as a sole proprietorship.

b.   Purchased $875 of office supplies on account.

c.   Purchased equipment of $25,000 with a down payment of $15,000, and signed a 3-year note for the balance, with interest at 12%.

d.   Performed services for customers for $5,800 cash.

e.   Paid $500 of the amount owed from transaction b.

f.   Performed services of $7,000 for customers on account.

g.   Collected $3,250 from customers on account.

h.   Paid the following expenses for October: rent $2,400, wages $3,300, and utilities $1,375.

i.   Robert withdrew $1,100 from the business for personal expenses.

Required:

a.   Prepare journal entries for the above transactions.

Date		Description	Post Ref	Debit	Credit
General Journal			Page ____		

3-17. (Journalizing Transactions)

The Darling Corporation completed the following transactions during the month of December.

a. Sold 10,000 shares of $1 par value common stock for $3 per share.

b. Purchased $1,650 of computer supplies on account.

c. Purchased equipment of $18,000 with a down payment of $12,000, and signed a 2-year note for the balance, with interest at 10%.

d. Performed services for customers for $7,200 cash.

e. Paid $700 of the amount owed from transaction b.

f. Performed services of $9,500 for customers on account.

g. Collected $4,675 from customers on account.

h. Paid the following expenses for December: rent $2,800, wages $4,500, and utilities $2,475.

i. Paid cash dividends of $4,000.

j. Purchased a two-year insurance policy for $4,800.

Required:

a. Prepare journal entries for the above transactions.

Date		Description	Post Ref	Debit	Credit

General Journal — Page _____

MODULE 4

THE ADJUSTING PROCESS

So far we've learned to record the results of business transactions in the general journal, transfer that information into general ledger accounts, and test the equality of our debits and credits by drawing a trial balance. That's quite an accomplishment! But recall that in Module 1 we said the recording process would produce useful accounting information that could be used to prepare financial statements. Is the information in the general ledger accounts presented in Module 3 ready to use in the preparation of financial statements for Amanda's Typing Service? Well, not quite.

Having recorded and posted the transactions which occurred during January is a good start, but before financial statements are prepared, another crucial step in the recording process must be completed. Each account should be reviewed to assure that the account balance reflects *all* the business activity of the company that has occurred, and *no more*. Often, last minute entries are required to adjust account balances accordingly. Recall that accrual accounting requires that revenues be recognized when earned, and that expenses be recognized in the periods they help generate revenues. In accounting, recognizing an item means:
(1) recording it in the accounting records, and (2) reporting it on the financial statements.

To help determine that all items are properly recognized, we should review the balances in the general ledger accounts. Only after we are certain that the account balances properly reflect the results of this period's business activity should we use that information in the preparation of financial statements.

A review of the account balances often results in modifications in the amounts reflected. This review and modification process is known as the **adjustment process**. The journal entries made in anticipation of the preparation of financial statements to modify account balances so that they accurately reflect the company's economic position and the results of its operations are called **adjusting entries**.

The adjustment process takes place at the end of the financial statement period, but before the financial statements are prepared. It may take days or weeks to determine all the adjustments necessary in order to have account balances which properly reflect the results of operations measured under accrual accounting guidelines. For instance, if a company's financial statement period ends December 31, the adjustment process may continue well into January or even later. The ongoing business transactions will be recorded and dated as they occur during January. The adjusting entries that are required will be entered back on the December page of the general journal, and will be dated December 31, even if they are actually being recorded in January. This practice is necessary because the adjusting entries relate to the period ending December 31, and must be considered in the account balances before financial statements are prepared. The transactions reflecting January business activity, and dated as such should not be considered during the preparation of the December 31 financial statements.

The adjusting process enhances accounting's ability to reflect reality. If accrual accounting is our basis to measure reality, we must be sure that we have recognized revenue in the period it is earned, and expenses in the period they helped to generate revenue. During the adjustment process, accounting records are reviewed to make sure that all items that should be recognized in the current period have been recorded. In addition, during the adjustment process, it is ascertained that no items that should be recognized in future periods appear in the current period's records. As we explore the process of reviewing accounts and determining if adjusting entries are needed, keep the purpose of the process in mind: The adjusting process is used to be certain that the revenues and expenses of the period and the company's financial position are properly reflected in the account balances before the information is used in financial statements. You will not be able to memorize the format of a finite set of adjusting entries. Each company's situation is different, and adjusting entries are a result of the business activity of the period and how it was recorded. To determine the necessary adjusting entries, you must be able to see what *has* been recorded and what *should* be recorded. The adjustment process is definitely a thinking process.

As we describe examples of some adjustments, we use T-accounts to illustrate the results. As you work with the examples and as you determine necessary adjustments in other settings, using T-accounts may be helpful. Even the most experienced record keepers use T-accounts to help them "see" what adjusting entries are needed. The adjustment process results in three basic types of adjusting entries: accruals, deferrals, and others.

ACCRUALS

These adjustments are made to recognize items that should be included in the income statement period, but have not yet been recorded. Accruals are recorded *before* the associated cash flow has taken place. Remember, accrual accounting recognizes revenues and expenses regardless of whether or not the cash has changed hands. In this way, the basic foundation of accrual accounting creates the need for accrual adjustments. There are two types of accruals: accrued revenues and accrued expenses.

Accrued Revenues

Accrued revenues result from adjustments made to record revenues which have been earned during the financial statement period but which have not yet been recognized. Again, accrual accounting requires that revenue be recognized when earned regardless of whether cash has been received or the customer has been billed. So, at the end of the accounting period, before financial statements are prepared, we must be certain that all revenue earned during the period has been recorded.

For example, Ace Cleaning Service's fiscal year ends on December 31. Ace has a $3,000 contract to clean the offices of Bowden and Company for a three-month period beginning

November 1, 1995. Assume that Ace intends to bill Bowden at the end of the contract period, on January 31, 1996. Normally, Ace Cleaning Service's bookkeeping department records revenue when the customer is billed for services performed. Accordingly, as of December 31, Ace *has not recorded* any revenue related to the Bowden contract.

As of December 31, has Ace received any cash from work done for Bowden? No. As of December 31, has Ace billed Bowden for any of the work done? No. But the basic guidelines of accrual accounting aren't concerned with the answers to either of those questions. Accrual accounting asks: As of December 31, has Ace *earned* any revenue from the work done for Bowden? The answer is: Because it has performed two of the three months of service it has earned $2,000 of the $3,000 contract amount. So, revenue of $2,000 should be shown on Ace's income statement for the period ending December 31.

Now, remember that none of this revenue has yet been recorded. So we must make a journal entry to record the $2,000 revenue. This is Ace's accrued revenue, revenue being recorded during the adjustment process to reflect amounts earned but not yet recorded. If our adjusting entry is to increase revenue by $2,000, we must credit Ace's Service Revenue account by that amount. But, we know debits must equal credits, so we need a debit for our adjusting entry. What has Ace received for the work completed? Certainly not cash, but Ace does have a legal claim to a payment from Bowden. Therefore, Ace should record an increase in Accounts Receivable as the debit portion of this adjusting entry. The complete adjusting entry to reflect Ace's accrued revenue is:

```
Accounts Receivable            2,000
        Service Revenue                2,000
```

The adjusting entry above will increase Accounts Receivable and Service Revenue so that these accounts provide a more accurate depiction of reality. The increase in Service Revenue will impact Ace's income statement, increasing net income by $2,000. The increase in net income will result in an increase in Retained Earnings of $2,000, but the company's balance sheet will remain in balance because the increase in Accounts Receivable will cause total assets to increase by $2,000 as well. When financial statements are prepared using these adjusted balances, the financial statements provide a more accurate picture of Ace's earnings for the period, and the company's actual financial position.

Accrued Expenses

Accrued expenses result from adjustments made to record expenses that have been incurred during the financial statement period, but which have not yet been recognized. That is, if an expense has been incurred, but, for whatever reason, has not been recorded, it should be recorded during the adjustment process. Before financial statements are prepared, we must be certain that all expenses supporting the earnings activity for that period are recorded.

For example, assume Ace Cleaning Service received a telephone bill for $200 on January 5, 1996. A review of the telephone bill reveals that it is for December's phone service. Because the bill was received in January, it was not recorded in December. Accordingly, as of December 31, 1995, Ace's Telephone Expense account did not reflect all the cost of telephone service for 1995. Remember, under accrual accounting, we are not concerned with whether or not the bill has been paid. Nor are we concerned with whether or not the payment is due. Accrual accounting asks: Was the expense incurred in this period to support revenue generating activity in this period?

To properly reflect the amount of telephone expense for 1995, Ace's Telephone Expense account must be increased by $200. In other words, $200 of telephone expense should be accrued. For our adjusting entry to increase the amount of expense recorded for the period by $200, we must debit Telephone Expense for that amount. Since debits must equal credits, we need a credit for the remaining portion of the entry. Ace spent no money on this phone bill, so Cash should not be credited. Instead, Ace must recognize that it owes the amount to the telephone company. Therefore, the credit portion of the adjusting entry must reflect an increase in the company's liabilities.

The company's debt to the telephone company must be paid soon, so clearly the account credited must be a current liability. However, in practice, the actual account credited may vary. Some companies use an account called Accrued Expenses to record the liabilities created as a result of accruing expenses during the adjustment process. For many companies, all current liabilities from relatively minor, ongoing operating expenses are recorded in the Accounts Payable account. In the purest sense, Accounts Payable should reflect only amounts owed to suppliers, so many companies put other accrued expenses in separate accounts. For purposes of illustration, we assume Ace has individual accounts for these items. Thus, Ace's adjusting entry to accrue the expense would be:

```
Telephone Expense                200
     Telephone Expense Payable        200
```

The adjusting entry above will increase Telephone Expense and Telephone Expense Payable, to more accurately reflect the cost of operating the company during the financial statement period. The increase in Telephone Expense will increase Ace's total expenses, causing the company's net income for the period to be lower than it would have been without the adjustment. The lower net income will be reflected on Ace's income statement, and it will also be seen in a lower amount being added to the company's retained earnings. In addition, the recording of the liability will cause an increase in Ace's total liabilities. Again, even though Ace has spent no cash related to this phone bill, the amount of expense and liability must be recorded to properly reflect the company's 1995 business activity.

Now you have seen basic examples of accruals of revenue and expense. As you explore the adjustment process, you will face a variety of situations requiring accruals. Several features of accruals will always hold true, regardless of the specific situation:

-- Accrual adjustments take place before the related cash flow has happened. In our examples, Ace's accrued revenue was recorded before the cash from Bowden was received, and the accrued expense was recorded before cash was spent to pay the telephone bill.

-- Accruals are based on the foundations of accrual accounting. In our examples, Ace's revenue was accrued because it was *earned*, and the accrued expense was recorded because it was incurred to support the business activities of the financial statement period.

-- Adjustments to reflect accruals never affect the Cash account. This was certainly the case in the accrual of revenues and expenses for Ace.

Keeping these characteristics of accruals in mind, we can move on to the second major type of adjustments, deferrals.

DEFERRALS

These are adjustments related to situations in which a transaction has already been recorded in the company's accounting records, but the recognition of revenue or expense must be reevaluated. As you recall, in the examples of accrued revenues and accrued expenses, no record of the activity had been made prior to the adjustment process. This is the biggest distinction between accruals and deferrals. Deferrals relate to items which have already been recorded in the company's records, but which require adjustment to properly reflect the amount of revenue or expense for the period. As we will see, when dealing with deferrals, how these initial entries are made will determine what adjustments will be necessary. As with accruals, there are two types of deferrals: deferred revenues and deferred expenses.

Deferred Revenues

As was the case when determining how to make accruals, we rely on the foundations of accrual accounting to guide the adjusting process when dealing with deferrals. When determining the amount of revenue a company should report in a particular period, the basic rule is to recognize the revenue that has been *earned*. That sounds simple enough, but sometimes transactions related to revenues are recorded *before* any revenue is earned. Then, during the adjustment process, entries must be made to properly reflect the amount of revenue actually earned during the period.

For example, assume Ace Cleaning Service signed a contract with a new customer near the end of its December 31 year-end. Since the new customer is a small business without established credit, Ace required payment in advance. Ace agreed to clean the offices of Kemp's Temps (a temporary employment service) from November 1, 1995 to January 31, 1996 for a total of $750. When Kemp's Temps paid Ace for the service on November 1, Ace recorded the receipt of cash as:

```
Cash                            750
       Service Revenue                  750
```

At the end of the accounting period, December 31, the Cash general ledger account and the Service Revenue account would still reflect the $750 paid by Kemp's Temps. The $750 in cash *was* received, so the Cash account does not require adjusting. However, based on accrual accounting, we know Ace should only report revenues that have been *earned*. As of December 31, Ace has performed cleaning service for November and December, two of the three months. Therefore, the Service Revenue account should reflect an amount corresponding to those two months' service only. Without any adjustment to the Service Revenue account, Ace would be overstating its revenues for the year.

To bring the Service Revenue account down to the proper amount, reflecting only two months' service, we should debit Service Revenue for the one month's cleaning fee that has not yet been earned. The debit to Service Revenue for $250 ($750/3) is only half of the adjusting entry. Now, we need to determine the credit portion of the adjustment. What does the $250 represent? As described before, it is the charge for one month's cleaning service that has not yet been earned. Think about the situation Ace is in as of December 31. As of that date, the company has earned $500 of the $750, but what about the other $250? Ace *owes* the service to Kemp's Temps or owes them a refund of the $250. In either case, the $250, one-month portion of the amount originally received and recorded represents something Ace *owes*. Therefore, the amount should be reflected in a liability account.

Amounts received in advance from customers, and not yet earned as of the financial statement date, are generally called **Unearned Revenue**. Don't let the name confuse you. Focus on the word "unearned". This key word indicates the amount cannot be reflected on the company's income statement as a revenue, and it is in fact a liability until the company either refunds the customer's money or performs the service necessary to earn the amount. Either action would allow the company to eliminate the unearned revenue liability. Now, we've determined the necessary adjustment for Ace to recognize the proper amount of revenue related to its business with Kemp's Temps:

```
Service Revenue                      250
      Unearned Revenue                        250
```

The adjusting entry above reduces Ace's revenues which would result in a lower net income than would have been reported without the adjustment. The lower net income figure will cause a lower retained earnings balance than would have been the case if the adjustment had not been made. In addition, recording the unearned revenue amount will increase Ace's total liabilities. But the main purpose of the adjusting process is to make the account balances reflect the company's true position according to the guidelines of accrual accounting. Let's use T-accounts to illustrate the impact of the adjusting entry on the account balances involved. In the following illustration, we indicate postings from the original entry (when the cash was received) by the letter O, and the postings from the adjusting entry by the letter A.

```
        Cash                 Service Revenue           Unearned Revenue
  (O)  750                          750 (O)                    250 (A)
                        (A)  250    _____
                                     500
```

To make certain you understand the events illustrated above, let's take one more look. On November 1, Ace received $750 from Kemp's Temps for three months' cleaning service. That transaction resulted in the recording of the original journal entry. Its effect is shown in the Cash account and Service Revenue. As of December 31, Ace realized it had not yet earned the entire amount, and could not report all $750 as revenue. Through an adjusting entry, one month's worth of the amount ($250) was removed from Service Revenue and recorded in a liability account, Unearned Revenue. The resulting balance in Service Revenue, $500, reflects the amount which Ace can properly report as revenue. The T-accounts above show that the adjusting entry served its intended purpose — the proper amount of revenue and liability are shown.

The adjustment described above was a direct result of the recording of a revenue before it was earned. In this case, the receipt of cash prompted the original transaction, which resulted in the need for an adjustment at the end of the financial statement period. Recall we said the adjustments related to deferrals are determined by *how* the initial activity is recorded. Because of this, in the case of deferrals, you must know how the original transaction was recorded before the proper adjustment can be determined. Let's take another look at the activity between Ace Cleaning Service and Kemp's Temps to see how this works.

On November 1, 1995 Ace Cleaning Service received $750 from Kemp's Temps for services to be provided during November, December and January. That is a fact. The facts can't be changed, but the way the company records the transaction can. Certainly, cash was received, and the Cash account must be debited for $750. Even that part of the entry can't be changed, but what about the credit? Recall in the earlier recording of this transaction, Ace recorded the entire amount in Service Revenue. Then, at the end of the period, the account balances were adjusted to reflect the proper amounts. But on November 1, what other account besides Service Revenue could Ace have used to reflect the payment received in advance from its customer? Since you already know that a portion of the $750 will end up in Unearned Revenue after the adjustment process is complete, that account is a logical one to choose. But also, think about what really happened on November 1. The cash was received before any service had been performed, so recording the entire amount as a liability at that point would be very logical. Ace Cleaning Service could have recorded the receipt of cash from Kemp's Temps on November 1 as:

```
Cash                            750
      Unearned Revenue                750
```

The entry above is no better or worse than recording the cash receipt as an increase in the Service Revenue account. Either way, adjustments are needed to bring the account balances to the point that they properly reflect Ace's position as of December 31. If the November 1 transaction had been recorded as shown above, prior to any adjusting entry, Ace's accounting records would have reflected a $750 liability as of December 31. But, in fact, some of that liability had been "paid-off" by performing two months' service for Kemp's Temps. How much should really be in the Unearned Revenue account? Only the amount related to the one month's service which has not yet been performed. So, the balance in Unearned Revenue *should be* only $250. Therefore, we must make an adjusting entry to reduce the liability by $500, the amount related to the two months of service Ace has already performed. To reduce Unearned Revenue, we debit the account for $500, but what should the credit portion of the adjusting entry be? Think about what the $500 represents — it represents the amount which Ace has earned as of December 31. Therefore, we should increase the company's Service Revenue account with a $500 credit. Now we have it — the adjusting entry needed on December 31 is:

```
Unearned Revenue                500
      Service Revenue                 500
```

This adjusting entry increases the amount of revenue recorded, which increases Ace's net income compared to what it would have been if the adjustment weren't made. The higher net income would result in a higher retained earnings balance than what the company would have had if the adjustment had not been made. The debit to Unearned Revenue reduces Ace's liabilities.

Now, let's once again use T-accounts to illustrate the impact of the original entry and the adjusting entry on the accounts affected. Again, O is for original entry; A is for adjusting entry.

```
        Cash              Service Revenue        Unearned Revenue
  ───────────────        ───────────────        ───────────────
  (O)  750                         500 (A)                750 (O)
                                                 (A)  500  ─────
                                                            250
```

Notice that the entire original amount was recorded as a liability. No revenue was recognized when the transaction was originally recorded. During the adjustment process, the amount Ace had earned as of December 31 was removed from the Unearned Revenue account and recognized as revenue.

Take a moment to compare this set of T-accounts with the previous ones. What is important for you to see is that the original transaction may be recorded in different ways, but after the necessary adjustments, all account balances should properly reflect the company's position. The ending balances in Unearned Revenue and Service Revenue are the same, regardless of the way the original transaction was recorded. Also notice that the two adjusting entries are very different. Whether the accounts are debited or credited, and the dollar amounts are different because of the difference in how the original entry was made.

The way original transactions are recorded impacts *all* adjustments related to deferrals. We explored Ace's experience with deferred revenues; now it's time to look into deferred expenses.

Deferred Expenses

Adjustments relating to deferred expenses are necessary when a company has recorded transactions related to expenses before the expenses are incurred. Accrual accounting requires that expenses be recognized during the periods when the benefit is received or the item is "used up" to support the earning activity of the company. When companies record expenses in advance, adjusting entries are often needed so that expenses for the period are properly reflected.

For example, assume Ace Cleaning Service recently moved its office. Because of the excess demand for its office space, the landlords require tenants to pay rent quarterly, in advance. Ace moved into its office space on December 1, and paid the landlord $1,500 for three months' rent. The entry to record the payment on Ace's books was:

```
        Rent Expense                    1,500
             Cash                               1,500
```

At the end of the accounting period, December 31, the Rent Expense account would still reflect the impact of this entry. But expenses should reflect what has been "used up" to support the operation of the business. The truth is that as of December 31, only a portion (one month's worth) of the $1,500 has been used up. The remaining two months' worth of rent will provide Ace with office space for the first two months of next year. The amount related to January and February rent should not be reported as an expense as of December 31 because it has not been used up. Rather, this amount will provide a future benefit, and therefore, should be shown as an asset.

An adjusting entry is required to reduce the Rent Expense account so that it only reflects the one month's worth of rent ($500) that has been used up. The amount related to two months' worth of rent ($1,000) must be removed from Rent Expense and shown as an asset because it will provide future benefit to Ace. As we described in Module 1, expenses paid in advance are called prepaid expenses. The Prepaid Rent account will be used to represent the asset Ace has as a result of paying this expense in advance. Thus, the adjusting entry related to Ace's payment of rent in advance is:

Prepaid Rent	1,000	
Rent Expense		1,000

This adjustment will reduce Ace's total expenses to the proper amount, causing a higher net income than the company would have reported without the adjustment. The higher net income would result in a higher retained earnings balance than the company would have had if the adjustment had not been made. The debit to Prepaid Rent causes an increase in Ace's total assets.

Let's take a look at how the original entry and the subsequent adjustment affected the account balances of Ace Cleaning Service. Only three accounts were affected:

```
        Cash                  Rent Expense              Prepaid Rent
_____    _____    _____
     | 1,500 (O)      (O) 1,500 |              (A) 1,000 |
     |                          | 1,000 (A)             |
     |                    _____|                       |
     |                      500 |                       |
     |                          |                       |
```

Notice when the $1,500 was paid, Ace recorded the entire amount as Rent Expense. Only $500 of the original amount had been used up by December 31, so the balance in the Rent Expense account should have been only $500. The $1,000 related to rent for January and February of the next year had to be removed from Rent Expense and reported as an asset expected to provide future benefit to the company. The adjusting entry did just that.

As was the case with deferred revenues, the original transactions related to deferred expenses can be recorded in two different ways. In the illustration above, we assumed Ace recorded the $1,500 paid on December 1 as rent expense. But what if Ace's bookkeeper, realizing the amount was for rent paid in advance, originally recorded the $1,500 payment as an increase to the asset account, Prepaid Rent, instead? Not a problem. Either original entry is fine. The important thing is that the account balances be adjusted to present the truth before financial statements are prepared. If the payment of rent in advance had been recorded as an increase in an asset account, the original entry on December 1 would have been:

```
      Prepaid Rent                      1,500
         Cash                                    1,500
```

In this case, on December 31, the asset account Prepaid Rent would reflect the entire $1,500, but that balance does not properly present the company's true position. One month's worth of rent has been used up, and only two months' worth should be considered an asset as of December 31. The amount related to December's rent ($500) should be taken out of the asset account and recorded as an expense. Rent Expense is debited to reflect the increase and Prepaid Rent is credited to reduce the balance in the asset account. The adjusting entry, then, is as follows:

```
      Rent Expense                       500
         Prepaid Rent                            500
```

After the impact of this adjusting entry, Ace's account balances should reflect the company's true position — one month's worth of rent was used up this period, and two months' worth have been paid for and will provide future benefit to the company.

Cash	Rent Expense	Prepaid Rent
1,500 (O)	(A) 500	(O) 1,500
		_____ 500 (A)
		1,000

As you can see, even when the original recording of expenses paid in advance is shown as an increase in assets (prepaid expenses), with proper adjustments, the account balances will reflect the company's true position. Take a moment to compare these T-accounts to those showing the original transaction recorded as a debit to Rent Expense. Again, the account being debited and the account being credited, as well as the dollar amounts of the two adjusting entries are different. Clearly, the proper adjustment for deferred expenses cannot be determined without knowing how the original transaction was recorded. Is one way of recording expenses in advance better than the other? No. What's important is that the accounts be properly adjusted before financial statements are prepared.

Now you have seen basic examples of adjustments related to both deferred revenue and deferred expense. As you continue to learn about the adjustment process, you will face a variety of situations requiring these types of adjustments. Several characteristics of adjustments related to deferrals will always hold true:

-- Adjustments related to deferrals of revenue or expense take place *after* the transaction was originally recorded. In our examples, Ace's adjustments related to transactions recording cash received in advance from a customer, and the recording of rent paid in advance.

-- Adjustments related to deferrals of revenue or expense are based on the foundations of accrual accounting. In our examples, Ace's adjustments recorded only the amount of revenue *earned* even when the related cash was received in advance, and only the amount of expense *incurred* even when the entire amount was recorded in advance.

$3,650. The resulting figure when an asset's accumulated depreciation is subtracted from its original cost is also referred to as the net asset amount, but often this figure is untitled on balance sheets.

Even though the balance sheet presentation of long-lived assets may be familiar to you, what you may not know is: What type of account is Accumulated Depreciation? It appears on the balance sheet, so it can't be a revenue or expense. In fact, if you look at the adjusting entry to record depreciation, you will see that as Depreciation Expense is increased with a debit, Accumulated Depreciation is credited, which increases that account, too. The balance in Accumulated Depreciation is increased every time more depreciation expense is recorded. In fact, by definition, accumulated depreciation is the amount of depreciation that has been recorded on the asset thus far. The account balance shows how much of the asset's original cost has been converted to expense. As time passes and depreciation expense is recorded, the balance in Accumulated Depreciation rises as well. So, what is this account that has a credit balance, but appears in the asset section of the balance sheet?

As shown in the excerpt from Ace's balance sheet, accumulated depreciation is a reduction of the asset. Accumulated Depreciation is referred to as a **contra-asset account**. As explained in Module 2, contra accounts follow debit/credit rules opposite of those applied to their related accounts. Thus, contra-asset accounts have normal balances opposite of assets — they are increased with credits. A contra-asset account works against the associated asset account in the sense that the balance in the contra-asset account is subtracted from the asset account when shown on a balance sheet.

Contra-asset accounts such as Accumulated Depreciation are always listed immediately following their corresponding asset account. Not only are the asset and contra-asset shown together on the balance sheet, but in the general ledger, the accumulated depreciation account associated with a particular asset is assigned an account number that would place it in the general ledger immediately following that asset account. At this point, Accumulated Depreciation may be the only contra-asset with which you are familiar. However, as you encounter others, you will find these characteristics to be true for them as well.

Now that we have learned about the adjustment process, and the types of adjusting entries that are made, let's apply what we have learned to the accounting records of Amanda's Typing Service. After adjusting entries have been recorded and posted to the ledger accounts, the account balances should provide the information needed to prepare financial statements. So, let's proceed to make the necessary adjusting entries for Amanda's Typing Service, and then prepare the company's financial statements.

THE ADJUSTING PROCESS FOR AMANDA'S TYPING SERVICE

In the examples from Ace Cleaning Service, the specific situations requiring adjusting entries were pointed out for you. But certainly in an actual business setting, the scenarios would not present themselves as clearly as they did in the examples. Recall that the adjustment process was described as a *review* of the account balances to determine if they properly reflected the company's activity for the period. Indeed, the adjustment process requires an evaluation of each account balance to determine if it needs any adjusting. Clearly, in order to determine the proper adjustments, the accountant would have to be familiar with the basic operation. The adjustment process is a thinking process. No two companies are the same, and certainly the reality of each company's specific transactions will be different. The adjusting entries will vary from business to business, but a clear understanding of the purpose of adjustments will serve you well as you try to evaluate account balances.

If we are to review the balance in each account, we could find that information in two different forms. Recall from Module 3 that after posting all the entries for the month, we recorded the ending balance of each account in the general ledger. After that, we summarized the account balances in the trial balance. The trial balance is a more concise presentation of the information we need, so our evaluation will begin there. It is common practice to rely on the information in a trial balance to begin the evaluation of account balances. Then, if more detailed information is needed, we will look to the general ledger or the journal. Let's begin our adjustment process for Amanda's Typing Service with a look at the trial balance prepared in Module 3.

Amanda's Typing Service Trial Balance As of January 31, 1996		
Cash	$ 1,300	
Accounts Receivable	2,100	
Supplies	300	
Prepaid Insurance	1,200	
Office Furniture	2,500	
Computer System	7,000	
Accounts Payable		$ 5,200
Notes Payable		5,000
Common Stock		3,000
Dividends	500	
Service Revenue		2,900
Wage Expense	1,100	
Delivery Expense	100	
	$16,100	$16,100

The account balances reflected above show the results of business activity through January 31, 1996. Let's assume that now, on February 2, 1996 we are ready to begin the adjustment process. Remember, our goal is to make any necessary adjustments so that we have account balances which properly reflect the business activity during the period ending January 31. Our examination of the account balances will proceed through the accounts one-by-one in the order presented in the trial balance above.

Cash — As we said earlier, accrual and deferral adjustments don't affect the Cash account. However, cash is an important asset and it is crucial that the account balance be reviewed to determine that it properly reflects the amount of cash held by the company as of the financial statement date. In the case of Amanda's Typing Service, our review indicates that no adjustment to the Cash account is necessary.

Accounts Receivable — Amanda's Typing Service follows the common practice of recording revenue and the corresponding receivable when a bill is issued to the customer. Bills are issued upon completion of each job. For steady customers, Amanda's delivers the work as soon as it is completed, and sends the customer a bill. One thing that must be ascertained is that all billings for work completed during the month were recorded during the month. As it turns out, a small job ($45) for one of the company's best customers was completed on January 30. Since that customer is having more work done during the first week in February, a separate bill for the January 30 work was not prepared. Once that fact is uncovered, an adjusting entry must be made to record the revenue earned by completion of the work on January 30. The necessary adjusting entry is:

General Journal				Page 3	
Date 1996		Description	Post Ref	Debit	Credit
Jan.	31	Accounts Receivable		45	
		Service Revenue			45
		Adjustment to record work			
		completed on Jan. 30			

In addition to jobs completed near the end of the accounting period, another common source of adjustments to Accounts Receivable is work that is only partially completed at the end of the period. In the case of Amanda's Typing Service, the medical clinic has agreed to pay $800 for transcripts of all the doctors' tapes generated during January. As of January 31, transcripts corresponding to three weeks of tapes have been prepared. Again, since bills are not issued until the work is completed, the clinic has not yet been billed, and no record of the work done has been reflected in the accounting records.

Under accrual accounting, we should recognize the revenue earned by January 31 on the company's financial statements. Therefore, an adjusting entry is necessary to record the portion of the $800 which has been earned. Since three of the four weeks' worth of tapes have been transcribed, 3/4 of the $800 should be recognized as revenue this period:

	31	Accounts Receivable		600	
		Service Revenue			600
		3 weeks of January tapes			
		from medical clinic			

Both of these examples affect Accounts Receivable. At the same time that Accounts Receivable is being adjusted, the Service Revenue account is also being brought to its proper balance. Are these adjustments accruals, deferrals, or others? These are accruals. We can tell because the entries are recording revenue that has been earned, but has not yet been recorded. The adjustments record the proper amount of revenue for the period in spite of the fact that a formal bill has not yet been sent to the customer.

Supplies — This is an asset account, so the current balance of $300 should reflect the amount offering future benefit to the company. If Amanda's Typing Service used up any supplies during the month, an amount should be shown in an expense account. The trial balance indicates that no balance exists in an expense account related to supplies. To determine if an adjustment to the Supplies account is necessary, you must determine if the balance reflects reality. The balance suggests that Amanda's Typing Service has $300 of supplies on hand, available to provide future benefit to the company. If an asset such as supplies is a significant item, and may materially affect the accounting information, a careful count of the amount of supplies on hand would be necessary. However, in many businesses, supplies are not tracked very closely, and at the end of the period, an evaluation of the supply room or supply closet is made to determine a fair amount to report in the asset account.

After examining the supplies inventory, it is determined that only $120 of supplies were on hand at the end of January, so the Supplies account must be adjusted to show an ending balance of $120. If the Supplies account has a debit balance of $300, but it *should* show a debit balance of $120, what adjustment is necessary? A credit to Supplies for $180 is necessary to bring the account down to its proper balance. But what account should be debited? What does the $180 represent? It is the amount of supplies no longer on hand, the amount "used up". Expense accounts reflect amounts of assets used up during the period, so the debit must be to Supplies Expense:

	31	Supplies Expense		180	
		Supplies			180
		adjustment to show actual			
		amount of supplies on hand			

What type of an adjustment is shown above? This entry relates to deferred expenses. As was the case with the example of Ace Cleaning Service's Prepaid Rent account, the adjustment results from the payment of expenses in advance. At the time supplies were purchased, the transaction was recorded as an increase in an asset account, Supplies. However, supplies are intended to be used to help generate revenue, so buying supplies before you need to use them is a form of paying for expenses in advance.

The trial balance did not show a Supplies Expense account for Amanda's Typing Service. Can we record an adjustment to an account not included on the trial balance? Certainly. Often, if an account balance is zero, the account is not even listed on the trial balance. But even if the company did not have an established Supplies Expense account, the adjustment situation clearly signaled a need for the account, and one would be created. During the adjustment process, new accounts or those with zero balances are often affected — you should not assume that adjusting entries will affect only accounts on the company's trial balance.

The fact that Amanda's Typing Service showed no balance in Supplies Expense actually provided important information. This adjustment situation related to deferred expense, and as you will recall, adjustments of this type are dependent on how the original entry is recorded. The fact that no balance existed in the Supplies Expense account suggests that if supplies were purchased during the period, those transactions were recorded as increases to the asset account Supplies rather than to Supplies Expense.

Prepaid Insurance — This one's too easy. You already know what to do! Prepaid Insurance is an asset account. If any of the insurance coverage expired or was "used up", the amount should be seen in an expense account. Amanda's Typing Service shows no such account on its trial balance, but we can create one. Now we have to determine how much insurance coverage expired during January. How could you find out the terms of an insurance policy? You may have to investigate. The company may have files on such items, and gathering the necessary information might mean digging through files. In a larger company, there may be someone assigned to insurance coverage for all the facets of the operation. Often the adjustment process leads to an exploration of records beyond the scope of the accounting records.

In the case of Amanda's Typing Service, where can we find details of the terms of the insurance coverage? Let's revisit the company's general journal. This excerpt from the journal shows the entry to record the purchase of the insurance policy:

	7	Prepaid Insurance	180	1,200	
		Cash	110		1,200
		Liability coverage for one year			

Here's an example of the information in the description being helpful. If the $1,200 is for an entire year, each month's worth of coverage cost $100 ($1,200/12). This suggests that as each month passes, $100 of the asset Prepaid Insurance should be converted to expense. The adjusting entry required would be:

	31	Insurance Expense		100	
		Prepaid Insurance			100
		one month's premium expired			

This adjustment relates to deferred expenses, just as the previous entry to record Supplies Expense did. Be sure you understand that this adjustment would be totally different if Amanda's Typing Service had recorded the initial purchase of the policy as an increase in

Insurance Expense instead of Prepaid Insurance.

The adjusting entry above raises another issue... As of January 31, was a month's worth of coverage used up? Technically, no. The general journal shows the policy was purchased on January 7, so only 25 days of coverage had expired by the end of the month. If the policy were purchased on January 7, and the $1,200 bought coverage for one year, how much of the prepaid insurance had expired as of January 31? A calculation could be performed to determine a more precise amount of insurance expense for the first month's operations. Should that be done? Let's consider the pros and cons of the issue.

First of all, why would the company want to record an entire month's insurance when it has only used up 25 days of coverage? Two reasons come to mind, both of which relate to the ease of recording. The adjusting entry could be described in the journal as reflecting the expiration of a month's worth of insurance coverage; then, if nothing had changed by the end of next month, a new calculation would be unnecessary. Each month for twelve months, $100 of the prepaid insurance would be converted to expense. This leads to the second reason the company may wish to record a full month's worth of insurance expense. Think about the life of the insurance policy. If the cost of only 25 days of coverage is expensed the first month, and for each of the next eleven months, a full month's worth is expensed, a few days' coverage will have to be expensed next January. Again, the primary reasons for wishing to record an entire month's worth of insurance expense relate to the inner workings of the recording process. But is that reason enough to do it?

Without performing the calculations, think about the impact of recording a whole month's worth of insurance expense instead of only 25 days' worth. If a whole month's worth is only $100, how much less could 25 days' worth be? If we changed the adjusting entry to reflect only 25 days of insurance coverage, what impact would there be on the company's financial statements? Would reducing the reported amount of insurance expense by a few dollars have any impact on someone's evaluation of the performance of Amanda's Typing Service?

The concept we have run into is known as materiality. During the recording process, every effort should be made to record amounts properly and precisely, but the concept of materiality allows us to make choices to record items in ways that forego some precision for efficiency *if* the decision makers relying on the financial statement information would not be affected by the choice. In this case, decisions made by the readers of the company's financial statements would not be affected by the overstatement of a few dollars of insurance expense — materiality allows this choice. It is important that you understand materiality is a judgment call, and that it is relative. In other words, if the situation we have encountered dealt with several hundred dollars instead of several dollars, some might argue the difference would be material. Certainly, if the amount involved were several thousand dollars, the difference would be material to Amanda's Typing Service. But a difference of even ten thousand dollars might not be a material difference to General Motors or IBM or any major corporation. The test of materiality is: In the context of the choice at hand, would it affect the decision made by someone relying on the financial statement information? In the case of Amanda's Typing Service, choosing to record the full month's insurance expense is acceptable because the difference is immaterial.

Office Furniture — When reviewing long-lived asset accounts, the obvious adjustment which needs to be made is to record depreciation. Previously recorded depreciation would be reflected in the Accumulated Depreciation account. However, since our adjustments are for the company's first month of operation, no depreciation has yet been recorded on the office furniture. To determine the amount of depreciation, we must know management's estimates of: (1) the asset's useful life, and (2) the asset's residual value. These estimates may be made and noted when the asset is purchased, or the issue may not even be considered until the need for the estimates arises.

In the case of Amanda's Typing Service, the necessary estimates were not made when the office furniture was purchased. Before depreciation can be recorded, management must establish estimates of the furniture's useful life and residual value. After careful consideration, it was decided that the office furniture should have an estimated useful life of five years. After five years of heavy use, it is estimated that it will have a residual value of $100. Using straight-line depreciation, we can calculate the monthly depreciation expense as:

$$\frac{\$2,500 - \$100}{5} \quad X \quad 1/12 \quad = \quad \$40$$

Again, the issue of materiality could be raised because the office furniture was bought on January 9, but clearly if $40 is an entire month's worth, the difference in reporting the exact amount would be immaterial. The adjusting entry needed is:

31	Depreciation Expense, Office Furn.		40	
	Accumulated Dep, Office F.			40
	5-yr. useful life; $100 residual			
	value; one month's recorded			

Since this is the first entry regarding the depreciation of the office furniture, it would result in the first activity in these two ledger accounts. Anticipating the depreciation of the furniture, the bookkeeper may have opened these ledger accounts when the items were purchased, or the ledger accounts may need to be created when this adjusting entry is posted. In any case, the fact that these accounts were not included on the company's trial balance will not prevent us from recording the entry.

Is this adjustment an accrual, a deferral, or an other? Recording of depreciation is neither an accrual or a deferral — it falls in the category of other adjustments.

Computer System — Another long-lived asset requiring an adjusting entry to record depreciation. The management of Amanda's Typing Service considered carefully the future use of the computer system, and decided with the changes in technology, the asset's estimated useful life should be only four years. At the end of four years, the computer system is expected to have a residual value of $1,000. Monthly depreciation is calculated as:

$$\frac{\$7,000 - \$1,000}{4} \quad X \quad 1/12 \quad = \quad \$125$$

The entry is nothing new:

General Journal				Page 4	
Date 1996		Description	Post Ref	Debit	Credit
Jan.	31	Depreciation Expense, Computer		125	
		Accumulated Dep., Computer			125
		4-year useful life; $1000 residual			
		value; one month's recorded			

From the entries related to the computer system and the office furniture, we can tell that the company's general ledger will have individual accounts for the depreciation expense and accumulated depreciation of each long-lived asset. Particularly with regard to accumulated depreciation, having separate accounts will be helpful when we prepare financial statements for Amanda's Typing Service. Think of how the assets will be shown on the balance sheet. Remember, the contra-asset account (accumulated depreciation) for each asset will be shown as a reduction of the cost of the asset.

Accounts Payable — The evaluation of Accounts Payable should determine if all the amounts owed for expenses incurred during the financial statement period were included in the account balance. Note that the balance should include amounts still owed for the expenses incurred in the period, not just the bills received during the period. Looking at the bills received in the first few days of the next period will help determine what amounts relate to the first period. Sometimes, talking with those employees who deal with the payment of the company's bills, you may be able to determine if bills expected to arrive in the next few days will be for expenses incurred during the first period. Whether the bills have been received or not, the amounts need to be included in Accounts Payable if the expenses supported the operations for the financial statement period.

After discussing the matter with Amanda, we discover that one amount the company owes was never recorded: the phone bill. It is important to record all the amounts Amanda's Typing Service owed as of January 31 before preparing financial statements. Even if the bill was not received in January, an entry to record January telephone costs must be made:

	31	Telephone Expense		56	
		Accounts Payable			56
		January service (accrued)			

This is an accrual of an expense. That is, we are recording an expense that has not yet been recorded. The entry above is similar to the one in the example of Ace Cleaning Service.

Note that Amanda's Typing Service has decided to record amounts owed for minor operating expenses in the Accounts Payable account rather than create separate liability accounts. As we said earlier, this decision is simply a matter of preference, and will depend on whether the company wishes to report separate liabilities for the various types of expenses. Either method is acceptable.

Notes Payable — Is the balance in this account an accurate reflection of the company's situation with regard to the amount borrowed from the bank? Yes and no. Since only one note was signed, the accuracy of the balance in Notes Payable is easy to verify. Yes, $5,000 is the amount borrowed from the bank, and it must be repaid in 18 months. No adjustment to Notes Payable is needed, but the existence of an outstanding loan should trigger a thought as we review these accounts.

When the loan is repaid, Amanda's Typing Service must pay the bank the $5,000 borrowed plus interest. Even though the interest will not be paid until the loan is repaid, interest expense is being incurred as each day passes. In other words, the company is being charged interest for each day it holds the borrowed funds. If the loan were repaid today, the amount due would be the $5,000 principal and a small amount of interest. If the company waits until the loan is due (in 18 months) the amount due will be the $5,000 plus 18 months' worth of interest. The point is that as each day passes, interest expense is incurred, and to get an accurate picture of the expenses incurred by Amanda's Typing Service to support the January operations, it is necessary to record the amount of interest expense related to holding the borrowed funds for the month.

Where would you find details of the terms of the loan such as the interest rate? Certainly, a copy of the actual promissory note Amanda signed on behalf of the company should be in the company's files. This information could also have been included in the description of the entry to record the loan transaction in the company's general journal. The records of Amanda's Typing Service include a file folder marked "Financing", a likely prospect for information about the bank loan. Indeed, from the information in the file we have determined that the $5,000 was borrowed at 9% interest. Since the funds were borrowed on January 3, we will record one month's interest, calculated as follows:

```
Principal    X    Rate    X    Time    =    Interest

 $5,000      X    .09     X    1/12    =    $37.50
```

In the calculation of interest, the principal is the amount which is earning interest revenue or incurring interest expense. In this case, the principal is the amount borrowed. Keep in mind that interest rates are always stated in annual terms. That is, the 9% above indicates how much interest expense would be incurred for *a year* (not for the life of the note). In other words, a 9% note incurs interest at the rate of 9% per year regardless of whether the note is for 6 months, nine months, or as in this case, eighteen months. In the calculation above, the interest for a year would be $5,000 X .09. However, since we wanted to determine only one month's interest, the time factor used was 1/12.

Now that we have calculated the *amount* of interest, we must determine what accounts should be affected and how they should be affected to indicate the impact of the interest. Think about what the adjusting entry must show. The entry should show that interest expense has been incurred, but not yet paid for. To show an increase, we debit Interest Expense. The unpaid interest is an amount the company *owes*, even though the bank doesn't expect payment of the interest until the loan is repaid. To reflect an increase in the amount a company owes, a liability account is credited. Therefore, the adjusting entry to record interest on funds borrowed by Amanda's Typing Service is:

	31	Interest Expense		37. 50	
		Interest Payable			37. 50
		$5,000 X .09 X 1/12			
		18-Month Note — First Friendly Bank			

What type of adjustment is shown above? This entry reflects an accrual. Interest expense is being recorded to show the amount incurred during the period but not yet paid.

Common Stock — Think about the entry reflected in this account. The company issued stock. This transaction reflected an exchange of ownership interest in the corporation for assets (in this case, cash). Since stockholders' equity accounts such as this one are not directly related to the recording of revenues or expenses, adjustments related to properly following the revenue and expense recognition guidelines of accrual accounting do not generally affect these accounts. In the case of Amanda's Typing Service, a review of the account balance determines that the issuance of stock, the only transaction recorded in this account, was recorded properly.

Dividends — Again, as a component of stockholders' equity, the Dividends account generally does not require adjustment, unless of course, an error has been discovered. However, in the case of Amanda's Typing Service, the single transaction recorded in the Dividends account is correct.

Service Revenue — Recall that two adjustments to this account were made as a result of the review of Accounts Receivable. Actually, the recording of receivables and revenue are so closely related that the same adjustments would likely have been determined if the review had been considered a review of the Service Revenue account. In any case, the important point is that all revenues earned during the period must be recorded during the period, regardless of whether the cash has been received.

In addition to being certain no revenues of the period were overlooked, it is crucial that prior to the preparation of financial statements, revenue accounts not include any amounts not yet earned. Recall the example of Ace Cleaning Service. In one scenario, when cash was received in advance from a customer, the company recorded the transaction as an increase in revenue. When the revenue account is reviewed during the adjustment process, this type of transaction should be examined to be certain that only the amount *earned* by the end of the period be left in that account. By talking to Amanda, it was determined that Amanda's Typing Service received no payments in advance from its customers, and no adjustments besides those uncovered during the review of Accounts Receivable are needed.

Wage Expense — Since wages are an ongoing expense, incurred throughout each period of operation, it is important that the proper amount of wage expense be reflected in the accounting records before the information is used in financial statements. How can we determine the proper amount that should be shown as January wage expense for Amanda's Typing Service?

The balance showing in Wage Expense is $1,100. A review of the general ledger account shows that only one entry was posted to that account. The entry recorded in the general journal is:

	25	Wage Expense	710	1,100	
		Cash	110		1,100
		Last payday – Jan. 24 for			
		work through Jan. 20			

In this case, the description written when the entry was recorded is quite helpful. Employees were last paid on January 24, and have been paid for their work through January 20. Paychecks are issued every two weeks, every other Wednesday, for work through the previous Saturday. The next payday is February 7. On that day, checks will be issued reflecting employees' work through February 3. A look at part of a calendar will help us see what adjustment is needed.

JANUARY

Sunday	Monday	Tuesday	Wednesday	Thursday	Friday	Saturday
	1	2	3	4	5	6
7	8	9	10	11	12	13
14	15	16	17	18	19	PAY PERIOD ENDS 20
21	22	23	PAYCHECKS ISSUED 24	25	26	27
28	29	30	31			

FEBRUARY

Sunday	Monday	Tuesday	Wednesday	Thursday	Friday	Saturday
					1	PAY PERIOD ENDS 2 ... 3
4	5	6	PAYCHECKS ISSUED 7	8	9	10
11	12	13	14	15	16	17
18	19	20	21	22	23	24
25	26	27	28	29	30	

The financial statements for the period ending January 31 must reflect the wages earned by employees through January 31. As of January 31, Amanda's Typing Service had incurred wage expense for employees' work from January 21 through January 31, even though the company will not pay the workers until February 7. Remember, under accrual accounting, expenses are recorded as incurred regardless of whether they have as yet been paid.

The information needed to adjust the Wage Expense account may be gathered from a payroll clerk or other company employee. For Amanda's Typing Service, a review of the time sheets for the company's part-time employees indicates from January 21 through January 31, they worked a total of 98 hours and earned $612.50. The appropriate adjusting entry is:

	31	Wage Expense		612.50	
		Wages Payable			612.50
		98 hours Jan. 21 - Jan.31			

The entry above reflects an accrual of expenses. Amanda's Typing Service incurred the expense during the income statement period, but as of January 31, the amount was unpaid. The unpaid amount is generally recorded in a liability account separate from the company's accounts payable because the nature of the debt is different — wages are owed to the company's own employees rather than other business entities.

Since seldom would the pay period and the income statement period end on the same day, the accrual of wages or salaries is quite common. Again, the purpose of the adjusting process is to make the account balances properly reflect the company's financial position as of the financial statement date. This accrual for Amanda's Typing Service results in the presentation of proper amounts for both wage expense and the associated liability.

Before we leave the topic of employees' wages, it is important to note that the example above is a good illustration of the accrual of basic wage expense, but the presentation is highly simplified. The payment of employees' wages is much more complex than the example suggests. Due to state and federal income tax, social security, and other complications, payroll records may become quite involved — even businesses of moderate size often have payroll clerks or separate departments whose sole function is the proper recording of all the issues related to the payment of employees. The example from Amanda's Typing Service is a simplistic illustration of the payroll process, but it serves well as a basic example of accruing wage expense.

Delivery Expense — As is the case with the review of any expense account, it is crucial that we determine if the account balance reflects all amounts incurred to support this period's operations, even if the expense will not be paid until next period. The $100 shown in the trial balance reflects the recording of a bill from Speedy Delivery Service received on January 30. Speedy prepares its bills on the last Tuesday of the month and has its delivery personnel deliver them that afternoon. Certainly a bill prepared on January 30 would include the deliveries made for *most* of January. However, during the adjustment process, it would be necessary to check with workers at Amanda's Typing Service to determine if Speedy Delivery Service had made other deliveries during the last few days of the month, not reflected on that bill. Again, our goal is to determine the proper amount of expense that was incurred to support January operations. After exploring the issue, we have determined that $100 is indeed the proper amount of delivery expense incurred in January — no adjustment is needed.

WRAPPING UP THE ADJUSTMENT PROCESS

The review of account balances during the adjustment process for Amanda's Typing Service resulted in the recording of nine adjusting entries in the company's general journal. Recall the purpose of these entries is to make the account balances reflect more accurately results of the company's activities during the period. The account balances, however, are not affected by the process of recording the entries in the journal. The impact of the adjustment process is not realized until the adjusting entries are posted to the general ledger accounts. After posting of the adjusting entries, account balances should reflect amounts which are appropriate for use in financial statements.

On the following pages you will find the general journal pages of Amanda's Typing Service showing the adjusting entries. As the posting reference column indicates, these entries have been posted to the general ledger accounts. An illustration of each of the company's general ledger accounts follows the general journal pages. As you can see, for each account affected by the adjusting entries, a new current balance has been entered.

Date 1996		Description	Post Ref	Debit	Credit
		General Journal			Page 3
Jan.	31	Accounts Receivable	130	45	
		Service Revenue	610		45
		Adjustment to record work			
		completed on Jan. 30			
	31	Accounts Receivable	130	600	
		Service Revenue	610		600
		3 weeks of January tapes			
		from medical clinic			
	31	Supplies Expense	715	180	
		Supplies	170		180
		adjustment to show actual			
		amount of supplies on hand			
	31	Insurance Expense	735	100	
		Prepaid Insurance	180		100
		one month's premium expired			
	31	Depreciation Expense, Office Furn.	720	40	
		Accumulated Dep, Office F.	215		40
		5-yr. useful life; $100 residual			
		value; one month's recorded			

Date 1996		Description	Post Ref	Debit	Credit
Jan.	31	Depreciation Expense, Computer	725	125	
		Accumulated Dep., Computer	225		125
		4-year useful life; $1000 residual			
		value; one month's recorded			
	31	Telephone Expense	750	56	
		Accounts Payable	310		56
		January service (accrued)			
	31	Interest Expense	780	37.50	
		Interest Payable	370		37.50
		$5,000 X .09 X 1/12			
		18-month Note — First Friendly BANK			
	31	Wage Expense	710	612.50	
		Wages Payable	330		612.50
		98 hours Jan. 21 – Jan. 31			

Name of Account: Cash

Account No.: 110

Date 1996		Description	Post Ref	Debit	Credit	Balance Debit	Balance Credit
Jan.	1	Issued stock (1000 shares)	GJ1	3,000			
	3	Note due in 18 months	GJ1	5,000		8,000	
	7		GJ1		1,200	6,800	
	9		GJ1		2,500	4,300	
	11	down payment on computer	GJ1		2,000		
	13		GJ2		200	2,100	
	25		GJ2	800		2,900	
	25		GJ2		1,100		
	31	dividend	GJ2		500	1,300	

Name of Account: Accounts Receivable

Account No.: 130

Date 1996		Description	Post Ref	Debit	Credit	Balance Debit	Balance Credit
Jan.	25		GJ2	2,100		2,100	
	31		GJ3	45			
	31		GJ3	600		2,745	

Name of Account: Supplies

Account No.: 170

Date 1996		Description	Post Ref	Debit	Credit	Balance Debit	Balance Credit
Jan.	5		GJ1	300		300	
	31		GJ3		180	120	

4-28 **THE ADJUSTING PROCESS**

Name of Account: Prepaid Insurance

Account No.: 180

Date 1996		Description	Post Ref	Debit	Credit	Balance Debit	Balance Credit
Jan.	7	liability coverage - 1 year	GJ1	1,200		1,200	
	31		GJ3		100	1,100	

Name of Account: Office Furniture

Account No.: 210

Date 1996		Description	Post Ref	Debit	Credit	Balance Debit	Balance Credit
Jan.	9	desk, table, file cabinet, 3 chairs	GJ1	2,500		2,500	

Name of Account: Accumulated Depreciation, Office Furniture

Account No.: 215

Date 1996		Description	Post Ref	Debit	Credit	Balance Debit	Balance Credit
Jan.	31		GJ3		40		40

Name of Account: Computer System

Account No.: 220

Date 1996		Description	Post Ref	Debit	Credit	Balance Debit	Balance Credit
Jan.	11	system from Carl's Computers	GJ1	7,000		7,000	

Name of Account: Accumulated Depreciation, Computer System

Account No.: 225

Date 1996		Description	Post Ref	Debit	Credit	Balance Debit	Balance Credit
Jan.	31		GJ4		125		125

Name of Account: Accounts Payable

Account No.: 310

Date 1996		Description	Post Ref	Debit	Credit	Balance Debit	Balance Credit
Jan.	5	Rebecca's Office Supplies	GJ1		300		
	11	Carl's Computers	GJ1		5,000		5,300
	13	Rebecca's Office Supplies	GJ2	200			5,100
	30	Speedy Delivery Service	GJ2		100		5,200
	31		GJ4		56		5,256

Name of Account: Wages Payable

Account No.: 330

Date 1996		Description	Post Ref	Debit	Credit	Balance Debit	Balance Credit
Jan.	31		GJ4		612.50		612.50

Name of Account: Interest Payable

Account No.: 370

Date 1996		Description	Post Ref	Debit	Credit	Balance Debit	Balance Credit
Jan.	31		GJ4		37.50		37.50

Name of Account: Notes Payable

Account No.: 410

Date 19 96		Description	Post Ref	Debit	Credit	Balance Debit	Balance Credit
Jan.	3	First Friendly Bank - 18mths	GJ1		5,000		5,000

Name of Account: Common Stock

Account No.: 510

Date 19 96		Description	Post Ref	Debit	Credit	Balance Debit	Balance Credit
Jan.	1	1000 Shares no-par	GJ1		3,000		3,000

Name of Account: Dividends

Account No.: 530

Date 19 96		Description	Post Ref	Debit	Credit	Balance Debit	Balance Credit
Jan.	31		GJ2	500		500	

Name of Account: Service Revenue

Account No.: 610

Date 19 96		Description	Post Ref	Debit	Credit	Balance Debit	Balance Credit
Jan.	25	Services for cash	GJ2		800		
	25	Services on account	GJ2		2,100		2,900
	31		GJ3		45		
	31		GJ3		600		3,545

Name of Account: Wage Expense

Account No.: 710

Date 19 96		Description	Post Ref	Debit	Credit	Balance Debit	Credit
Jan. 25		through Jan. 20	GJ2	1,100		1,100	
	31		GJ4	612.50		1,712.50	

Name of Account: Supplies Expense

Account No.: 715

Date 19 96		Description	Post Ref	Debit	Credit	Balance Debit	Credit
Jan.	31		GJ3	180		180	

Name of Account: Depreciation Expense, Office Furniture

Account No.: 720

Date 19 96		Description	Post Ref	Debit	Credit	Balance Debit	Credit
Jan.	31		GJ3	40		40	

Name of Account: Depreciation Expense, Computer System

Account No.: 725

Date 19 96		Description	Post Ref	Debit	Credit	Balance Debit	Credit
Jan.	31		GJ4	125		125	

Name of Account: Delivery Expense

Account No.: 730

Date 1996	Description	Post Ref	Debit	Credit	Balance Debit	Balance Credit
Jan. 30		GJ2	100		100	

Name of Account: Insurance Expense

Account No.: 735

Date 1996	Description	Post Ref	Debit	Credit	Balance Debit	Balance Credit
Jan. 31		GJ3	100		100	

Name of Account: Telephone Expense

Account No.: 750

Date 1996	Description	Post Ref	Debit	Credit	Balance Debit	Balance Credit
Jan. 31		GJ4	56		56	

Name of Account: Interest Expense

Account No.: 780

Date 1996	Description	Post Ref	Debit	Credit	Balance Debit	Balance Credit
Jan. 31		GJ4	37.50		37.50	

Now that the adjusting entries have been posted, the account balances may be used in the preparation of financial statements for Amanda's Typing Service. However, before we proceed, it is important to be certain that the equality of debits and credits has been maintained. Our best assurance in that regard is a trial balance. Recall that a trial balance can be drawn at any time; preparing one upon completion of the adjustment process is a common practice. In fact, the preparation of an *adjusted* trial balance is a standard procedure in the recording process. The adjusted trial balance gathers the account balances together and offers a concise format from which we can prepare financial statements. From the general ledger accounts on the previous pages, the adjusted trial balance for Amanda's Typing Service was prepared. It is shown below.

Amanda's Typing Service
Adjusted Trial Balance
As of January 31, 1996

Account	Debit	Credit
Cash	$ 1,300	
Accounts Receivable	2,745	
Supplies	120	
Prepaid Insurance	1,100	
Office Furniture	2,500	
Accumulated Depreciation, Office Furn.		$ 40
Computer System	7,000	
Accumulated Depreciation, Computer		125
Accounts Payable		5,256
Wages Payable		612.50
Interest Payable		37.50
Notes Payable		5,000
Common Stock		3,000
Dividends	500	
Service Revenue		3,545
Wage Expense	1,712.50	
Supplies Expense	180	
Depreciation Expense, Office Furniture	40	
Depreciation Expense, Computer	125	
Delivery Expense	100	
Insurance Expense	100	
Telephone Expense	56	
Interest Expense	37.50	
	$17,616.00	$17,616.00

This trial balance includes all the accounts added to the company's general ledger as a result of the adjustment process. Even most of the accounts which were present in the first trial balance now have different balances. As the trial balance indicates, debits equal credits. Again, this trial balance offers assurance that we have maintained the equality of debits and credits, but does not provide assurance that the entries made were correct.

To illustrate the impact of the adjustment process on the records of Amanda's Typing Service, the original trial balance, referred to as the *unadjusted* trial balance, is shown below. Take a moment to compare the two trial balances.

Amanda's Typing Service Unadjusted Trial Balance As of January 31, 1996		
Cash	$ 1,300	
Accounts Receivable	2,100	
Supplies	300	
Prepaid Insurance	1,200	
Office Furniture	2,500	
Computer System	7,000	
Accounts Payable		$ 5,200
Notes Payable		5,000
Common Stock		3,000
Dividends	500	
Service Revenue		2,900
Wage Expense	1,100	
Delivery Expense	100	
	$ 16,100	$ 16,100

Note the information that would not even be present if financial statements were prepared from the account balances reflected in the unadjusted trial balance instead of those in the adjusted trial balance. Indeed, the financial statements presented in Module 1 reflected the unadjusted balances, using only information from the basic transactions of the company. They did not include the information provided as a result of the adjustment process.

PREPARING FINANCIAL STATEMENTS

The construction of financial statements is something with which you have already had experience. At this point, you need to see how statement preparation fits into the overall recording process. Account balances shown in the adjusted trial balance should reflect results of all the transactions recorded during the period, and all the adjusting entries made during the adjustment process, so these balances are ready for use in financial statements. Based on the figures shown in the adjusted trial balance for Amanda's Typing Service, the following financial statements were prepared:

Amanda's Typing Service
Income Statement
For the Month of January, 1996

Service Revenue		$3,545
Less:		
Wage Expense	$1,712.50	
Supplies Expense	180.00	
Depreciation Expense	165.00	
Delivery Expense	100.00	
Insurance Expense	100.00	
Telephone Expense	56.00	
Interest Expense	37.50	
Total Expenses		2,351
Net Income		$1,194

Amanda's Typing Service
Statement of Retained Earnings
For the Month of January, 1996

Retained Earnings January 1, 1996	$ 0
Add: Net Income	1,194
	$1,194
Less: Dividends	500
Retained Earnings January 31, 1996	$ 694

Amanda's Typing Service
Balance Sheet
January 31, 1996

Assets:

Current Assets:		
Cash	$1,300	
Accounts Receivable	2,745	
Supplies	120	
Prepaid Insurance	1,100	
Total Current Assets		$ 5,265
Long-term Assets:		
Office Furniture	$2,500	
Less: Accumulated		
Depreciation	40	$ 2,460
Computer System	$7,000	
Less: Accumulated		
Depreciation	125	6,875
Total Long Term Assets		$ 9,335
Total Assets		$14,600

Liabilities:

Current Liabilities:		
Accounts Payable	$5,256.00	
Wages Payable	612.50	
Interest Payable	37.50	
Total		
Current Liabilities		$ 5,906
Long-term Liabilities:		
Notes Payable		5,000
Total Liabilities		$10,906
Owners' Equity:		
Common Stock	$3,000	
Retained Earnings	694	
Total Owners' Equity		3,694
Total Liabilities and		
Owners' Equity		$14,600

These financial statements represent achievement of the goal of the adjustment process — the determination of account balances which properly reflect the results of the company's activities for the period and its financial position as of the balance sheet date. Results of the adjusting entries provide valuable information to the readers of the financial statements. Without these entries, many of the account balances would be incorrect, and many others would not even be shown. Six new expense accounts were added to the company's records as a result of the adjustment process. The income statement above shows five new expenses, because the balances of the two depreciation expense accounts have been combined. Two liability accounts were created during the process, as well. In addition, the balance sheet now indicates how much of the original cost of each long-lived asset has been converted to expense thus far, by showing accumulated depreciation.

The preparation of financial statements may seem to be the end of the recording process. If, in fact, the business were going to operate for only this one financial statement period, we might be able to prepare these statements and call it quits. However, assuming that the business will continue activity in future periods, additional steps in the recording process must be completed. Module 5 explores the process of bringing the recording process of one period to a close and getting the accounting records ready for activity in the next. Before moving into that topic, two other aspects of the recording process should be introduced. In the sections that follow, we will explore the use of worksheets and the recording of correcting entries.

WORKSHEETS — VALUABLE OPTIONAL TOOLS

Let's recap the steps taken thus far in recording business activity for Amanda's Typing Service:

** Record transactions in the general journal and post the entries to general ledger accounts.

** Prepare a trial balance (the unadjusted trial balance) to determine if debits equal credits.

** Record the necessary adjusting entries and post them to the general ledger accounts.

** Prepare an adjusted trial balance to again check for equality of debits and credits.

** Use the account balances from the adjusted trial balance to prepare financial statements for the period.

These steps have been followed thus far, and we have seen the process in great detail. Recording transactions in the journal and posting the entries to the ledger accounts are steps dealing with permanent records of the company and formal documents that are parts of the accounting system. In contrast, the trial balances are simply tools used to make the process easier. The unadjusted trial balance checked our debits and credits and then helped guide our review of the account balances during the adjustment process. The adjusted trial balance assured us that our debits and credits were equal and then provided the balances we needed for the preparation of financial statements.

Like the trial balances themselves, the worksheet is a tool often used to make the recording process easier. Use of a worksheet is optional, and using it will have no impact on the actual accounting records maintained in the journal and ledger. If a worksheet is to be used, it is first created when the unadjusted trial balance is drawn. A worksheet serves as a road map through the subsequent steps of the recording process we have completed thus far. In no way does it affect the recording of the entries in the journal or the posting of them to the ledger, but using a worksheet *may* take the place of preparing separate trial balances.

Worksheets may be completed manually, or on a computer. The computer may be helpful in the completion of the routine parts of the worksheet, and using a computerized form of a worksheet may reduce errors. However, the computer cannot analyze the account balances or determine if an account balance properly reflects results of the company's activity for the period. Even if you use spreadsheet software to help in your completion of a worksheet, it is important that you understand how the worksheet is constructed, and how it can help you. Let's examine the construction of a worksheet. The worksheet illustration is followed by a list of explanations corresponding to the numbered items.

1. 2. 3. 4. 5.

ACCOUNT TITLES	Trial Balance DEBIT	Trial Balance CREDIT	Adjustments DEBIT	Adjustments CREDIT	Adjusted Trial Balance DEBIT	Adjusted Trial Balance CREDIT	Income Statement DEBIT	Income Statement CREDIT	Balance Sheet DEBIT	Balance Sheet CREDIT
Cash	XX				XX				XX	
Land	XX				XX				XX	
Supplies	XX			X	X				X	
Accounts Payable		XX				XX				XX
Common Stock		XX				XX				XX
Retained Earnings		XX				XX				XX
Salaries Expense	XX				XX		XX			
Rent Expense	XX			X	X		X			
Revenue		XXX				XXX		XXX		
Interest Expense			X		X		X			
Interest Payable				X		X				X
Supplies Expense			X		X		X			
Prepaid Rent			X		X				X	
TOTALS	XXX	XXX	XX	XX	XXXX	XXXX	XX	XXX	XXXX	XXX
							NI			NI
							XXX	XXX	XXXX	XXXX

1. In the first column, the account titles are entered. Some companies enter each account from the general ledger, whether or not it currently has a balance. The advantage of this approach is that few accounts, if any, will have to be added as a result of the adjustment process. Then, since the accounts in the ledger are numbered in a manner reflecting their order in the financial statements, the list of accounts on the worksheet will be in a more useful order. The other approach is to simply enter the names of accounts showing balances after the transactions of the period have been recorded and posted. Then, if accounts are affected by adjustments, they are simply added at the bottom of the list. This approach was used by Amanda's Typing Service for the company's first worksheet. In fact, most of the accounts which were first affected during the adjustment process had not yet been created in the company's ledger when the worksheet was begun.

2. The first set of debit/credit columns is used for the current, unadjusted balances of the accounts. This trial balance would be the same as what we have called the unadjusted trial balance. That is, we list the balance of each general ledger account after all transactions of the period have been posted, but before any adjustments have been made. As was the case with the unadjusted trial balance prepared separately, debits must equal credits. Certainly, if the column totals are not equal, any errors must be corrected before proceeding with the rest of the worksheet.

3. In the set of columns entitled "Adjustments", the same types of adjusting entries we have discussed throughout this module would be entered. If a worksheet is being used, the adjusting entries are determined and placed in these columns during the adjustment process. The totals in the debit and credit columns must equal, just as any entries recorded would have an equal amount of debits and credits.

The worksheet offers an environment in which account balances and the impact of adjusting entries can be readily seen, which many people find makes the adjustment process much easier. The investigations necessary to uncover adjustments for Amanda's Typing Service were minimal, but often determining necessary adjustments may be a much more complex process. Since the worksheet is just an informal tool, adjustments entered here may be changed and reentered easily if a mistake is made. Recording adjustments on a worksheet has no impact on the ledger account balances; once the appropriate adjusting entries are determined, they must be recorded in the company's journal and posted to the ledger.

4. The adjusted trial balance is a familiar item. In a non-worksheet situation, it was a list of account balances drawn from the general ledger, reflecting the transactions of the period and all the adjusting entries recorded. In a worksheet environment, the balances will reflect the same impacts and should be the same numbers. However, instead of coming from the ledger accounts, the balances in the adjusted trial balance columns of a worksheet are a result of following each account balance across the worksheet from left to right.

The initial balance of each account was shown in the first set of debit/credit columns. If no adjustment to an account was made, the balance entered in the adjusted trial balance columns should be the same as what was shown in the beginning trial balance. Care should be taken to bring debit balances across as debits and credit balances across as credits — careless errors are easy to make! If an adjustment to the account was entered in the second set of debit/credit columns, the adjusted trial balance amount for that account must reflect the impact of the adjustment. Here, too, care must be taken to properly determine the adjusted balance of each account.

The two columns of the adjusted trial balance must be equal before moving on in the worksheet. The adjusted trial balance is simply a blend of the beginning trial balance and the adjustments. If the beginning trial balance columns show an equal amount of debits and credits, and the adjustment columns do as well, the adjusted trial balance columns certainly should. In other words, if the first two sets of debit/credit columns are in balance, and the adjusted trial balance columns aren't equal, an error in moving account balances across and entering them in the adjusted trial balance must have been made.

Just as was the case with the adjusted trial balance prepared separately, the balances in the adjusted trial balance columns of a worksheet are those used in the preparation of financial statements.

5. The final two sets of columns are discussed together because they are completed simultaneously. As we said, the account balances in the adjusted trial balance columns are those used in financial statements. After the adjusted trial balance columns are totaled and deemed to be correct, the balance in each account is transferred to its appropriate place in either the income statement or balance sheet columns. The balances maintain the type of balance they showed in the adjusted trial balance. That is, debits are moved to the debit columns of either the income statement or balance sheet; credit balances are moved to either the credit column of the income statement or the credit column of the balance sheet.

A working knowledge of the accounts and what accounting elements they represent is important. If accounts are revenues or expenses, they will be moved into the income statement columns. All asset, liability and owners' equity accounts appear in the balance sheet columns. Notice from the illustration that in general the balance sheet items appeared first, followed by the income statement accounts. This results from the initial trial balance listing accounts in the order they appear on the company's chart of accounts and in the general ledger. However, care should be taken not to become lazy about deciding whether an account belongs in the income statement columns or with the balance sheet accounts. Notice that because of adjusting entries which added accounts that weren't in the initial trial balance, balance sheet accounts may appear near the bottom of the worksheet.

When the income statement columns are totaled, debits and credits are NOT equal — that's good. Likewise, when the balance sheet columns are totaled, debits and credits are NOT equal — that's also good. For the first time, we have encountered a situation in which "out of balance" is good. Look at what accounts are in the income statement columns — revenues are in the credit column and expenses are in the debit column. Given the accounts in each column, we wouldn't expect the debit and credit columns of the income statement section of the worksheet to be equal. These two columns should be "off", and they should be off by an amount equal to the difference between the revenues and the expenses, net income. Think about how this works in the balance sheet columns of the worksheet. The debits and credits in these columns will also be out of balance by an amount equal to the net income of the period. Why? Because the owners' equity accounts don't reflect the addition of net income. For instance, for a corporation, the amount shown in retained earnings is the beginning balance, not yet increased by this period's earnings. Remember, on a balance sheet, the amount shown in owners' equity is the ending balance, as calculated and presented on the statement of owners' equity.

So, when the income statement and balance sheet columns of the worksheet are totaled, expect them NOT to show an equal amount of debits and credits. The two sets of columns SHOULD however, be out of balance by the *same amount*. As indicated on the illustration, adding the net income figure to the debit column of the income statement and the credit column of the balance sheet should bring both sets of columns into balance.

With the account balances properly sorted into two sets of columns, financial statement preparation from the worksheet information is easy. As the income statement is prepared, only items from the income statement columns of the worksheet should be used. After the bridge statement (in this case, the statement of retained earnings) is completed, the ending balances in owners' equity accounts can be used in conjunction with the other account balances from the balance sheet columns of the worksheet to prepare the company's balance sheet.

Preparation of a worksheet is not difficult, and in many ways makes some aspects of the recording process easier to complete and easier to understand. Now that we've described the worksheet process in an abstract setting, let's apply what we've learned, and prepare a worksheet for Amanda's Typing Service. Remember, the process begins with the unadjusted trial balance, so the information in the first set of debit/credit columns matches that shown in the trial balance prepared after the January transactions were recorded, but before the adjusting entries were made. If a worksheet were used, the adjusting entries would have been determined in much the same way as they were earlier in this module. However, the adjustments would have been first noted on the worksheet, and only after it was determined the entries were appropriate, would they have been recorded in the journal and posted to the ledger accounts.

Note that the figures shown on the adjusted trial balance in the worksheet are the same as those presented earlier on the separate adjusted trial balance. That is as expected. Preparation of a worksheet should not alter the outcome of the recording process. Indeed, the net income figure shown on the worksheet is the same as that presented on the income statement prepared earlier.

Amanda's Typing Service – For the Month Ended January 31, 1996

ACCOUNT TITLES	Trial Balance DEBIT	Trial Balance CREDIT	Adjustments DEBIT	Adjustments CREDIT	Adjusted Trial Balance DEBIT	Adjusted Trial Balance CREDIT	Income Statement DEBIT	Income Statement CREDIT	Balance Sheet DEBIT	Balance Sheet CREDIT
Cash	1,300				1,300				1,300	
Accounts Receivable	2,100		600 / 45		2,745				2,745	
Supplies	300			180	120				120	
Prepaid Insurance	1,200			100	1,100				1,100	
Office Furniture	2,500				2,500				2,500	
Computer System	7,000				7,000				7,000	
Accounts Payable		5,200		56		5,256				5,256
Notes Payable		5,000				5,000				5,000
Common Stock		3,000				3,000				3,000
Dividends	500				500				500	
Service Revenue		2,900		600 / 45		3,545		3,545		
Wage Expense	1,100		612.50		1,712.50		1,712.50			
Delivery Expense	100				100		100			
Supplies Expense			180		180		180			
Insurance Expense			100		100		100			
Depreciation Exp, Furn			40		40		40			
Accumulated Dep, Furn				40		40				40
Depreciation Exp, Comp.			125		125		125			
Accumulated Dep, Comp				125		125				125
Telephone Expense			56		56		56			
Interest Expense			37.50		37.50		37.50			
Interest Payable				37.50		37.50				37.50
Wages Payable				612.50		612.50				612.50
Totals	16,100	16,100	1,796	1,796	17,616	17,616	2,351	3,545	15,265	14,071
							1,194			1,194
							3,545	3,545	15,265	15,265

Using a worksheet to help in the completion of the adjustment process and the preparation of financial statements is optional. One thing that is NOT optional is the correction of errors. Since nobody's perfect, it is likely that at some point, you will uncover an error you made or one made by someone else. Given the steps of the recording process that we have explored thus far, you might guess that correcting errors is not simply a matter of erasing and replacing entries. But since the existence of errors is a distinct possibility, it is important that you know how to properly deal with them.

ERRORS AND THEIR CORRECTION

As entries are made in the journal, debits and credits must be kept equal; the errors discussed in this section assume that this basic rule was not violated. After journal entries are posted to the ledger accounts, if a trial balance doesn't show an equal amount of debits and credits, an error was made in the posting process. In this case, the ledger accounts should be reviewed and postings should be corrected.

If a journal entry records an equal amount of debits and credits, but does not properly reflect the transaction involved, a correcting entry must be made. Errors can occur any time, and can be discovered any time. When an error is discovered, a correcting entry should be recorded in the general journal immediately. The description of the correcting entry should explain the nature of the error, and refer to which entry was incorrect.

The review of account balances performed as part of the adjustment process may uncover errors. If an error is discovered during the adjustment process, the correcting entry is made at that time, and is posted to the ledger accounts along with the adjusting entries. If a worksheet is being used, correcting entries determined during the adjustment process are shown in the adjustment columns of the worksheet, and then recorded and posted along with the adjusting entries.

As you can imagine, there is a wide variety of possible errors. The specific details of each error can vary, and so there are an endless number of different correcting entries. When an error is discovered, it is important to determine what *was* recorded and what *should have been* recorded. Then, the proper correcting entry can be determined.

As we explore several examples of errors and their correction, we will use T-accounts to illustrate the impacts of the entries. When determining necessary correcting entries, you may find it helpful to use T-accounts to "see" the effects of entries on account balances.

To illustrate the thinking process involved in determining correcting entries, we offer examples of several of the most common types of errors: (1) transactions may be recorded for the wrong amount, (2) the wrong accounts may be debited or credited, (3) the entry may be recorded "backwards", or (4) an entry may be recorded twice.

Our four examples are all based on the same scenario. The scenario involves Barton Company, which is about to record a $1,200 invoice for work it performed for Marlin Manufacturing. Barton should have recorded the bill as follows:

```
        Accounts Receivable          1,200
            Revenue                          1,200
```

In each section that follows, it is assumed that a different error was made in the recording of this transaction. The proper correcting entries are illustrated and discussed.

(1) transactions may be recorded for the wrong amount. Assume that the Barton Company recorded the transaction with Marlin Manufacturing as if the bill were for $2,100 instead of the proper amount of $1,200. A correcting entry is needed. First, what entry *was* made? The entry made in error was:

```
Accounts Receivable            2,100
     Revenue                            2,100
```

What entry *should have been* made? The entry should have been:

```
Accounts Receivable            1,200
     Revenue                            1,200
```

By focusing on what was done and what should have been done, we can determine the necessary corrective action. In this case, the correct accounts were affected, but each one was affected by $2,100 instead of $1,200. In order to bring Accounts Receivable and Revenue down to the correct amount, $900 must be taken out of each account balance. Therefore, the correcting entry would be:

```
Revenue                          900
     Accounts Receivable                900
```

Did the correcting entry above have the intended impact? Let's post the two entries that were made (the original "wrong" entry and the correcting entry) to T-accounts to see if their combined effect is the same as what *should have been* done in the first place. (E) indicates the error and (C) indicates the correcting entry:

```
       Accounts Receivable                          Revenue
   (E)  2,100 |                                    |  2,100  (E)
             |   900  (C)            (C)    900    |
        1,200 |                                    |  1,200
```

As the T-accounts illustrate, the combined effect of the original entry and the correcting entry is the same as the entry that should have been made.

(2) the wrong accounts may be debited or credited. Now, let's assume that when the $1,200 bill to Marlin Manufacturing was sent, the transaction was recorded as a debit to Accounts Payable instead of a debit to Accounts Receivable, but the correct dollar amount was recorded. A correcting entry is needed. First, what entry *was* made? The entry was recorded as:

```
Accounts Payable               1,200
     Revenue                            1,200
```

What entry *should have been* made? The entry should have been:

```
     Accounts Receivable            1,200
          Revenue                           1,200
```

By comparing what was done and what should have been done, we can determine the necessary corrective action. In this case, the dollar amounts are correct, and Revenue was properly credited. The error appears in the debit portion of the entry. Accounts Payable was debited when it should not have been affected at all, and no debit to Accounts Receivable was made. In order to bring Accounts Payable and Accounts Receivable to their correct amounts, $1,200 must be added to the asset account and $1,200 must be taken out of the liability account. Therefore, the correcting entry would be:

```
     Accounts Receivable            1,200
          Accounts Payable                  1,200
```

Did the correcting entry above have the intended impact? Let's post the two entries that were made (the original "wrong" entry and the correcting entry) to T-accounts to see if their combined effect is the same as what *should have been* done in the first place. (E) indicates the error and (C) indicates the correcting entry:

```
   Accounts Payable                Revenue              Accounts Receivable
 ─────────────────          ─────────────────       ─────────────────
 (E)  1,200 |                          |  1,200  (E)     (C)  1,200 |
      ───── | 1,200  (C)               |                           |
            |  -0-                     |                           |
```

As the T-accounts illustrate, the combined effect of the original entry and the correcting entry is the same as the entry that should have been made in the first place. The correcting entry resulted in the proper amount in both Accounts Receivable and Revenue and the elimination of the effect of the mistaken entry on Accounts Payable.

(3) the entry may be recorded "backwards". This time assume that Barton Company recorded the proper amount of the transaction ($1,200) and chose the correct accounts to use, but accidentally recorded the entry as a debit to Revenue and a credit to Accounts Receivable. In this case, the original entry was:

```
     Revenue                        1,200
          Accounts Receivable               1,200
```

The entry that *should have been* made is:

```
     Accounts Receivable            1,200
          Revenue                           1,200
```

Notice that the two accounts affected by the original entry and the two accounts that should have been affected are the same, so the correcting entry will involve only these two accounts. Correction in this case is a combination of undoing what was done, and doing what should have been done. For example, Revenue was reduced by $1,200 in the original entry, but it should have been increased by $1,200. So, our correcting entry must increase Revenue by a total of $2,400 to undo the effect of the original entry and record the increase that *should* have been recorded. The same logic holds true for the impact on Accounts Receivable. Thus, the correcting entry should be:

```
Accounts Receivable          2,400
     Revenue                           2,400
```

Will this correcting entry result in correct balances in both accounts affected? Let's see:

```
              Revenue                    Accounts Receivable
         _____         _____
 (E) 1,200 |                                   | 1,200 (E)
  _____  | 2,400 (C)       (C) 2,400 |  _____
           | 1,200                1,200 |
```

After the impact of the correcting entry, both Accounts Receivable and Revenue show proper balances, the balances that would have shown if the original entry had been made properly.

(4) an entry may be recorded twice. Duplication of an entry certainly results in the need for a correction. When the $1,200 bill to Marlin Manufacturing was sent, the transaction was inadvertently recorded twice. Even though the nature of this type of error may be different, the thinking process to determine the necessary correction is the same. First, what entry *was* made? Actually, in this case, two entries were made:

```
Accounts Receivable          1,200
     Revenue                           1,200

Accounts Receivable          1,200
     Revenue                           1,200
```

What entry *should have been* made? A single entry should have been recorded:

```
Accounts Receivable          1,200
     Revenue                           1,200
```

In this case, it is necessary to undo the impact of the duplication. That is, we need to eliminate the effect of one of the original entries. In order to "undo" the effect of one of the original entries, we simply record the opposite impact in each account. In the original entry, Accounts Receivable was debited for $1,200. To eliminate the effect of this entry we simply credit Accounts Receivable for $1,200. This same strategy will correct the balance in the Revenue account as well. Therefore, the correcting entry would be:

```
Revenue                      1,200
     Accounts Receivable               1,200
```

The correcting entry above should undo the impact of *one* of the original entries, thus eliminating the effect of duplication. Did it have the intended impact? Let's post the two entries that were originally made and the correcting entry to T-accounts to see if their combined effect is the same as what *should have been* done in the first place.

Accounts Receivable			Revenue		
(E) 1,200				1,200	(E)
(E) 1,200				1,200	(E)
_____	1,200	(C)	(C) 1,200	_____	
1,200				1,200	

As the T-accounts illustrate, the combined effect of the original entries and the correcting entry is the same as the single entry that should have been made.

CONCLUSION

Just as the adjustment process requires analysis and thought, so does the process of correcting errors. We provided four examples of common errors, but this is only a sample of what is possible. In the recording of journal entries, Murphy's Law holds true: Whatever can go wrong, will go wrong! Whatever the error, following a careful thought process and using T-accounts to verify the results is a good approach.

In this module, we explored steps in the recording process culminating in the preparation of financial statements — we've come a long way! But if Amanda's Typing Service is to continue operating in future periods, the accounting records for the first period must be closed, and the system must be made ready for the recording of next period's activity. Module 5 will guide you through that part of the recording process.

APPLY WHAT YOU HAVE LEARNED

4-1. (Recording Accrued Revenue)

Home Care Services provides in-home services for the elderly and disabled. On November 1, 1995, Home Care entered into a three-month contract with Martha Todd to care for Martha's elderly mother while Martha was overseas on business. The contract is for $6,000 per month, and the total amount of $18,000 is to be paid by Martha to Home Care at the end of three months when Martha returns from overseas.

Required: Prepare the adjusting entry for Home Care Services at December 31, 1995.

4-2. (Recording Accrued Revenue)

On December 1, 1995, Pitman Photo performed specialty photography services for a preferred customer. The customer gave Pitman a note in the amount of $25,000 with interest at 12%. The principal plus interest is due at the end of three months. The transaction was recorded by Pitman as follows:

```
Dec 1      Notes Receivable          25,000
              Service Revenue                  25,000
```

Required: Prepare the adjusting entry for Pitman Photo to record accrued interest at December 31, 1995.

4-3. (Recording Accrued Expense)

Brad's Super Sports pays total wages of $3,600 per week on Saturday of each week. Wages are $600 per day for 6 days, Monday through Saturday. Wages through Saturday, September 27 have been paid, and the next payday will be Saturday, October 4.

Required: Prepare the adjusting entry for accrued wages on Tuesday, September 30.

4-4. (Recording Accrued Expense)

On October 1, 1995, Flo's Boutique borrowed $10,000 from Niagara First at 12% interest per year. The principal plus interest is due at the end of four months.

Required: Prepare the adjusting entry for accrued interest on December 31, 1995.

4-5. (Preparation and Effects of Adjusting Entries)

Ralph Brito Custom Photography is about to prepare its financial statements for 1994. The following information is available:

a.   As of December 31, 1994, photography services totaling $1,450 had been performed for customers, but not yet billed.

b.   The telephone bill of $180 was received On January 5, 1995. The bill is for December telephone service.

c.   A physical count revealed that the cost of photographic supplies on hand at December 31, 1994 was $250. Prior to any adjusting entries, the Photographic Supplies account had a December 31, 1994 balance of $450.

d.   Employees were paid $1,500 on January 4, 1995 for work performed December 28, 29, and 30, and January 2 and 3. Employees earned wages evenly during the five day period.

Required:

I.   Prepare the appropriate adjusting entries for Ralph Brito Custom Photography.

II.   In the space provided below, indicate the effect of each adjustment on the financial statement items. Use the following code:

        I means the entry made the item increase
        D means the entry made the item decrease
        NE means the entry had no effect on the item

Adjusting Entry	Total Assets	Revenue	Expenses	Net Income
a.				
b.				
c.				
d.				

4-5. Working Papers

Date		Description	Post Ref	Debit	Credit
General Journal				Page	

4-6. (Preparation and Effect of Adjusting Entries)

Ace Lawn Care is about to prepare its financial statements for 1994. The following information is available:

a. During the last week of December, Ace Lawn Care cut 32 lawns. Of these, 14 lawn jobs totaling $1,080 were for cash customers, and the remaining 18 lawn jobs totaling $1260 were for charge customers who will be billed during the first week in January 1995. The transactions for the cash customers were recorded during December. However, the transactions for the customers that will be billed during the first week of January, 1995 have not been recorded.

b. A bill from Mobile Oil totaling $128 was received on January 5, 1995. The bill is for gasoline used during December by the lawn care service.

c. At December 31, 1994, Ace had trash bags and other supplies costing $190 on hand. Prior to any adjusting entries, the balance in the Supplies account as of December 31, 1994 is zero.

d. Employees were paid $1,200 on January 2, 1995 for work performed during the last week in December.

Required:

I. Prepare the appropriate adjusting entries for Ace Lawn Care.

II. In the space provided below, indicate the effect of each adjusting entry on the financial statement items. Use the following code:

  I means the entry made the item increase
  D means the entry made the item decrease
  NE means the entry had no effect on the item

Adjusting Entry	Net Income	Total Assets	Total Liabilities	Owners' Equity
a.				
b.				
c.				
d.				

Date		Description	Post Ref	Debit	Credit

General Journal   Page _____

4-7. (Preparation and Effect of Adjusting Entries)

L. Jones Trucking operates a small fleet of delivery trucks and is preparing financial statements for its July 31, 1995 fiscal year end. The information below pertains to 1995.

a. On June 1, L. Jones Trucking received advance payment of $300 for three months of daily delivery service between two law offices located in south Florida.
    NOTE: The entry on June 1 could have been made two different ways. HOW that entry was made determines what the appropriate adjusting entry is. Provide the two possible June 1 entries, and the adjusting entry for each. In the chart below, the two possible adjusting entries for this scenario are identified as a1. and a2.

b. By July 31, L. Jones Trucking had completed one half of the work required to transport material between two warehouses. The customer will be billed $800 when the work is complete. (No entries relating to this transaction had been recorded.)

c. On August 14, L. Jones Trucking received $180 bill from Mobile Oil for bill for gasoline used in its delivery trucks. Of the $180, $120 pertains to gasoline used during July, and the remaining $60 was used in August.

d. The Prepaid Insurance account is used to record all payments of insurance. The annual insurance policy was renewed on March 1, with full payment of $6,240 being made at that time. As of July 31, the balance in the Prepaid Insurance account is $6,240.

e. The Supplies Expense account is used to record all purchases of supplies. As of July 31, the Supplies account has a balance of zero and supplies of $230 are on hand.

Required: I.   Prepare the appropriate adjusting entries.

II. In the space provided below, indicate the effect of each adjusting entry on the financial statement items. Use the following code:

I means the entry made the item increase
D means the entry made the item decrease
NE means the entry had no effect on the item

Adjusting Entry	Cash	Revenue	Expenses	Net Income
a1.				
a2.				
b.				
c.				
d.				
e.				

4-8. (Identification of Entry Type and Preparation of Adjusting Entries)

Molina Security Service has a contract for $200 to provide security services to Quick Shot Photo Supplies for a two-month period beginning December 1, 1994. Quick shot will be billed at the end of the contract period.

Required:

a. 1. In preparation of Molina Security Services' December 31, 1994 financial statements, what type of adjusting entry is required? (accrual, deferral, or other)

_____

2. In the space provided below, prepare the appropriate adjusting entry for Molina Security Service.

b. 1. In preparation of Quick Shot Photo Supply's December 31, 1994 financial statements, what type of adjusting entry is required? (accrual, deferral, or other)

_____

2. In the space provided below, prepare the appropriate adjusting entry for Quick Shot Photo Supply.

4-9. (Identification of Entry Type and Preparation of Adjusting Entries)

Gary Steinmann's Charter Boat Company rents dock space from the Holiday Isle Resorts located in the Florida Keys. On November 1, 1994, Steinmann paid Holiday Isle Resorts $360 for 3 months' dockage in advance.

Required:

a.   1.   In preparation of Gary Steinmann's Charter Boat Company's fiscal year-end statements dated November 30, 1994, what type of adjusting entry is required? (accrual, deferral, or other)

       _____

      2.   With respect to Gary Steinmann's Charter Boat Company, the November 1 payment could have been recorded two different ways. Each way would have resulted in a different adjusting entry. In the space for the November 1 entries, provide the two possible original entries for Gary Steinmann's Charter Boat Company. In the space adjacent to the original entries, provide the appropriate adjusting entries for each method.

November 1	Adjusting Entry
November 1	Adjusting Entry

b.   1.   In preparation of Holiday Isle Resorts annual financial statements dated December 31, 1994, what type of adjusting entry is required? (accrual, deferral, or other)

       _____

      2.   Holiday Isle Resorts could have recorded the November 1 receipt of payment in one of two ways. Each way would have resulted in a different adjusting entry. In the space for the November 1 entries, provide the two possible adjusting entries for Holiday Isle Resorts. In the adjacent space, provide the appropriate adjusting entries for each method.

November 1	Adjusting Entry
November 1	Adjusting Entry

4-10. (Depreciation)

Natacha's Nouvelle Creations purchased some high-tech art design equipment on January 1, 1995 for $35,000. Natacha believes the equipment will be useful for 5 years, and will be worth $3,000 at the end of 5 years.

Required:

a. Prepare the depreciation adjusting entry at December 31, 1995.

b. What is the book value of the equipment on December 31, 1995?

$_____

4-11. (Adjusting Entries from Trial Balance)

Anderson Engineering began operations in January 1995. At the end of January, the unadjusted trial balance is:

Anderson Engineering
Unadjusted Trial Balance
January 31, 1995

	Debit	Credit
Cash	$22,600	
Accounts Receivable	9,000	
Supplies	500	
Equipment	11,000	
Accounts Payable		$ 9,000
Notes Payable		12,000
Common Stock		10,000
Dividends	500	
Service Revenue		16,500
Wages Expense	900	
Rent Expense	2,500	
Utilities Expense	500	
Totals	$47,500	$47,500

Additional information:

a. Service revenue of $1,000 has been earned but has not yet been billed.

b. Supplies inventory is $125.

c. Equipment has a 5 year life and a $2,000 residual value.

d. The telephone bill of $130 for January is unpaid.

e. Interest on notes payable is 12%.

f. Wages of $300 are owed.

Required:

Prepare adjusting entries at the end of January.

Date		Description	Post Ref	Debit	Credit

General Journal — Page ____

4-12. (Preparation of an Adjusted Trial Balance)

Required:

Using the information from Problem 4-11, prepare an adjusted trial balance for Anderson Engineering.

Anderson Engineering Adjusted Trial Balance January 31, 1995		

4-13. (Preparation of Financial Statements from Adjusted Trial Balance)

Required:

Using the adjusted trial balance from Problem 4-12, prepare the financial statements for Anderson Engineering.

4-14. (Deferred Revenue)

On August 1, 1995, The Buffalo Bills Football Club received $26,000 for season tickets for the 1995 NFL football season. The Bills play 10 home games from September through December, 1995. This transaction was recorded as follows:

Aug 1 Cash   26,000
                   Unearned Revenue   26,000

Required:

a.   Assuming the Bills play 3 home games in September, 1995, give the adjusting entry at September 30, 1995.

b.   At the end of September, 1995, how much of the $26,000 should be reported as:

        a liability on the balance sheet? $_____

        a revenue on the income statement? $_____

4-15. (Deferred Revenue)

On August 1, 1995, The Buffalo Bills Football Club received $26,000 for season tickets for the 1995 NFL football season. The Bills play 10 home games from September through December, 1995. This transaction was recorded as follows:

Aug 1   Cash   26,000
                Ticket Revenue   26,000

Required:

a.   Assuming the Bills play 3 home games in September, 1995, give the adjusting entry at September 30, 1995.

b.   At the end of September, 1995, how much of the $26,000 should be reported as:

        a liability on the balance sheet? $_____

        a revenue on the income statement? $_____

4-16. (Deferred Expense)

Kelly's Synchronized Swimming paid $6,000 rent for an indoor swimming facility in advance on June 1 for three months ($2,000 per month for June, July, and August). The transaction was recorded as follows:

June 1 Prepaid Rent 6,000
            Cash   6,000

Required:

a.   Prepare the adjusting entry at June 30.

b.   At the end of June, how much of the $6,000 rent should be reported as:

        an asset on the balance sheet? $_____

        an expense on the income statement? $_____

4-17. (Deferred Expense)

Kelly's Synchronized Swimming paid $6,000 rent for an indoor swimming facility in advance on June 1 for three months ($2,000 per month for June, July, and August). The transaction was recorded as follows:

June 1 Rent   Expense   6,000
            Cash   6,000

Required:

a.   Prepare the adjusting entry at June 30.

b.   At the end of June, how much of the $6,000 rent should be reported as:

        an asset on the balance sheet? $_____

        an expense on the income statement? $_____

4-18. (Deferred Expense, Two Approaches)

Jean's Goat Farm paid $14,400 for a three year insurance policy on January 1. The policy provides insurance coverage for her farm for the next three years.

Required:

a.   Show two possible ways of recording the purchase of the insurance policy on January 1, and show the corresponding adjusting entry for December 31 in the adjacent box.

January 1	Adjusting Entry
January 1	Adjusting Entry

4-19. (Deferred Revenue, Two Approaches)

On September 1, 1995, Mike's Underwater Photography received $12,000 cash in advance for deep-sea color photography services to be performed over the next three months. Mike estimates that the project will require a total of six dives during the three months, with an equal amount of photography services done with each dive. Mike made two dives in September, 1995.

Required:

a.   Show two possible ways of recording the receipt of the $12,000 cash advance on September 1, 1995 and show the corresponding adjusting entry for September 30,1995 in the adjacent box.

September 1	Adjusting Entry
September 1	Adjusting Entry

4-20. (Depreciation)

Dianne's Dream World purchased equipment for $25,000 on September 1, 1995. The equipment has an estimated useful life of 4 years, and a residual value of $1,000.

Required:

a.   Prepare the depreciation adjusting entry at December 31, 1995.

b.   What is the book value of the equipment on December 31, 1995?
                 $_____

4-21. (Depreciation)

Audrey's Auto Place built a showroom some years ago at a cost of $500,000. The showroom has a useful life of 20 years, and a residual value of $20,000. Audrey's Balance Sheet at December 31, 1995 shows the showroom as follows:

```
Long-term Assets:
     Auto Showroom                        $500,000
     Less Accumulated Depreciation         120,000
     Book Value                           $380,000
```

Required:

a.   Assuming that depreciation has been properly recorded for 1995, what is the amount of depreciation expense for the year 1995?
                 $_____

b.   Give the journal entry that was made to record depreciation for 1995.

c.   How old is the showroom at December 31, 1995? _____

4-22. (Comprehensive Problem)

Mandy's Small Animal Hospital began operations in June 1995. At the end of June, the unadjusted trial balance is:

Mandy's Small Animal Hospital
Unadjusted Trial Balance
June 30, 1995

	Debit	Credit
Cash	$ 6,000	
Accounts Receivable	3,000	
Supplies	700	
Equipment	15,000	
Accounts Payable		$ 3,800
Unearned Revenue		4,000
Notes Payable		2,000
Common Stock		10,000
Dividends	2,500	
Service Revenue		13,500
Wages Expense	2,900	
Rent Expense	2,700	
Utilities Expense	500	
Totals	$33,300	$33,300

Additional information:

a. Service revenue of $1,000 has been earned but has not yet been billed.
b. Supplies inventory at the end of June is $300.
c. Equipment has a 4-year life and a $3,000 residual value.
d. A utilities bill of $200 for June is unpaid and has not been recorded.
e. Interest on notes payable is 12%.
f. Wages of $300 are owed at the end of June.
g. On June 1, Mandy paid rent of $2,700 in advance for three months ($900 per month for June, July, and August).
h. $1,000 of the Unearned Revenue has been earned during the month of June.
i. On June 2, supplies were purchased for $700 cash. The transaction was incorrectly recorded as a debit to Supplies and a credit to Accounts Payable.
j. During June, a transaction for $4,000 of services to a customer on account was incorrectly recorded as $400.

Required:

1. Prepare adjusting entries at the end of June.

2. Prepare correcting entries for the errors.

3. Prepare an adjusted trial balance.

4. Prepare an income statement, a statement of retained earnings, and a balance sheet.

4-23. (Preparation of a Worksheet and Financial Statements)

The following *unadjusted* account balances are for the fiscal year ended July 31, 1995 for General Automotive Repair:

Cash	3,400
Accounts Receivable	5,200
Auto Parts	2,300
Supplies	480
Truck	22,000
Accumulated Depreciation — Truck	4,000
Accounts Payable	2,200
Notes payable — Non-Current	5,000
Common Stock	1,000
Additional Paid-In Capital	3,000
Retained Earnings	?
Dividends	2,250
Service Revenue	203,000
Wage Expense	65,000
Rent Expense	24,000
Parts Expense	95,000
Supplies Expense	1,120
Utilities Expense	5,200

Other information:

The cost of supplies on hand at July 31, 1995 was $200.

The cost of parts on hand at July 31, 1995 was $1,300.

Wages owed to employees as of July 31, 1995 was $940.

The truck is depreciated using the straight-line method and has a residual value of $2,000 with an estimated economic useful life of 5 years.

As of July 31, 1995, service has been completed for customers totaling $890 which has not been billed or recorded.

On August 3, a utility bill is received for July's utilities totaling $250.

The Note Payable pertains to a loan received on May 1, at 12%.

Required:

a.   Prepare a worksheet for General Automotive Repair for the fiscal year ended July 31, 1995. Assign Retained Earnings the amount needed to make the debit and credit columns of the unadjusted trial balance equal.

b.   Prepare financial statements for General Automotive Repair for the year ended July 31, 1995.

ACCOUNT TITLES	Trial Balance		Adjustments		Adjusted Trial Balance		Income Statement		Balance Sheet	
	DEBIT	CREDIT	DEBIT	CREDIT	DEBIT	CREDIT	DEBIT	CREDIT	DEBIT	CREDIT

THE ADJUSTING PROCESS

4-24. (Preparation of a Worksheet and Financial Statements)

The following are *unadjusted* account balances for Hinds Pet Grooming Service as of December 31, 1995:

Cash	8,400
Accounts Receivable	3,100
Grooming Supplies	430
Computer System	2,200
Accumulated Depreciation — Computer	500
Accounts Payable	200
Notes payable — Non-current	2,000
Common Stock, $1 par	500
Additional Paid-in Capital	3,000
Retained Earnings	?
Service Revenue	45,600
Wage Expense	32,200
Rent Expense	1,200
Grooming Supplies Expense	5,600

Other information:

The cost of grooming supplies on hand at December 31, 1995 was $390.

Wages owed to employees as of December 31, 1995 were $220.

The computer is depreciated using the straight-line method and has a residual value of $200 with an estimated economic useful life of 4 years.

As of December 31, 1995, pet grooming services totaling $380 have been completed for customers, but not yet been billed or recorded.

The Note Payable pertains to a loan from Friendly Bank on June 1, 1995 at 9%.

Required:

a. Prepare a worksheet for Hinds Pet Grooming Service for the year ended December 31, 1995. Assign Retained Earnings the amount needed to make the debit and credit columns of the unadjusted trial balance equal.

b. Prepare financial statements for Hinds Pet Grooming Service for the year ended December 31, 1995.

ACCOUNT TITLES	Trial Balance		Adjustments		Adjusted Trial Balance		Income Statement		Balance Sheet	
	DEBIT	CREDIT	DEBIT	CREDIT	DEBIT	CREDIT	DEBIT	CREDIT	DEBIT	CREDIT

THE ADJUSTING PROCESS

4-25. (Errors and Their Correction)

Bea Careful made the following errors in recording transactions:

a.   Purchased office supplies for cash of $1,667. The transaction was recorded for the wrong amount of $1,776.

b.   Purchased equipment on account for $2,000. The transaction was recorded as a debit to Equipment and a credit to Cash.

c.   Performed $3,600 of services for a customer on account. The transaction was recorded as a debit to Service Revenue and a credit to Accounts Receivable.

d.   Purchased a two-year insurance policy for $2,400 cash. The transaction was recorded twice.

Required:

For each of the above errors:

1.   Prepare the journal entry that *should have been made*.

2.   Prepare the *correcting entry*.

4-26. (Errors and Their Correction)

Johnny Be Good made the following errors in recording transactions:

a.   Purchased office supplies on account for $1,333. The transaction was recorded as a debit to Accounts Payable and a credit to Office Supplies.

b.   Purchased equipment on account for $2,000. The transaction was recorded as a debit to Equipment and a credit to Accounts Payable for $200.

c.   Performed services of $3,600 for a customer on account. The transaction was recorded twice.

d.   Purchased a two-year insurance policy for $2,400 cash. The transaction was recorded as a debit to Wages Expense and a credit to Cash.

Required:

For each of the above errors:

1.   Prepare the journal entry that *should have been made*.

2.   Prepare the *correcting entry*.

3.   Post the error (E) and the correcting entry (C) to T-accounts.

MODULE 5

ENDING THE BUSINESS YEAR - THE CLOSING PROCESS

Thus far, we have explored the recording of business transactions and the recording of the entries necessary to adjust account balances prior to the preparation of financial statements. Regular entries to record business activity are made continuously, throughout the life of the business. The adjustment process and preparation of financial statements takes place as often as the business finds it necessary.

At a minimum, businesses generally prepare financial statements once a year. But many times, owners or lenders require financial statement information more often than annually. In the case of Amanda's Typing Service, the financial statements prepared in Module 4 were for the company's first month of business. Financial statements which are prepared monthly or quarterly are called interim financial statements. **Interim financial statements** are those prepared for a period which is shorter than the company's business year.

The business year, a 12-month period for which financial statements are prepared is called a **fiscal year**. A company's fiscal year may or may not correspond to a calendar year. In other words, the business year may cover a 12-month period other than January 1 to December 31. The use of a non-calendar fiscal year is permissible by accounting rules, and offers the advantage of allowing companies to prepare financial statements during a slow business period. For example, many major retailers adopt a fiscal year ending January 31, allowing the companies to get the holiday rush behind them before having to gather together their financial statement information. Although the term *fiscal year* actually refers to *any* business year, it is often used to refer only to non-calendar business years.

As the days, weeks and months pass, hundreds, if not thousands of business transactions are recorded. Whenever financial statements are to be prepared, adjusting entries are made in order to provide more accurate financial information. An interim income statement provides revenue and expense information for whatever period it is designed to cover. An interim balance sheet presents the financial position of the company as of a particular date, the end of the interim period.

The income statement prepared at year-end should reflect an accumulation of all the revenue and expense activity for the year. The year-end balance sheet should reflect the financial position of the company with respect to the amounts of assets, liabilities and equity as of the end of the fiscal year. Differences in the nature of the items shown on these two financial statements are important.

Dollar amounts for revenues and expenses shown on the annual income statement represent an accumulation of all the revenues earned and all the expenses incurred during the year. That is, service revenue of $100,000 does not mean that there is a pile of revenue worth $100,000 in a company warehouse somewhere, but rather, it merely means that if you added up all the service revenue *earned* during the year, the total would be $100,000. The same can be said for expenses. For example, if supplies expense of $5,000 is shown on the income statement, it does not mean that there is a pile of $5,000 worth of supplies expense laying around the company somewhere, but rather, if the cost of all the supplies *used* by the company were added up, the total would be $5,000.

In contrast to the amounts on the income statement, the dollar amounts on the year-end balance sheet represent what the company has, what it owes, and the owners' equity as of the end of the year. For example, if the balance sheet shows merchandise inventory $24,000, that means that as of the balance sheet date, $24,000 of inventory was owned by the company. Likewise, an accounts payable balance of $15,000 means that the company has a $15,000 debt for accounts payable at year end. Balance sheet amounts reflect the company's position at a point in time rather than reflecting an accumulation over a period.

What happens at the beginning of a new business year? How should the amounts reflected on the financial statements at the end of one year be treated as the company begins a new business year? The answer depends on the nature of the items in question. As we've discussed, the nature of items on the income statement is quite different from the nature of balance sheet items. For this reason, treatment of the two groups of items at the end of the business year differs.

Should the service revenue earned on the first day of the new year be added to the amount of service revenue from the last year? Well, not really. Instead, it would be better to start off with a clean slate for revenues each year. That way, when one looked at a revenue account, it would include the revenue earned to date in the current year. It would not reflect the revenue earned in past years. As it turns out, all income statement accounts should start out each year with a clean slate, a zero balance.

Income statement accounts are called **temporary accounts** because the amounts entered in these accounts are eliminated at the very end of the accounting year. That is, income statement accounts are used only temporarily — ultimately, the account balances are eliminated to make way for the next year's entries. Temporary accounts are also called **nominal accounts**.

In contrast to amounts shown on the income statement, amounts shown on the balance sheet do not reflect an accumulation throughout the year. Rather, balance sheet items reflect the dollar amount corresponding to something that exists as of the balance sheet date. The dollar amounts on the balance sheet should not start off at zero each year, but rather the ending balance from one year should become the beginning balance of the next.

Balance sheet accounts represent balances of things the company has, owes, or the balance of owners' equity. For example, the cash account represents the amount of cash the company has. If the company has $1,000 cash on the last day of the business year, for instance, midnight, December 31, 1994, then the company will have the same amount of cash at 12:01 A.M., January 1, 1995. Likewise, if the company has a liability for accounts payable totaling $2,000 at 11:59 P.M. on December 31, it will have the same liability at 12:01 A.M. January 1. Accordingly, these accounts should not start at zero at the beginning of the new year, but rather the ending balance from one year should become the beginning balance of the next.

Balance sheet accounts are called **permanent accounts** because the balances in these accounts are not eliminated at the end of the year. Balances in permanent accounts certainly may change as a result of business activity, but they are not eliminated simply because the end of the business year has arrived. The balance in each balance sheet account represents something that the company has (an asset), or owes (a liability), or the ownership interest (an equity). Just because a new year begins does not change the company's financial position, nor should the account balances representing its financial position be changed. Permanent accounts are also called **real accounts**.

Based on our discussion, the ending of one business year and the beginning of the next impacts temporary and permanent accounts differently. The process which takes place at the end of the year to prepare account balances for the next year's activity is called the **closing process**. As its name implies, the closing process is the last step performed in the accounting records each business year. This process closes out the past year's temporary account balances, in preparation for the next year's entries.

Closing an account means bringing the account balance to zero. In order to close an account, an entry opposite of the account's current balance must be made. When accounts are closed, their balances are transferred *somewhere*, which indicates the other portion of the entry. During the closing process, the **Income Summary** account is used as the offset account to the debit and credit entries required to zero-out the revenue and expense accounts. Thus, during the closing process, we will close revenues and expenses *to* Income Summary.

The entire closing process can be described in four simple steps:

1. Close all revenue accounts to Income Summary.

2. Close all expense accounts to Income Summary.

3. Close Income Summary to Retained Earnings.

4. Close the Dividends account to Retained Earnings.

Now, let's look at each step in more detail, describing its purpose and illustrating the basic format of the necessary journal entry.

Step   1.   Close all revenue accounts to Income Summary.

As you know, revenue accounts have credit balances. Accordingly, to decrease a revenue account to zero will require a debit entry equal to the balance in the account. Thus, a debit entry to a revenue account in an amount equal to the account balance will close the account.

The revenue accounts are to be closed *to* Income Summary, so that account must be credited. For Step 1., each revenue account must be debited for the amount of its account balance, and Income Summary must be credited for the total. The basic format of the first closing entry is:

```
        Revenue A                    XX
        Revenue B                    XX
            Income  Summary                   XXXX
```

Posting this entry will reduce all revenue account balances to zero, closing each account, and will transfer their balances to the Income Summary account.

Step   2. Close all expense accounts to Income Summary.

As you know, expense accounts have debit balances. Accordingly, to decrease an expense account to zero will require a credit entry equal to the balance in the account. Thus, a credit entry to an expense account in an amount equal to the account balance will close the account. The expense accounts are to be closed *to* Income Summary, so that account must be debited. For Step 2., each expense account must be credited for the amount of its account balance, and Income Summary must be debited for the total. The basic format of the second closing entry is:

```
        Income Summary               XXX
            Expense A                        X
            Expense B                        X
            Expense C                        X
```

Posting this entry will reduce all expense account balances to zero, closing each account, and will transfer their balances to the Income Summary account.

Step   3. Close Income Summary to Retained Earnings.

This step requires that Income Summary be closed, completing the entire life-cycle of this account. Income Summary is a tool account used only to gather account balances and facilitate the closing process. To close the Income Summary account we need to know its balance.

Notice that in Step 1., the balances in all revenue accounts were closed to Income Summary. In Step 2., the balances in all expense accounts were closed to Income Summary. A T-account illustrating the impact of Steps 1 and 2 on Income Summary may be helpful:

```
                        Income Summary

(Step 2. expenses closed         │  XXXX  (Step 1. revenues closed
      to Income Summary)   XXX    │             to Income Summary)
                           ───────┼───────
                                  │   X    Balance after Steps 1 and 2
```

The balance in the Income Summary account after Steps 1 and 2 of the closing process is equal to the difference between revenues and expenses (net income or net loss for the year).

When revenues are larger than expenses, Income Summary has a credit balance after Steps 1 and 2. This credit balance represents the income for the period and it should be added to retained earnings. To accomplish this addition to retained earnings, Income Summary is closed by a debit equal to the balance in Income Summary, and the Retained Earnings account is credited for the same amount. The basic format of the entry to close the Income Summary account and increase Retained Earnings by the current period's net income is shown below:

```
Income Summary                      X
       Retained Earnings                  X
```

The entry above is one of the most interesting in accounting because it is that magical entry that adds the period's income to Retained Earnings and thus increases shareholders' equity by the amount of earnings. Retained Earnings has a normal credit balance, so the entry above would increase the account balance.

Step   4. Close the Dividends account to Retained Earnings.

The Dividends account has a normal debit balance and is a temporary account. To close the Dividends account, a credit entry equal to the account balance is made. To close the account *to* Retained Earnings, a corresponding debit entry is made. Debiting Retained Earnings causes a decrease in its account balance, which is the consequence of declaring dividends.

```
Retained Earnings                   XX
       Dividends                           XX
```

This entry too is quite interesting because it reduces Retained Earnings by the amount of income distributed to shareholders. Keep in mind that retained earnings is composed of all the income earned by the company from the beginning of its existence, less the income distributed to owners (dividends).

Note that all companies will prepare closing entries to complete Steps 1, 2, and 3 of the closing process. Step 4, however, is only necessary if dividends were declared during the business year. Closing the Dividends account must be recorded separately from the closing of revenues and expenses, because a distribution to owners has no effect on the company's net income. For this reason, Dividends is closed directly to Retained Earnings. The entry made in Step 4 of the closing process has no impact on Steps 1, 2, or 3 and has no impact on the activity in Income Summary.

After all closing entries have been recorded and posted, all revenue accounts, all expense accounts, the Income Summary account and the Dividends account should each have a balance of zero. In addition, the Retained Earnings account balance should agree with the ending retained earnings amount shown on the bridge statement (the statement of retained earnings or the statement of stockholders' equity.)

THE CLOSING PROCESS FOR AMANDA'S TYPING SERVICE

To see the closing process in action, let's apply the 4-step process to Amanda's Typing Service. Recall that the accounting information and financial statements for Amanda's Typing Service developed in Module 4 were for January 1996 only. Because January is not the end of the company's business year, closing entries were not made at that time. Rather, closing entries would be made at the end of the company's business year which, for Amanda's is December 31. To illustrate the closing process, let's assume that on December 31, 1996, the end of Amanda's Typing Service's first year of business, the adjusted trial balance for the company appeared as follows:

Amanda's Typing Service
Adjusted Trial Balance
As of December 31, 1996

Cash	$ 13,242	
Accounts Receivable	5,240	
Supplies	590	
Office Furniture	2,500	
Accumulated Depreciation, Office Furn		$ 480
Computer System	7,000	
Accumulated Depreciation, Computer		1,500
Accounts Payable		4,200
Wages Payable		342
Interest Payable		450
Notes Payable		5,000
Common Stock		3,000
Dividends	6,000	
Service Revenue		45,800
Wage Expense	20,850	
Supplies Expense	220	
Depreciation Expense, Office Furn	480	
Depreciation Expense, Computer	1,500	
Delivery Expense	900	
Insurance Expense	1,200	
Telephone Expense	600	
Interest Expense	450	
	$ 60,772	$ 60,772

Now, let's go through the 4-step closing process for Amanda's Typing Service.

Step 1. Close all revenue accounts to Income Summary.

In the case of Amanda's Typing Service, the only revenue account shown in the trial balance is Service Revenue. To close this $45,800 account balance *to* Income Summary, a debit of $45,800 is made to Service Revenue and a credit of the same amount is made to Income Summary, as shown below:

General Journal				Page 5	
Date 1996		Description	Post Ref	Debit	Credit
Dec.	31	Service Revenue		45,800	
		Income Summary			45,800
		To close revenues for the year			

As a consequence of the above entry, the balance in Service Revenue is zero, and Income Summary has a credit balance of $45,800. If the company had more than one revenue account, each would have been debited for the amount of its credit balance, and the total would have been credited to Income Summary.

Step 2 - Close all expense accounts to Income Summary.

In the case of Amanda's Typing Service, there are several expense accounts to close. The entry to close Amanda's expense accounts is shown below:

	31	Income Summary		26,200	
		Wage Expense			20,850
		Supplies Expense			220
		Depreciation Exp, Office F.			480
		Depreciation Exp, Computer			1,500
		Delivery Expense			900
		Insurance Expense			1,200
		Telephone Expense			600
		Interest Expense			450
		To close expenses for the year			

As a result of the closing entry above, the balance in all expense accounts is zero and now the Income Summary account reflects a total of two entries.

Step   3. Close Income Summary to Retained Earnings.

In order to close Income Summary, we must first determine the account's balance. The balance in Income Summary can be determined by examining the closing entries we have made thus far for Amanda's Typing Service. Although not required, it may be helpful to post the entries from Steps 1 and 2 to a T-account for Income Summary.

```
                        Income Summary
                     ─────────────────────────
                        │  45,800  (Step 1)
    (Step 2)  26,200    │
                     ─────────────────────────
                        │  19,600  Balance after Steps 1 and 2
```

As indicated above, the balance in the Income Summary account after Steps 1 and 2 of the closing process is a credit balance of $19,600. This credit balance represents the income for the period and it should be added to retained earnings. To accomplish this addition to retained earnings, Income Summary is closed by a debit of $19,600 and the Retained Earnings account is credited for the same amount, as shown below:

	31	Income Summary		19,600	
		Retained Earnings			19,600
		Close Income Summary; add income to R/E			

As a result of the closing entry above, the Income Summary account has a zero balance and the balance in Retained Earnings has been increased by $19,600, net income for the year.

Step   4. Close the Dividends account to Retained Earnings.

In the case of Amanda's Typing Service, the Dividends account has a debit balance of $6,000. Therefore, to close Dividends to Retained Earnings requires a $6,000 debit to Retained Earnings and a credit to Dividends in the same amount. The entry to complete Step 4 of the closing process is:

	31	Retained Earnings		6,000	
		Dividends			6,000
		Close dividends; reduce Retained E.			

As a result of the closing entry above, the Dividends account has a zero balance, and the balance in Retained Earnings has been reduced by $6,000, the amount of dividends declared during the year.

RESULTS OF THE CLOSING PROCESS

Once all the closing entries are posted to the general ledger, the balances in all the revenue accounts, all the expense accounts, the Income Summary account, and the Dividends account will equal zero. Also, the Retained Earnings account balance will reflect the addition of the period's net income, and the reduction caused by the distribution of earnings to shareholders in the form of dividends.

To illustrate the effects of the closing process on the general ledger accounts of Amanda's Typing Service, T-accounts have been prepared. Beginning balances in the T-accounts are those assumed in the adjusted trial balance of December 31, 1996. A closing entry was made for each of the four steps of the closing process. Numbers shown in parentheses indicate the entry (1-4) from which the posting was made.

Note that Amanda's Typing Service had no beginning balance in Retained Earnings because the year illustrated was the company's first year of operation. Retained Earnings is a permanent account, and for most established businesses, the account will carry a balance throughout the year. Therefore, in most cases, Retained Earnings will have a balance prior to the impact of the closing entries.

Cash		Accounts Receivable		Supplies		Office Furniture	
13,242		5,240		590		2,500	

Accumulated Dep., Office Furn		Computer System		Accumulated Dep., Comp. System		Accounts Payable	
	480	7,000			1,500		4,200

Wages Payable		Interest Payable		Notes Payable		Common Stock	
	342		450		5,000		3,000

Dividends		Service Revenue		Wage Expense		Supplies Expense	
6,000	6,000 (4)	(1) 45,800	45,800	20,850	20,850 (2)	220	220 (2)
-0-			-0-	-0-		-0-	

Dep. Expense Office Furn		Dep. Expense Comp. System		Delivery Expense		Insurance Expense	
480	480 (2)	1,500	1,500 (2)	900	900 (2)	1,200	1,200 (2)
-0-		-0-		-0-		-0-	

Telephone Expense		Interest Expense		Income summary		Retained Earnings	
600	600 (2)	450	450 (2)		45,800 (1)		19,600 (3)
-0-		-0-		(2) 26,200		(4) 6,000	
				(3) 19,600			13,600
				-0-			

After the closing entries have been posted to the general ledger, a trial balance should be prepared. A trial balance prepared immediately following the posting of the closing entries is called a post-closing trial balance. At this point in the recording process, only balance sheet accounts reflect account balances other than zero. If shown at all, income statement accounts reflect zero balances.

The post-closing trial balance for Amanda's Typing Service is shown below:

Amanda's Typing Service Post-closing Trial Balance As of December 31, 1996		
Cash	$ 13,242	
Accounts Receivable	5,240	
Supplies	590	
Office Furniture	2,500	
Accumulated Depreciation, Office Furn.		$ 480
Computer System	7,000	
Accumulated Depreciation, Computer		1,500
Accounts Payable		4,200
Wages Payable		342
Interest Payable		450
Notes Payable		5,000
Common Stock		3,000
Retained Earnings		13,600
	$28,572	$28,572

Now our account balances are ready for the beginning of the new business year. The balance sheet accounts reflect the same amounts as they did prior to the closing entries with the exception of the Retained Earnings account. Also, the income statement accounts have been closed to zero to provide a clean slate to record revenues and expenses in the next period.

Closing entries are made only at the end of the business year after adjusting entries have been recorded and financial statements have been prepared. Are closing entries made at the end of each accounting period? Well, they are if the accounting period is defined as the company's business year. Often however, a more casual use of the term "accounting period" is made, referring to a month or a quarter of the business year. At the end of these periods, adjusting entries are often made and interim financial statements are often prepared. In casual conversation, the process of adjusting account balances and preparing financial statements may be referred to as "closing". However, the formal closing process as we have described it in this module is generally completed only at the end of the business year — not at the end of interim periods.

Closing entries are the final ones recorded in the accounting records at the end of the business year. In the next module, we explore an optional accounting procedure performed at various times throughout the business year.

THE CLOSING PROCESS FOR PROPRIETORSHIPS AND PARTNERSHIPS

The closing process can be completed in four simple steps. The examples within the module illustrated the process for a corporation. Closing entries for proprietorships and partnerships are not very different from what you have already seen.

Steps 1 and 2 of the closing process would be exactly the same, regardless of the form of business involved. In Step 3, however, Income Summary would be closed to capital accounts. For a proprietorship, with only one capital account, the closing entry for Step 3 would be:

```
Income Summary              XX
     A. Wells, Capital            XX
```

The effect of this entry would be the same as what was described earlier — Income Summary would be closed and its balance would be transferred to an equity account. This entry increases the owner's capital account by the net income earned during the year.

A partnership will have more than one capital account, but the same approach is taken to Step 3 of the closing process:

```
Income Summary              XX
     A. Wells, Capital            X
     J. Wells, Capital            X
```

This entry, too, would bring the balance in Income Summary to zero. The earnings for the year would be shared by the partners in whatever proportion was outlined in the partnership agreement. Each partner's share of the year's earnings would increase his or her capital account.

Step 4 of the closing process would also be a bit different for proprietorships and partnerships. Recall this step is only completed if distributions are made to the owners. In a corporation, owners get distributions in the form of dividends. In proprietorships and partnerships, distributions to owners are called drawings or withdrawals. Drawings or Withdrawals accounts are temporary accounts with normal debit balances. They function much the same way as a Dividends account. Thus, if the owner of a proprietorship has taken drawings during the year, Step 4 of the closing process would be:

```
A. Wells, Capital              X
     Drawings (or Withdrawals)      X
```

This entry would have an effect similar to what has already been described. The Drawings account balance would be zero, and the owner's capital account would be reduced by the amount of the drawings for the year.

In a partnership setting, the balance in each partner's Drawings account will be closed to the partner's Capital account. In our example, if each partner made withdrawals during the period, the entry would be:

```
A. Wells, Capital            XX
J. Wells, Capital             X
     A. Wells, Drawings            XX
     J. Wells, Drawings             X
```

As expected, this entry would close the Drawings accounts and reduce the Capital accounts of each partner.

After all the closing entries have been recorded and posted to the general ledger, account balances for a proprietorship or partnership will be similar to those described for a corporation. The balances in all the revenue accounts, all the expense accounts, the Income Summary account, and the Drawings accounts will equal zero. Also, all capital account balances will reflect the addition of the period's net income, and the reduction caused by the distributions to owners in the form of drawings. These capital account balances should agree with the ending capital account amounts shown on the company's statement of capital.

APPLY WHAT YOU HAVE LEARNED

5-1. (Identify Temporary and Permanent Accounts)

Required:
Identify the following accounts as either temporary or permanent.

ACCOUNT	T = TEMPORARY P = PERMANENT
Accounts Payable	
Accounts Receivable	
Accumulated Depreciation	
Additional Paid-in Capital	
Cash	
Common Stock	
Depreciation Expense	
Dividends	
Elsie Cow, Withdrawals	
Elsie Cow, Capital	
Equipment	
Expired Insurance	
Interest Payable	
Interest Expense	
Interest Income	
Notes Payable	
Prepaid Rent	
Rent Expense	
Rent Revenue	
Retained Earnings	
Service Revenue	
Supplies	
Supplies Expense	
Wages Payable	
Wages Expense	

5-2. (Real and Nominal Accounts, Normal Balance)

Required:

Identify the following accounts as either *Real* or *Nominal* accounts, and indicate the normal balance of each account.

ACCOUNT	R = REAL N = NOMINAL	NORMAL BALANCE Debit or Credit
Accounts Payable		
Accounts Receivable		
Accumulated Depreciation		
Additional Paid-in Capital		
Cash		
Common Stock		
Depreciation Expense		
Dividends		
M. Smart, Drawings		
M. Smart, Capital		
Office Furniture		
Expired Insurance		
Interest Payable		
Interest Expense		
Unearned Revenue		
Notes Payable		
Prepaid Rent		
Rent Expense		
Rent Revenue		
Retained Earnings		
Service Revenue		
Supplies		
Supplies Used		
Wages Payable		
Wages Expense		

5-3. (Closing Entries from T-accounts)

Revenues		Expenses		Income Summary	
	7,000	3,000			

Dividends			Retained Earnings	
1,200				6,000

Required:

Using the information from the above t-accounts:

a. How much is net income? $_____

b. Enter the four closing entries in the t-accounts above.

c. What is the new balance in Retained Earnings after closing? $_____

5-4. (Basic Closing Entries — Corporation)

The adjusted trial balance for Michelle's Personal Parties at December 31, 1995 is:

Michelle's Personal Parties
Adjusted Trial Balance
December 31, 1995

	Debit	Credit
Cash	$ 5,000	
Supplies	3,000	
Equipment	15,000	
Accounts Payable		$ 2,500
Common Stock		12,000
Retained Earnings		3,500
Dividends	1,200	
Service Revenue		24,000
Rent Expense	1,800	
Food Expense	16,000	
Totals	$42,000	$42,000

Required: a.   Prepare the entry to close the revenue account.

         b.   Prepare the entry to close the expense accounts.

   c.   What is the balance in *Income Summary* after entries a. and b.? $_____
           What does this balance represent? _____

   d.   Give the entry to close the *Income Summary* account.

   e.   Give the entry to close the *Dividends* account.

5-5. (Post-Closing Trial Balance and Statement of Retained Earnings)

Required:

a.   Using the information from Problem 5-4, prepare a post-closing trial balance for Michelle's Personal Parties.

b.   Prepare a retained earnings statement for Michelle's Personal Parties for the period ended December 31, 1995.

5-6. (Corporate Closing Entries)

The adjusted trial balance for Ralph's Rodent Ridder is:

Ralph's Rodent Ridder
Adjusted Trial Balance
December 31, 1995

	Debit	Credit
Accounts Payable		$15,000
Accounts Receivable	$12,000	
Accumulated Depreciation		2,200
Cash	1,100	
Common Stock		25,000
Depreciation Expense	3,500	
Dividends	6,500	
Equipment	5,000	
Interest Revenue		1,200
Notes Receivable	10,000	
Prepaid Rent	3,200	
Rent Expense	2,400	
Retained Earnings		5,400
Service Revenue		21,500
Supplies	3,000	
Supplies Expense	1,800	
Truck Fleet	30,000	
Unearned Revenue		8,200
Totals	$78,500	$78,500

Required:

a. In the space provided, prepare closing entries for Ralph's Rodent Ridder at December 31, 1995.

b. How much is net income for 1995? $_____

c. What is the new balance in Retained Earnings at December 31, 1995 after closing?
$_____

5-7. (Post-Closing Trial Balance)

Required:
Using the information from Problem 5-6, prepare a post-closing trial balance for Ralph's Rodent Ridder.

5-8. (Basic Closing Entries — Proprietorship)

Christopher Rules is an electronic communications service for legal precedents. The company's adjusted trial balance at September 30, 1995, the close of its fiscal year is:

```
             Christopher Rules
          Adjusted Trial Balance
            September 30, 1995

                              Debit      Credit
Cash                        $ 7,000
Accounts Receivable          12,000
Accounts Payable                       $ 8,000
Christopher, Capital                     2,000
Christopher, Withdrawals      6,000
Service Revenue                         50,000
Wages Expense                32,000
Electricity Expense           3,000
Totals                      $60,000    $60,000
```

Required: a.   Prepare the entry to close the revenue account.

b.   Prepare the entry to close the expense accounts.

c.   What is the balance in *Income Summary* after entries a. and b.?
$_____
What does this balance represent? _____

d.   Give the entry to close the *Income Summary* account.

e.   Give the entry to close the *Withdrawals* account.

5-9. (Post-Closing Trial Balance and Statement of Capital)

Required: a.   Using the information from Problem 5-8, prepare a post-closing trial balance for Christopher Rules.

b.   Prepare a capital statement for Christopher Rules for the year ended September 30, 1995.

5-10. (Partnership Closing Entries and Post-Closing Trial Balance)

An alphabetical list of adjusted account balances for *Mike & Jean's Hawaiian Connection* as of August 31, 1995 is:

Accounts Receivable	15,000
Accounts Payable	14,000
Cash	8,700
Insurance Expense	1,200
Interest Revenue	1,600
Jean, Drawings	1,500
Jean, Capital	5,000
Mike, Capital	3,000
Mike, Drawings	2,000
Prepaid Insurance	5,600
Rent Expense	4,800
Service Revenue	36,000
Supplies Expense	1,300
Supplies	5,700
Unearned Revenue	4,200
Wages Expense	18,000

Required:

a.   Prepare an adjusted trial balance.

b.   In the space below, prepare closing entries, assuming that Mike and Jean share profits and losses equally.

c.   How much is net income for the fiscal year ended August 31, 1995?
$_____

d.   What are the new balances in Mike and Jean's Capital accounts after closing?

Mike, Capital $_____   Jean, Capital $_____

e.   Prepare a post-closing trial balance.

5-11. (Corporate Closing Entries, Post-Closing Trial Balance, and Financial Statements)

The adjusted trial balance for Anderson Engineering at the end of its first fiscal year of operations is:

Anderson Engineering
Adjusted Trial Balance
January 31, 1995

	Debit	Credit
Cash	$22,600	
Accounts Receivable	10,000	
Supplies	125	
Equipment	11,000	
Accumulated Depreciation		$ 150
Accounts Payable		9,130
Wages Payable		300
Notes Payable		12,000
Interest Payable		120
Common Stock		10,000
Dividends	500	
Service Revenue		17,500
Wages Expense	1,200	
Supplies Expense	375	
Depreciation Expense	150	
Telephone Expense	130	
Interest Expense	120	
Rent Expense	2,500	
Utilities Expense	500	
Totals	$49,200	$49,200

Required:

a.   Prepare closing entries.

b.   Prepare a post-closing trial balance.

c.   Prepare the three financial statements.

5-12. (Proprietorship Closing Entries, Post-Closing Trial Balance, and Financial Statements)

The adjusted trial balance for Smith's Income Tax Service at the end of its fiscal year is:

Smith's Income Tax Service
Adjusted Trial Balance
July 31, 1995

	Debit	Credit
Cash	$ 1,000	
Accounts Receivable	2,250	
Supplies	260	
Prepaid Insurance	1,100	
Equipment	1,500	
Accum. Deprec., Equipment		$ 50
Computer System	2,200	
Accum. Deprec., Computer		55
Accounts Payable		1,730
Wages Payable		200
Smith, Capital		7,000
Smith, Withdrawals	2,500	
Service Revenue		5,750
Wages Expense	2,000	
Supplies Expense	540	
Insurance Expense	100	
Deprec. Exp., Equipment	50	
Deprec. Exp., Computer	55	
Telephone Expense	80	
Rent Expense	1,000	
Utilities Expense	150	
Totals	$14,785	$14,785

Required:

a.   Prepare closing entries.

b.   Prepare a post-closing trial balance.

c.   Prepare the three financial statements.

5-13. (Closing Entries and Post-Closing Trial Balance — Corporation)

The adjusted trial balance below reflects account balances (in random order) resulting from a year of operations.

Filadora Futures
Adjusted Trial Balance
December 31, 1995

	Debit	Credit
Accounts Payable		$ 17,400
Accounts Receivable	$ 30,000	
Accumulated Depreciation		5,400
Cash	47,400	
Common Stock		22,000
Depreciation Expense	5,400	
Dividends	6,000	
Equipment	33,000	
Interest Payable		4,400
Interest Expense	4,400	
Notes Payable		36,000
Retained Earnings		10,000
Rent Expense	18,500	
Service Revenue		90,000
Supplies	4,500	
Supplies Expense	2,500	
Telephone Expense	4,700	
Utilities Expense	18,000	
Wages Payable		3,600
Wages Expense	14,400	
Totals	$188,800	$188,800

Required:

a.   Prepare closing entries.

b.   Prepare a post-closing trial balance.

MODULE 6

REVERSING ENTRIES

At the end of each business year, adjusting entries are made to bring account balances to their proper amounts before financial statements are prepared. Then, the formal closing process described in Module 5 is performed. Adjusting entries are also often recorded when interim financial statements are to be prepared (e.g., monthly or quarterly). In the periods following the recording of adjusting entries, care must be taken. *Most* entries recorded in the next period are unaffected by the adjusting entries, but, in some cases, adjusting entries directly affect the recording of subsequent transactions.

What happens when the bookkeeper makes an entry that relates to an item for which an adjustment was previously made? As an example, assume that an adjusting entry was made to record $200 as the estimated telephone expense for December 1994. When the telephone bill is actually received in January, the bookkeeper cannot correctly record the bill without reviewing the amount that was already recorded as part of the previous period's adjustment process. When the actual telephone bill is received, the bookkeeper will record the bill along with all the other routine bills received. If the amount of the actual telephone bill is $220, the entire $220 must be paid, but only an additional $20 of telephone expense needs to be recorded. In this way, the subsequent entry has been affected by an adjusting entry made in a previous period.

In this module, we refer to the entries to record regular, ongoing transactions in the new accounting period as routine entries. One big problem arising in the recording process is that the bookkeeper seldom knows if, and how, the previous period's adjusting entries affect each of the routine entries being made to record transactions in the current period. There are several possible reasons why this situation exists. First, the adjusting entries are often made by someone other than the person who is responsible for the routine recording of business transactions. Often, bookkeepers record routine transactions throughout the period, but an accountant may be brought in to determine the necessary adjusting entries before financial statements are prepared. Second, too many adjusting entries may be involved for it to be realistic to expect the bookkeeper to remember the effects of each one. Keep in mind the examples related to Amanda's Typing Service are useful illustrations, but the recording process for a real company will be much more involved. Third, often considerable time passes before the routine entries which relate to a previous period's adjusting entries are made. Especially if adjusting entries are prepared only once a year, the related, subsequent entries may be recorded months later.

The effort required to consider the impact of past adjusting entries before making new entries can be considerable. In addition to being a hardship on the bookkeeping staff, situations requiring such a review of past accounting records open the door to accounting errors. With the following example, we can see how an error can occur if the bookkeeper fails to consider the impact of a previous adjusting entry.

On November 1, 1994, Carol Jean's Engineering Co. borrowed $12,000 from the local bank at 10% interest, agreeing to pay the interest costs when the loan is repaid on February 1, 1995. On December 31, 1994, the company recorded the following adjusting entry to accrue two months' interest expense
($12,000 X 10% X 2/12 = $200):

```
 1994
Dec. 31    Interest Expense                 200
                Interest Payable                     200
```

If, when February 1, 1995 arrives, the bookkeeper erroneously makes the routine entry to record the interest payment without regard to the adjusting entry, the subsequent entry would be made as follows:

```
 1995
Feb. 1     Interest Expense                 300
                Cash                                 300
```

Because the previous adjusting entry was not considered, the entry above to record the payment of interest creates two serious problems. First, $200 of the $300 was already recognized as expense in the previous period. Therefore, interest expense is overstated. Second, the liability account, Interest Payable, remains on the books even though the $200 of interest, which was owed as of December 31, 1994, was paid on February 1, 1995.

In order to record the interest payment correctly, the bookkeeper must consider the adjusting entry when determining the accounts and amounts to debit and credit. In doing so, the bookkeeper would determine that Interest Payable should be reduced to zero by a debit, and that Interest Expense should only be debited for the one month's interest not yet recognized. Therefore, the correct entry would be:

```
 1995
Feb. 1     Interest Payable                 200
           Interest Expense                 100
                Cash                                 300
```

Compared to the simpler (but incorrect) February 1 entry first suggested, this entry is a bit cumbersome. And, as you might imagine, the process of reviewing adjusting entries and account balances as routine entries are made is tedious, time-consuming, and generally hated by all bookkeepers. In this example, it may be much better to take steps so that even if adjusting entries have been made, the subsequent payment of interest can be routinely recorded as a straightforward debit to Interest Expense and credit to Cash. Creating a setting in which routine transactions do not require a review of earlier adjusting entries is precisely the purpose of using reversing entries. **Reversing entries** are entries made at the very beginning of an accounting period to "undo" the impact of selected adjusting entries made in the previous period.

The use of reversing entries is optional. Although reversing entries offer definite advantages, some companies do not use them and, instead, require their bookkeeping personnel to take special care when making routine entries. The use of reversing entries is very popular, however, because it allows entries to be made in a routine fashion without regard to the effects of adjusting entries recorded earlier. Certainly, most medium and large companies use reversing entries, so time spent understanding them is worthwhile.

As the name implies, a reversing entry is simply a reversal of an adjusting entry that has already been recorded. Reversing entries are extremely easy to make because all the accountant has to do is to reverse the debits and credits originally recorded in the adjusting entry. Reversing entries are the very first entries made in the new accounting period. In this setting, the accounting period may be a new business year or simply the next quarter or month. Reversing entries may be used in any period subsequent to one in which adjusting entries were recorded. Let's take another look at the December 31, 1994 interest expense adjusting entry for Carol Jean's Engineering Co. The entry is shown below:

```
1994
Dec. 31    Interest Expense            200
                Interest Payable              200
```

To reverse an entry, we simply debit the accounts and amounts that were originally credited, and credit the accounts and amounts that were originally debited. In this case, the reversing entry corresponding to the adjusting entry above is:

```
1995
Jan. 1     Interest Payable            200
                Interest Expense              200
```

The reversing entry above is dated January 1, 1995, the first day of the next accounting period, regardless of whether December 31, 1994 was the end of the entire business year or the end of an interim period. Note that all that is necessary in order to prepare a reversing entry is to "reverse" the debits and the credits recorded in an adjusting entry. Obviously, the procedure to *make* reversing entries is so simple that little time, and almost no study, is required to master the skill.

There are, however, two challenges relative to reversing entries. The first challenge is understanding the mechanics of *how* reversing entries work, which will also lead to a better understanding of why they are useful. The second challenge is determining *which* adjusting entries should be reversed and which should not. Not all adjusting entries should be reversed — only certain ones are "reversible".

HOW REVERSING ENTRIES WORK

Before you can understand the mechanics of reversing entries and how they benefit the recording process, it is critical that you understand the three categories of adjusting entries described in Module 4, and the effects of the closing process described in Module 5. If you do not understand these topics, you may need to take time now to review them. To explore in detail how reversing entries work, we will continue to use the interest accrual entry for Carol Jean's Engineering Co. as our example.

As mentioned earlier, reversing entries are useful in any period subsequent to one in which adjusting entries were recorded. In the first scenario, we will assume that the December 31, 1994 entry was an adjustment made at the end of the business year. Thus, the adjustment process would be followed by the closing process. In the second scenario, we will examine the usefulness of reversing entries in a period following an interim period in which adjusting entries were recorded. In both cases, we will use T-accounts to show the impact of the entries on the accounts involved.

To begin the first scenario, let's look at the adjusting entry made on December 31, 1994. The adjusting entry to accrue two months' worth of interest expense is shown below. (A = Adjusting entry)

```
        Interest Expense              Interest Payable
                        |                          |
  A      200            |                          |   200      A
                        |                          |
```

Now, let's look at the impact of closing entries. Interest Payable is a liability account, a real account, and therefore, is not closed during the closing process. Of the accounts shown above, only Interest Expense is affected by the closing process. The impact of the closing entries on Interest Expense is shown below. (C = Closing entry)

```
        Interest Expense              Interest Payable
                        |                          |
  A      200            |                          |   200      A
          _____   200  |   C                      |
          -0-           |                          |
```

As the T-accounts indicate, the post-closing balance in Interest Expense is zero, and the liability account, Interest Payable, still shows a $200 credit balance. This is how the accounts would begin the new year *regardless* of whether or not reversing entries are used. That is, the use of reversing entries has no impact on the adjusting process or the closing process. In fact, a company could wait until the balances above are entered as beginning balances for the next period before even deciding whether or not to use reversing entries.

Our next step is to follow the routine entries made to record the payment of interest in the next accounting period. First, we will examine the situation assuming reversing entries are not used, and then, we will examine the same situation, but we will assume that reversing entries are used.

Let's see what happens when reversing entries are NOT used. In this case, the bookkeeper must review the accounts to help determine the correct entry to record the February 1 interest payment. In addition to a decrease in cash of $300, as we stated earlier, Interest Payable should be eliminated, and Interest Expense should be increased by $100. The entry to record the subsequent payment of interest is shown in the T-accounts below. (S = Subsequent entry)

```
        Interest Expense                    Interest Payable

  A        200                                        200      A
                    200      C            S    200
          -0-                                        -0-
  S        100
```

```
                        Cash

                                300      S
```

Note that Interest Expense reflects $100, which is the interest expense for the one month of 1995, and the balance in Interest Payable is eliminated, which is appropriate because the company no longer owes the bank any interest. The payment of interest reduced Cash by $300, which must be reflected in the recording of the transaction. Of course, it can be assumed that the Cash account had a balance prior to this entry. The T-account for Cash is shown only to show the complete subsequent, routine entry, in this case, the payment of interest.

Before moving on to the next part of our illustration, be certain you understand why the $100 debit balance in Interest Expense and the zero balance in Interest Payable are the correct balances after the impact of the interest payment. Whether or not reversing entries are used, account balances must be correct once the series of entries ending with the routine entry, referred to here as the subsequent entry, is complete. Thus, we must expect that our illustration of the example using a reversing entry will conclude with the same balances in Interest Expense and Interest Payable as indicated above.

Now let's see what happens when reversing entries ARE used. Remember, the use of reversing entries does not change the adjusting or closing process, so the impacts of the December 31 adjusting and closing entries shown in the T-accounts below are the same as in the first situation. After the closing process, Interest Expense would have a zero balance, and Interest Payable would show a $200 credit balance. Remember, a reversing entry is the exact opposite of an adjusting entry made in the previous period. The reversing entry, which would be the first entry of the next accounting period, is illustrated below.
(R = Reversing entry)

```
        Interest Expense                    Interest Payable

  A        200                                        200      A
                    200      C            R    200
          -0-                                        -0-
                    200      R
```

Note that the reversing entry causes a curious *credit* balance in the Interest Expense account. The reversing entry also eliminates the balance in the Interest Payable account, even though the company has not yet paid the interest it owes. It is a good thing that financial statements are not being prepared now, because the account balances do not properly reflect the company's financial position. However, as we will soon see, even though the account balances after the reversing entry seem a bit odd, these balances, in combination with a simple, routine, subsequent entry, will result in correct account balances.

On February 1, 1995, the entry to record the payment of interest must be made. Because the reversing entry was made, the bookkeeper need not review account balances, or consider the impact of the adjusting entry. Instead, a normal, routine, subsequent entry can be made to record the payment of interest, as shown below. (S = Subsequent entry)

Interest Expense		Interest Payable	
A 200			200 A
	200 C	R 200	
-0-			-0-
	200 R		
S 300			
100			

Cash	
	300 S

With the impact of the reversing entry in place, the subsequent payment of interest on February 1, 1995, can be recorded with a simple debit to increase Interest Expense and credit to decrease Cash. Note that after this entry, Interest Payable shows its proper zero balance, and Interest Expense has the correct $100 debit balance, reflecting the one month's interest expense incurred in 1995. The entry to record the payment of interest reflected a decrease in Cash of $300, as did the comparable entry made when it was assumed that reversing entries were not made. Indeed, the use of reversing entries cannot change the reality that the company paid $300 in this transaction.

In the example illustrated above, the entry on February 1, the subsequent entry, was made without the bookkeeper having to review past adjusting entries or account balances. With reversing entries in place, simple instructions to record interest payments as increases in the Interest Expense account would suffice. Thus, reversing entries offer considerable savings in time, while reducing the likelihood of recording errors.

Our examples thus far have explored the use of reversing entries after the end of an accounting period in which closing entries are made. As you recall from Module 5, generally, closing entries are made annually. When interim financial statements are prepared, adjusting entries are usually recorded, but closing entries are generally not made. Do reversing entries work when adjusting entries are made, but closing entries are not? Yes, they do. Reversing entries work equally well when closing entries are not made. Let's look at the interest accrual entry for Carol Jean's Engineering Co. once more, but this time we will assume that the company's fiscal year end is June 30. In that case, the December 31 adjustment was made for the preparation of quarterly, interim financial statements. Accordingly, no closing entries would be made at December 31, 1994.

Let's walk through the example again, under these new set of assumptions. As we will see, reversing entries can also save valuable time following adjusting entries made at the end of interim periods. The December 31, 1994 adjusting entry to accrue two months' of interest expense (illustrated below) would be the same regardless of whether the company chose to use reversing entries. (A = Adjusting entry)

```
    Interest Expense              Interest Payable
   ─────────────────            ─────────────────
   A    200     │                     │   200    A
               │                     │
```

Since December 31, 1994 is the end of an interim period, we are assuming that the adjusting process and the preparation of financial statements are not followed by the recording of closing entries. Instead, the next accounting period, in this case, the next quarter, begins on January 1, 1995, and the accounts would begin the new accounting period with the balances indicated above.

Our example will follow the same pattern as before. First, we will assume the company does NOT use reversing entries. Then, we can explore the results if the company does use them.

If no reversing entry is made, the next activity relevant to our example is the February 1, 1995 payment of interest. In this case, the bookkeeper must consider the impact of the adjusting entry made earlier and the current balances in the accounts, before making the entry. If no reversing entry had been made, the subsequent entry to record the payment of interest would have to properly separate the total amount debited between two accounts, as illustrated below. (S = Subsequent entry)

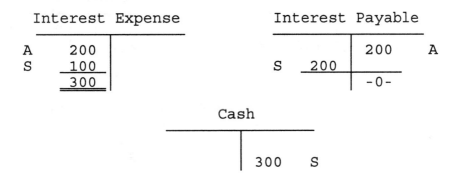

The entry to record the interest payment properly records $100 of interest expense, increasing the balance to $300. This result is different from that of our first example because of the absence of the closing entries. At the end of interim periods, if closing entries are not made, balances in temporary accounts such as revenues and expenses are not brought to zero. Rather, the account balances are maintained as the next period begins, and the balances accumulate toward the annual amounts to be reflected in the account balances at the end of the business year. As indicated above, the subsequent entry reduced the balance in the liability account, Interest Payable, to zero.

The $300 debit balance in Interest Expense and the zero balance in Interest Payable after the payment of interest on February 1, 1995 are correct. However, with the use of reversing entries, those balances can be achieved with a much simpler approach to the routine, subsequent entry reflecting the payment of interest.

Now, let's examine the impact of a reversing entry on the company's recording of its subsequent, routine entry. As we said, the adjusting process on December 31, 1994 would be the same regardless of the company's policy regarding reversing entries. Since no closing entries were made at the end of the interim period, the account balances at the beginning of the new period were those resulting from the adjusting process. If the company uses reversing entries, they will be the first ones recorded in the new period, as illustrated below.

(R = Reversing entry)

```
        Interest Expense              Interest Payable
                      |                            |
  A      200          |                            |  200     A
                      |  200    R       R    200   |
         -0-          |                            |  -0-
                      |                            |
```

As you can see, the reversing entry brings both account balances to zero. This result is logical, because the adjusting entry was the only activity in each account prior to the reversing entry. By definition, the reversing entry will "undo" the impact of the adjusting entry. Thus, after the adjusting entry and its corresponding reversing entry, both accounts show zero balances. As a result of the reversing entry, the account balances do not properly reflect the company's financial position, but this situation is only temporary. With the impact of the reversing entry in place, the subsequent entry to record the payment of interest on February 1, 1995, can be recorded simply, as shown below. (S = Subsequent entry)

```
        Interest Expense              Interest Payable
                      |                            |
  A      200          |                            |  200     A
                      |  200    R       R    200   |
         -0-          |                            |  -0-
  S      300          |                            |
```

```
                Cash
                  |
                  |  300    S
                  |
```

After the simple recording of the February 1 payment of interest, the accounts reflect the same balances achieved earlier. Interest Expense reflects the $300 incurred to date, and Interest Payable has a zero balance, because the company owes no interest at this point in time. Again, the impact on the Cash account was the same regardless of whether the company used reversing entries. However, because the reversing entry was used, the bookkeeper could record the interest payment without modifying the entry to accommodate the effect of the adjusting entry made in December.

In accounting periods following the recording of adjusting entries, reversing entries can be useful tools. The examples shown thus far have illustrated that when reversing entries are used, the bookkeeper does not need to review adjusting entries in order to properly record subsequent, routine transactions. For reversing entries to work properly though, only certain adjusting entries should be reversed. Reversing all adjusting entries would lead to erroneous account balances and require a host of correcting entries. We will now discuss how to tell which adjusting entries should be reversed, and which should not.

DETERMINING WHICH ENTRIES SHOULD BE REVERSED

In order for the accounting system to function properly, only certain entries should be reversed. If all adjusting entries are reversed, the resulting erroneous account balances would require a host of correcting entries or worse — inaccurate accounting information. So, even if a company wishes to take full advantage of the benefits of reversing entries, not all the adjustments made should be reversed. The big question, then, is: Which adjusting entries should be reversed? In other words, which adjustments are reversible?

The following rule will guide you in determining which adjusting entries should be reversed:

> **Reverse ALL accrual adjusting entries, and any deferral adjusting entry which changed an asset or liability account from a zero balance.**

You will recall from Module 4 that there are three types of adjusting entries: accruals, deferrals, and others. Being able to identify adjusting entries as belonging to one of these three categories is crucial to the use of the guideline stated above.

With respect to accrual entries, little discussion is needed, because *if* the adjusting entry is an accrual, it is reversible.

If the adjusting entry is a deferral, it should only be reversed if it changed an asset or liability account from a zero balance. Another way of stating this guideline is: Deferral adjustments are reversible if the asset or liability account involved had a zero balance *before* the adjustment was recorded. In these situations, the reversing entry will bring the asset or liability account back to its pre-adjustment balance of zero. So, the guideline can also be stated as: Deferral adjustments are reversible if the reversing entry would bring the asset or liability account to a zero balance.

Recall in Module 4, we saw how companies can originally record transactions related to deferred revenue or deferred expense in either an income statement (nominal) account, or a balance sheet (real) account. We went on to show that either technique works equally well, because during the adjustment process, the accountant would make entries changing the account balances to reflect the reality of the situation as of the financial statement date. How these original transactions are recorded impacts not only the adjusting entries that must be made, but also whether those adjusting entries are reversible.

Let's explore an example of deferred expense. Marcus Models prepares its financial statements on a calendar year basis. However, the company signed the lease on its office space on February 1, agreeing to pay $1,800 per quarter, paid in advance at the beginning of each quarter. Therefore, during 1994, the company paid rent on February 1, May 1, August 1, and November 1. Regardless of how the payment transactions were recorded throughout the year, after the adjustment process, the balances in Rent Expense and Prepaid Rent should reflect the true financial position of the company. As of December 31, 1994, the adjusted account balances of Marcus Models should indicate 11 months' of rent ($6,600) in Rent Expense, and 1 month's rent ($600) in Prepaid Rent. Before any adjustments on December 31, 1994, three situations are possible with regard to the rent payments: (1) Each payment could have been recorded as an increase (debit) to Rent Expense, (2) Each payment could have been recorded as an increase (debit) to Prepaid Rent, or (3) The four payments could have been recorded in a mixture of the ways described in (1) and (2). In each case, a deferral adjustment would be required to bring the account balances to their proper amounts. Let's see in which cases the adjusting entry would be reversible.

(1) Each payment could have been recorded as an increase (debit) to Rent Expense. If this were the case, before any adjustment were made, Rent Expense would reflect all four payments ($7,200), and the Prepaid Rent account would have a zero balance. The required adjusting entry would be:

```
1994
Dec. 31    Prepaid Rent                  600
                Rent Expense                    600
```

This deferral adjustment would reduce the balance in the expense account by $600 and increase the asset account, Prepaid Rent, from zero to $600. Because all the payments were recorded as increases to Rent Expense, the Prepaid Rent account had a zero balance prior to adjustment. Therefore, following the guideline regarding reversing entries, this adjusting entry could be reversed.

(2) Each payment could have been recorded as an increase (debit) to Prepaid Rent. If this procedure were followed throughout the year, the balance in Prepaid Rent at year-end, prior to any adjustments would reflect all four payments ($7,200), and the Rent Expense account would have a zero balance. The required adjusting entry would be:

```
1994
Dec. 31    Rent Expense                6,600
                Prepaid Rent                  6,600
```

This deferral adjustment would reduce the balance in the asset account, Prepaid Rent, to indicate the amount that had been "used up" during the year. This 11-month portion would be reflected in the Rent Expense account. Looking back at the guideline for reversing entries, would this adjusting entry be reversible? No. Only deferral adjustments which changed an asset or liability account from a zero balance would be reversible. In this case, the asset account, Prepaid Rent, had a $7,200 balance prior to the adjusting entry, so this situation does not meet the guidelines. The adjusting entry above is correct, but even if the company wished to use reversing entries as often as possible, they should not reverse this adjustment.

(3) The four payments could have been recorded in a mixture of the ways described in (1) and (2). Examples in Module 4 assumed that for each type of transaction, the company decided to record the activity in one way or another. In other words, management may decide that all payments of rent in advance should be recorded as expense or all payments of rent in advance should be recorded as increases to an asset account. In a perfect world, the situations described in (1) and (2) would occur. But, realistically, at the end of the year, accounting records may indicate that some of the four rent payments were recorded as expense as some were entered into the asset account. This situation is *not* unusual. If the rent payments in our example were recorded in a mixture of ways, at the end of the year, both Rent Expense and Prepaid Rent would have balances. An adjusting entry would certainly be necessary to bring each account to its proper balance.

What is important to note in regard to reversing entries is that the mixture of entries throughout the year would result in an adjusting entry that would NOT be reversible. The Prepaid Rent account would have a balance other than zero prior to the adjustment, so the adjusting entry would not be changing the asset account from a zero balance. And certainly, the reversal of the adjustment would not bring the asset account to a zero balance.

By exploring the three situations above, we have seen how to apply the guideline to determine if a deferral adjustment should be reversed. In situation (1), all the original transactions were recorded as increases to Rent Expense. Thus, at year-end, Prepaid Rent, an asset account, had a zero balance before the adjusting entry. In this case, the adjusting entry can be reversed, and reversing it would bring the asset account back to a zero balance. In situation (2), all the original transactions were recorded as increases to Prepaid Rent, so the asset account definitely had a balance prior to the year-end adjustment. Therefore, the adjusting entry should not be reversed. In situation (3), specific numbers were not determined, but the recording of at least *some* of the original transactions in the Prepaid Rent account meant that its balance at year end would not be zero. Thus, the adjusting entry in this situation should not be reversed.

Determining if deferral adjustments are reversible is not difficult — simply apply the guidelines, and evaluate the situation. Determining if adjustments in the third major category, "others" are reversible is even simpler. Looking back at the basic guideline for determining which adjustments are reversible, we see no mention of this type of adjustment. That's because they are not reversible. So, if you have identified an adjusting entry as neither an accrual or a deferral, but rather a member of the third category, do not reverse it.

Before being able to say if an adjusting entry should be reversed, you must be able to correctly identify it as an accrual a deferral, or an other. Then, in very concise terms, the guidelines for reversing entries are:

> Accruals — Yes, they are all reversible.
>
> Deferrals — Maybe, further details must be known.
>
> Others — No, these should not be reversed.

Recall that the use of reversing entries is optional. These entries may be very helpful, but not all adjusting entries should be reversed. Let's assume that Amanda's Typing Service wishes to use reversing entries whenever possible. We can review the adjusting entries made by the company at the end of January to determine which ones should be reversed.

REVERSING ENTRIES — AMANDA'S TYPING SERVICE

Let's assume that Amanda has opted to use reversing entries for her typing service business. We will now review each one of the company's adjusting entries which were originally presented in Module 4 and determine which ones should be reversed. Reversing entries are the very first entries in the next accounting period, whether it is the next interim period, or a new business year. In the case of Amanda's Typing Service, the reversing entries would be the first ones entered in the next interim period, beginning February 1, 1996.

As each adjusting entry is considered, the following question should be asked, and then the appropriate steps should be taken:

IS THE ADJUSTING ENTRY AN ACCRUAL, A DEFERRAL, OR AN OTHER?

IF it's an accrual, it's reversible.

IF it's a deferral, it's only reversible if it changed an asset or liability account from a zero balance.

IF it's an other, it's not reversible.

Adjusting Entry #1

General Journal				Page 3	
Date 1996		Description	Post Ref	Debit	Credit
Jan.	31	Accounts Receivable	130	45	
		Service Revenue	610		45
		Adjustment to record work completed on Jan. 30			

IS THE ADJUSTING ENTRY AN ACCRUAL, A DEFERRAL, OR AN OTHER?

It's an accrual, so it is reversible. Amanda's Typing Service would record the reversing entry below on February 1, 1996:

General Journal				Page 6	
Date 1996		Description	Post Ref	Debit	Credit
Feb	1	Service Revenue		45	
		Accounts Receivable			45
		to reverse adjustment of accrued revenue			

Adjusting Entry #2

	31	Accounts Receivable	130	600	
		Service Revenue	610		600
		3 weeks of January tapes			
		from medical clinic			

IS THE ADJUSTING ENTRY AN ACCRUAL, A DEFERRAL, OR AN OTHER?

This entry, too, represents an accrued revenue, so it is reversible. The reversing entry is shown below:

	1	Service Revenue		600	
		Accounts Receivable			600
		to reverse accrual adjustment			

Adjusting Entry #3

	31	Supplies Expense	715	180	
		Supplies	170		180
		adjustment to show actual			
		amount of supplies on hand			

IS THE ADJUSTING ENTRY AN ACCRUAL, A DEFERRAL, OR AN OTHER?

As indicated in Module 4, this entry is related to a deferred expense and accordingly, is classified as a deferral adjusting entry. So, it might be reversible. We must investigate further. A review of the account balances just prior to the adjusting entries offers the information we need. The purchase of supplies was recorded as an increase in an asset account, Supplies, rather than as an increase in Supplies Expense. The Supplies account had a $300 debit balance before the adjusting process began, and the adjusting entry above reduced the balance to the proper amount. Because the asset account did not have a zero balance before the adjusting entry, the adjusting entry should not be reversed.

Adjusting Entry #4

31	Insurance Expense	735	100		
	Prepaid Insurance	180			100
	one month's premium expired				

IS THE ADJUSTING ENTRY AN ACCRUAL, A DEFERRAL, OR AN OTHER?

Adjusting entry #4 is a deferral entry. Accordingly, before determining if it should be reversed, more information is needed. The credit to Prepaid Insurance reduces the balance in that asset account. Logically, then, we would expect that Prepaid Insurance *had* a balance prior to the adjusting entry. Indeed, the payment for an entire year's worth of insurance coverage was recorded as a debit to Prepaid Insurance, and prior to the adjusting entry, the account showed a debit balance of $1,200. Reversing the adjusting entry would certainly not bring the asset account back to a zero balance; a reversing entry should not be made for this deferral adjustment.

Adjusting Entries #5 and #6

These two adjustments are almost identical, and will require the same thought process to determine if they can be reversed.

31	Depreciation Expense, Office Furn	720	40		
	Accumulated Dep., Office F.	215			40
	5-yr. useful life; $100 residual				
	value; one month's recorded				
31	Depreciation Expense, Computer	725	125		
	Accumulated Dep., Computer	225			125
	4-year useful life; $1,000 residual				
	value; one month's recorded				

ARE THE ADJUSTING ENTRIES ACCRUALS, DEFERRALS, OR OTHERS?

As you should recall from Module 4, adjusting entries to record depreciation are categorized as "others". Are they reversible? NO — Adjusting entries in this third category should not be reversed.

Adjusting Entry #7

	31	Telephone Expense	750	56	
		Accounts Payable	310		56
		January service (accrued)			

IS THE ADJUSTING ENTRY AN ACCRUAL, A DEFERRAL, OR AN OTHER?

This adjusting entry is an accrual, recognizing an expense that had not yet been recorded. Once we determine this adjustment is an accrual, the hard part is over — all accruals are reversible. The reversing entry is shown below:

	1	Accounts Payable		56	
		Telephone Expense			56
		to reverse expense accrual			

The adjusting entry to record the phone bill was made so that financial statements could be prepared. The recording of vendor invoices during the adjusting process often lacks the required approvals and other formalities required when an invoice is recorded in a routine fashion. This reversing entry takes the phone bill back off the books, so it can be recorded with a routine entry along with all the other bills recorded in February.

Adjusting Entry #8

	31	Interest Expense	780	37.50	
		Interest Payable	370		37.50
		$5,000 X .09 X $\frac{1}{12}$			
		18-month note — First Friendly Bank			

IS THE ADJUSTING ENTRY AN ACCRUAL, A DEFERRAL, OR AN OTHER?

This adjusting entry shows an accrued expense. Since it is an accrual, the adjusting entry may be reversed. The reversing entry is shown below.

	1	Interest Payable			37.50	
		Interest Expense				37.50
		to reverse accrual Adjustment				

As with the example for Carol Jean's Engineering Co., this reversing entry will allow the bookkeeper for Amanda's to make the routine entry to record the payment of interest without having to review the adjusting entries that have affected the Interest Payable and Interest Expense accounts.

Adjusting Entry #9

	31	Wage Expense	710	612.50	
		Wages Payable	330		612.50
		98 hours Jan. 21 – Jan. 31			

IS THE ADJUSTING ENTRY AN ACCRUAL, A DEFERRAL, OR AN OTHER?

This entry is an accrual, recognizing wage expense that had been incurred, but had not yet been recorded. All the accruals made by Amanda's Typing Service should be reversed; the company's last reversing entry is shown below.

	1	Wages Payable			612.50	
		Wage Expense				612.50
		to reverse expense Accrual				

Now we have completed the review of adjusting entries and determined which should be reversed. Once you have determined what *type* of adjusting entry is being considered, deciding whether or not it is reversible is not too difficult. With the illustration from

Amanda's Typing Service, you saw how reversing entries are recorded. We are confident that you found the reversing entries to be the simplest of all accounting entries to prepare.

After recording the reversing entries in the general journal, Amanda's Typing Service would post them to the general ledger. Reversing entries are posted to the general ledger in a similar fashion as other entries — the only difference is that reversing entries are always the first entries posted in the new accounting period.

In this and preceding modules, we have simplified our examples by limiting them to service companies. The accounting for merchandising companies is a little more complicated because of the involvement of merchandise inventory and the calculations of cost of goods sold. We will explore these issues in our next module.

APPLY WHAT YOU HAVE LEARNED

6-1. (Which Adjusting Entries Should Be Reversed?)

Required:

For each of the adjusting entry situations described in the table below, indicate what type of adjusting entry is needed, and whether or not the adjusting entry should be reversed.

Adjusting Entry Descriptions	Type A = Accrual D = Deferral O = Other	Reverse? Y = Yes N = No
Depreciation		
Expense incurred before cash is paid		
Rent Paid in Advance. Original payment of rent was recorded as *Rent Expense*		
Rent Paid in Advance. Original payment of rent was recorded as *Prepaid Rent*		
Revenue earned before cash is received		
Supplies used. Original purchase of supplies was recorded in *Supplies Expense* account		
Supplies used. Original purchase of supplies was recorded in *Supplies* account		
Interest expense incurred but not paid		
Cash Received in Advance. Original receipt of cash was recorded as *Unearned Revenue*		
Cash Received in Advance. Original receipt of cash was recorded as *Service Revenue*		

6-2. (Reversing Accrued Wages)

Brad's Super Sports pays total wages of $3,600 per week on Saturday of each week. Wages are $600 per day for 6 days, Monday through Saturday. The last pay day in September was Saturday, September 27, and the next pay day will be Saturday, October 4. The following adjusting entry for two days' accrued wages was made on Tuesday, September 30:

```
Sep 30    Wages Expense         1,200
               Wages Payable              1,200
```

Required: a.   Prepare journal entries for the following:

Oct 1 Reversing entry for accrued wages

Oct 4 Payment of weekly wages

b.   How much of the wages paid on October 4 should be reported as wages expense for:

September? _____   October? _____

6-3. (Reversing Accrued Interest)

On October 1, 1995, Flo's Boutique borrowed $10,000 from Niagara First at 12% interest per year. The principal plus interest is due at the end of four months. On December 31, 1995, the following adjusting entry was made to record accrued interest:

```
Dec 31    Interest Expense        300
               Interest Payable            300
```

Required: Prepare journal entries for the following:

a.   Reversing entry on January 1, 1996.

b.   Payment of the principal plus interest on February 1, 1996.

c.   If Flo's Boutique did not make the reversing entry in part a., what would the entry be on February 1, 1996 when the company paid the principal plus interest?

6-4. (Reversing Accrued Revenue)

Home Care Services provides in-home services for the elderly and disabled. On November 1, 1995, Home Care entered into a three-month contract with Martha Todd to care for Martha's elderly mother while Martha was overseas on business. The contract is for $6,000 per month, and the total amount of $18,000 is to be paid by Martha to Home Care at the end of three months when Martha returns from overseas. On December 31, 1995, Home Care Services made the following adjusting entry:

```
Dec 31     Accounts Receivable        12,000
               Service Revenue                    12,000
```

Required: Prepare journal entries for the following:

     a.   Reversing entry on January 1, 1996.

     b.   Receipt of the $18,000 cash by Home Care on February 1, 1996.

     c.   If Home Care Services did not make the reversing entry in part a., what would the entry be on February 1, 1996 when Home Care received the $18,000 cash?

6-5. (Reversing Accrued Revenue)

On December 1, 1995, Pitman Photo performed specialty photography services for a preferred customer. The customer gave Pitman a Note Receivable in the amount of $25,000 with interest at 12%. The principal plus interest is due at the end of three months. Pitman made the following adjusting entry on December 31, 1995:

```
Dec 31     Interest Receivable        250
               Interest Revenue                250
```

Required: Prepare journal entries for the following:

     a.   Reversing entry on January 1, 1996.

     b.   Receipt of the principal plus interest on March 1, 1996.

     c.   If Pitman Photo did not make the reversing entry in part a., what would the entry be on March 1, 1996 when Pitman received the principal plus interest?

6-6. (Deferred Revenue Adjustment — Reversible or Not?)

On August 1, 1995, The Buffalo Bills Football Club received $26,000 for season tickets for the 1995 NFL football season. The Bills play 10 home games from September through December, 1995. This transaction was recorded as follows:

```
Aug 1      Cash                        26,000
                Unearned Revenue                26,000
```

The Bills played 3 home games in September, 1995, and the following adjusting entry was made at September 30, 1995:

```
Sep 30     Unearned Revenue             7,800
                Ticket Revenue                   7,800
```

Required: a.   Should the above adjusting entry be reversed? Why or why not?

b.   If a reversing entry should be made, give the reversing entry.

6-7. (Deferred Revenue Adjustment — Reversible or Not?)

On August 1, 1995, The Buffalo Bills Football Club received $26,000 for season tickets for the 1995 NFL football season. The Bills play 10 home games from September through December, 1995. This transaction was recorded as follows:

```
Aug 1      Cash                        26,000
                Ticket Revenue                  26,000
```

The Bills played 3 home games in September, 1995, and the following adjusting entry was made at September 30, 1995:

```
Sep 30     Ticket Revenue              18,200
                Unearned Revenue                18,200
```

Required: a.   Should the above adjusting entry be reversed? Why or why not?

b.   If a reversing entry should be made, give the reversing entry.

6-8. (Deferred Expense Adjustment — Reversible or Not?)

Kelly's Synchronized Swimming paid $6,000 rent for an indoor swimming facility in advance on June 1 for three months ($2,000 per month for June, July, and August). The transaction was recorded as follows:

```
June 1      Prepaid Rent    6,000
                 Cash                  6,000
```

On June 30, the following adjusting entry was made:

```
June 30    Rent Expense         2,000
                 Prepaid Rent              2,000
```

Required: a.   Should the above adjusting entry be reversed? Why or why not?

b.   If a reversing entry should be made, give the reversing entry.

6-9. (Deferred Expense Adjustment — Reversible or Not?)

Kelly's Synchronized Swimming paid $6,000 rent for an indoor swimming facility in advance on June 1 for three months ($2,000 per month for June, July, and August). The transaction was recorded as follows:

```
June 1      Rent Expense    6,000
                 Cash                  6,000
```

On June 30, the following adjusting entry was made:

```
June 30    Prepaid Rent         4,000
                 Rent Expense             4,000
```

Required: a.   Should the above adjusting entry be reversed? Why or why not?

b.   If a reversing entry should be made, give the reversing entry.

6-10. (Deferred Expense Adjustment — Reversible or Not?)

Jean's Goat Farm paid $14,400 for a three-year insurance policy on January 1, 1995. The policy provides insurance coverage for her farm for the next three years. The transaction was recorded as follows:

```
Jan 1        Prepaid Insurance     14,400
                  Cash                        14,400
```

On December 31, 1995, the following adjusting entry was made:

```
Dec 31       Insurance Expense      4,800
                  Prepaid Insurance          4,800
```

Required: a. Should the above adjusting entry be reversed? Why or why not?

b. If a reversing entry should be made, give the reversing entry.

6-11. (Deferred Expense Adjustment — Reversible or Not?)

Jean's Goat Farm paid $14,400 for a three-year insurance policy on January 1, 1995. The policy provides insurance coverage for her farm for the next three years. The transaction was recorded as follows:

```
Jan 1        Insurance Expense     14,400
                  Cash                        14,400
```

On December 31, 1995, the following adjusting entry was made:

```
Dec 31       Prepaid Insurance      9,600
                  Insurance Expense          9,600
```

Required: a. Should the above adjusting entry be reversed? Why or why not?

b. If a reversing entry should be made, give the reversing entry.

6-12. (Deferred Revenue Adjustment — Reversible or Not?)

On September 1, 1995, Mike's Underwater Photography received $12,000 cash in advance for deep-sea color photography services to be performed over the next three months. Mike estimates that the project will require a total of six dives during the three months, with an equal amount of photography services done with each dive. Mike made two dives in September, 1995. The original transaction was recorded as follows:

```
Sep 1       Cash                          12,000
                    Unearned Revenue                 12,000
```

On September 30, 1995, the following adjusting entry was made:

```
Sep 30      Unearned Revenue         4,000
                    Service  Revenue                   4,000
```

Required: a. Should the above adjusting entry be reversed? Why or why not?

        b. If a reversing entry should be made, give the reversing entry.

6-13. (Deferred Revenue Adjustment — Reversible or Not?)

On September 1, 1995, Mike's Underwater Photography received $12,000 cash in advance for deep-sea color photography services to be performed over the next three months. Mike estimates that the project will require a total of six dives during the three months, with an equal amount of photography services done with each dive. Mike made two dives in September, 1995. The original transaction was recorded as follows:

```
Sep 1       Cash                          12,000
                  Service Revenue                     12,000
```

On September 30, 1995, the following adjusting entry was made:

```
Sep 30      Service Revenue          8,000
                    Unearned Revenue                  8,000
```

Required: a. Should the above adjusting entry be reversed? Why or why not?

        b. If a reversing entry should be made, give the reversing entry.

6-14. (Reversing Entries)

Anderson Engineering began operations in January 1995. At the end of January, the company's unadjusted trial balance was:

```
             Anderson Engineering
            Unadjusted Trial Balance
               January 31, 1995
```

	Debit	Credit
Cash	$22,600	
Accounts Receivable	9,000	
Supplies	500	
Equipment	11,000	
Accounts Payable		$ 9,000
Notes Payable		12,000
Common Stock		10,000
Dividends	500	
Service Revenue		16,500
Wages Expense	900	
Rent Expense	2,500	
Utilities Expense	500	
Totals	$47,500	$47,500

Anderson made the following adjusting entries at January 31, 1995:

Accounts Receivable	1,000	
Service Revenue		1,000
Supplies Expense	375	
Supplies		375
Deprec. Expense, Equipment	150	
Accum. Deprec., Equipment		150
Prepaid Rent	1300	
Rent Expense		1300
Interest Expense	120	
Interest Payable		120
Wages Expense	300	
Wages Payable		300

Required:

Prepare reversing entries for February 1, 1995.

6-15. Smith's Income Tax Service reversing entries

The *unadjusted* and the *adjusted* trial balances for Smith's Income Tax Service at July 31, 1995 are:

	Unadjusted Trial Balance Debit	Unadjusted Trial Balance Credit	Adjusted Trial Balance Debit	Adjusted Trial Balance Credit
Cash	$ 1,000		$ 1,000	
Accounts Receivable	2,000		2,250	
Supplies	800		260	
Prepaid Insurance	1,200		1,100	
Equipment	1,500		1,500	
Accum. Deprec., Equipment				$ 50
Computer System	2,200		2,200	
Accum. Deprec., Computer				55
Accounts Payable		$ 1,730		1,730
Wages Payable				200
Smith, Capital		7,000		7,000
Smith, Withdrawals	2,500		2,500	
Service Revenue		5,500		5,750
Wages Expense	1,800		2,000	
Supplies Expense			540	
Insurance Expense			100	
Deprec. Exp., Equipment			50	
Deprec. Exp., Computer			55	
Telephone Expense	80		80	
Rent Expense	1,000		1,000	
Utilities Expense	150		150	
Totals	$14,230	$14,230	$14,785	$14,785

Required:

a.   Determine the adjusting entries that Smith's Income Tax Service made at July 31, 1995.

b.   Prepare the reversing entries for Smith's Income Tax Service for August 1, 1995.

MODULE 7

THE RECORDING PROCESS FOR MERCHANDISING COMPANIES

Thus far, this book has explored the recording process from the perspective of a service company. Now, we will explore the recording process for a merchandising company. Many of the procedures used in the recording of activities for a merchandising company are the same as the ones we have already seen. For instance, merchandisers will have original transactions, adjusting entries, and closing entries. Merchandisers may choose to use reversing entries, also. Merchandisers post their journal entries to ledger accounts and prepare trial balances. As was the case with service firms, worksheets *may* be used in the recording process of merchandising firms.

The most notable distinction between a merchandiser and a service firm such as Amanda's Typing Service is the existence of the products that the merchandiser buys for resale. The recording process for a merchandising firm must consider the added complexities of keeping track of the cost of the products as they flow in and out of the business. In this module, we will focus on the aspects of the recording process for merchandisers which are different from those for service companies.

Throughout this module, account titles and terms not used by service firms will be introduced. For instance, the revenue account used by merchandise companies to record the sale of goods is called **Sales** or sometimes, **Sales Revenue**. In order to keep customers happy with prompt availability of products, merchandisers typically stockpile merchandise to sell. The stockpile of ready-to-sell products held by a merchandising firm is called **merchandise inventory**, or simply **inventory**. The dollar amount of inventory reported on the balance sheet represents the cost of merchandise bought by the firm, but not yet sold. The cost of merchandise inventory which was sold during the period is shown on the income statement as an expense called **cost of goods sold**.

There are two basic systems to record transactions involving the purchase and sale of merchandise — the perpetual inventory system and the periodic inventory system. The procedures to record most of the transactions related to inventory differ between the two systems. Accordingly, we will discuss in detail the entries made under each system.

Note that in the presentation of the recording process under each inventory system, we describe and illustrate entries representing the *purest* form of the system. That is, the entries presented as components of the perpetual inventory system assume a *purely* perpetual inventory system, and those offered as illustrations of the periodic inventory system represent the use of a *purely* periodic system. Why is this situation noteworthy? Because in other settings in your accounting education, and in real business settings, you will likely be confronted with accounting systems using a hybrid of the two. For instance, many companies use a basic perpetual inventory system, but in order to accumulate specific information that management may find useful, they adopt procedures from the periodic system for specific types of transactions such as returns of merchandise. In any case, a clear understanding of the procedures in each system will serve you well, even if you are faced with a system using a mixture of features from the periodic inventory system and the perpetual inventory system.

For each inventory system, the following topics are discussed:

— Buying Merchandise

— Purchase Discounts

— Purchase Returns and Allowances

— Freight Costs Related to Merchandise

— Recording Sales

— Sales Discounts

— Returned Merchandise and Sales Allowances

— Accounts Used in the System

— Financial Statements

— Closing Entries

In addition, any issues or topics unique to each system are discussed. At the end of the module, worksheets used under each inventory system are illustrated. However, the use of worksheets and the inclusion of this material is optional.

In the event that you only need to explore one of the two inventory systems, you will find the coverage of transactions for each system to be totally independent of the information regarding the other system. Additionally, if you do explore both systems, they can be covered in either order. In order for the information to have these features, for topics in which the procedures under the two systems are identical, the explanations are duplications.

PERPETUAL INVENTORY SYSTEM

The perpetual system gets its name from the fact that when this system is used, a running balance (also called a perpetual balance) of the inventory on hand is maintained in the accounting records. Under the perpetual system, accounting entries are made to change the Inventory account every time merchandise is received or shipped out. So, accounting records are perpetually updated for the purchase and sale of merchandise.

BUYING MERCHANDISE

When the perpetual inventory system is used, the Inventory account is increased when merchandise is purchased. As an example, assume that Speace Electrical Supply purchases $4,500 worth of merchandise on account. The entry to record the purchase would increase both Inventory and Accounts Payable as shown below:

```
Inventory                    4,500
        Accounts Payable              4,500
```

PURCHASE DISCOUNTS

Suppliers commonly offer a discount for the prompt payment of invoices. **Sales terms**, also called **terms of sale** are indicated on each invoice to inform the customer when the supplier expects payment and if any prompt-payment discounts are applicable to the transaction. Sales terms are generally stated in an abbreviated fashion. For example, terms of "2 10, N 30" are common. In words, these terms are described as "2 percent, 10 days, net 30 days." *In this context*, the term *net* refers to the full invoice amount, ignoring any discount. Thus, 2 10, N 30 means a 2% discount is allowed if the buyer pays the invoice within 10 days; otherwise, the entire amount of the invoice is due within 30 days. Unless otherwise indicated, the days start counting at the invoice date. If the abbreviation "EOM" is included in the sales terms, the days start counting at the End Of the Month of the sale. Although sales terms vary, the following key is useful for most popular sales terms.

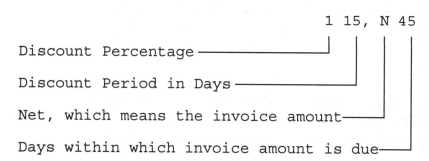

NOTE: It is common business practice to use the postmark on the envelope to prove the date payment was made. That is, in order to earn the discount, the buyer must *send* payment by the end of the discount period.

The table below includes a sample of various sales terms.

TERMS	Discount	Discount Allowed If Paid Within	Invoice Amount Is Due Within	When Days Start Counting
2 10, N 30	2%	10 Days	30 Days	Invoice Date
1 10, N 45	1%	10 Days	45 Days	Invoice Date
2 10 EOM, N 30 EOM	2%	10 Days	30 Days	End of Month of Sale
3% 15, Net 30 Days	3%	15 Days	30 Days	Invoice Date
Net 10 Days	None		10 Days	Invoice Date
Net 30	None		30 Days	Invoice Date
N 30	None		30 Days	Invoice Date
Net 10 EOM	None		10 Days	End of Month of Sale
N 30 EOM	None		30 Days	End of Month of Sale

From the buyer's point of view, discounts offered for the prompt payment of invoices are called **purchase discounts**. There are two methods used to account for purchase discounts — the gross method and the net method. We have already seen how purchases of merchandise on account are recorded under the perpetual inventory system — the Inventory account and Accounts Payable are both increased. However, the *amount* for which a purchase of merchandise is recorded depends on the method used to deal with purchase discounts.

GROSS METHOD

When the gross method is used, the purchase is originally recorded at the **gross invoice amount**. In this context, recording a purchase at the gross amount means recording the full invoice price without deducting the discount. As an example, assume that Speace Electrical Supply purchased $10,000 of merchandise from a supplier with terms of 2 10, N 30. The purchase would be recorded at its gross amount, $10,000, as shown below:

```
Inventory                      10,000
        Accounts Payable                10,000
```

If the invoice is paid within the discount period, Speace would not pay the supplier $10,000. Rather, Speace would send the supplier the invoice amount less the amount of the discount, as calculated below:

Gross invoice amount	$10,000
Less the 2% discount	− 200
Amount paid	$ 9,800

Although only $9,800 would be remitted to the supplier, the payment would fully settle the $10,000 debt owed by Speace. The difference between the amount paid and the invoice amount is the amount of the purchase discount.

Under the gross method, the original purchase of this merchandise was recorded as a $10,000 increase in Inventory. If Speace pays the invoice within the discount period, the purchase discount amount is recorded as a reduction of the cost of inventory. An entry to record payment of the $9,800 is shown below:

Accounts Payable	10,000	
Cash		9,800
Inventory		200

Notice that Cash is decreased with a credit for the $9,800 paid and Accounts Payable for this purchase is appropriately reduced to zero with a debit of $10,000. The difference ($200) is credited to Inventory.

When a buyer fails to pay an invoice within the discount period, the entire invoice amount must be paid. In this case, under the gross method, the amount of cash paid equals the amount originally recorded when the merchandise was purchased. In the example of Speace's purchase of $10,000 of merchandise, the transaction was recorded as an increase in Inventory and an increase in Accounts Payable for $10,000. If Speace misses the discount period and pays the full invoice amount, the entry is a debit to Accounts Payable for $10,000 and a credit to Cash for the same amount, as shown below:

Accounts Payable	10,000	
Cash		10,000

Under the gross method, the original purchase was recorded ignoring any possible discount, so when the discount is missed, the entry simply reduces Accounts Payable and Cash. Because the original purchase of the inventory increased the Inventory account by the full $10,000, payment of the bill requires no change in Speace's Inventory account.

NET METHOD

When the net method is used, the purchase of inventory is recorded at the **net invoice amount**. *In this context*, the net amount refers to the gross invoice amount less any discount offered for prompt payment. Using the previous example from Speace Electrical Supply, the purchase of $10,000 of merchandise with terms of 2 10, N 30 using the net method under a perpetual inventory system would be recorded as:

```
Inventory                       9,800
        Accounts Payable                9,800
```

The entry to record the purchase under the net method increases Accounts Payable by the net invoice amount. That is, the amount owed is recorded as the amount which is due *IF* the discount is taken.

Then if the purchaser pays within the discount period, recording payment under the net method is a simple matter of reducing Cash by the amount paid and reducing Accounts Payable by an equal amount. In the example of Speace Electric, if payment is made within the discount period, the company only needs to send the supplier $9,800 to settle the bill from the purchase of $10,000 of merchandise. If Speace used the net method to record the purchase, payment of the invoice within the discount period would be a simple matter of eliminating the Accounts Payable for this invoice with a $9,800 debit and decreasing Cash with a credit of $9,800. The entry is shown below:

```
Accounts Payable                9,800
        Cash                            9,800
```

If, however, Speace pays this invoice after the discount period has expired, the amount owed is not the amount originally recorded in Accounts Payable under the net method. If a buyer does not pay within the discount period, no discount is allowed, and the supplier expects payment of the full invoice amount. If Speace makes payment after the discount period has expired, the company must pay the entire $10,000 invoice amount. In this case, the entry should decrease Cash by the $10,000 paid and eliminate the $9,800 Accounts Payable for this invoice. The $200 difference between the cash paid of $10,000 and the $9,800 originally recorded in Accounts Payable is the amount of the purchase discount forfeited by Speace for not paying within the discount period. This amount is debited to an account called **Purchase Discounts Lost**, as seen in the entry below:

```
Accounts Payable                9,800
Purchase Discounts Lost          200
        Cash                           10,000
```

Lost discounts are usually considered part of the cost of financing the company's operations. The balance in Purchase Discounts Lost is generally classified as a type of interest expense and may be included in the "other expense" section of an income statement.

GROSS METHOD VS. NET METHOD — A COMPARISON

A summary of the entries to record purchases on account and subsequent payment of the invoices using the gross and net method under the perpetual inventory system is offered below:

Entries Related to a $10,000 Purchase — Terms 2 10, N 30 When the Perpetual Inventory System is Used		
	GROSS METHOD	NET METHOD

Invoice Date 2-1-95	Inventory 10,000
	   Accounts Payable 10,000
		Inventory 9,800
		   Accounts Payable 9,800

IF Payment Is Made 2-10-95	Accounts Payable 10,000
	   Cash 9,800
	   Inventory 200
		Accounts Payable 9,800
		   Cash 9,800

IF Payment Is Made 2-30-95	Accounts Payable 10,000
	   Cash 10,000
		Accounts Payable 9,800
		 Purch. Disc. Lost 200
		   Cash 10,000

As you examine the table above, notice that not all accounts are affected by the choice of recording method. The credits to Cash are the same under the two methods. A choice between the gross and net methods of recording purchases *cannot* impact the amount that must be paid for the items, but it can affect the balances of accounts other than Cash. Under the gross method, Inventory will be increased by the net amount ($9,800) if the company pays within the discount period. If the discount is not taken, the company's Inventory account reflects an increase of $10,000 for the purchase of this merchandise. Under the net method, Inventory is increased *only* by the net amount — regardless of whether or not the discount is received. Some would argue this lower amount more accurately reflects the cost of the inventory, because the company *could* buy it for the net amount.

Notice the information made available in the accounting records as a result of the use of the two methods. Under the gross method, no information is kept to tell financial statement users (or management) whether the company routinely takes advantage of prompt-payment discounts offered by suppliers or if it usually pays for purchases of merchandise after the discount period. In contrast, the net method of recording purchases highlights the magnitude of purchase discounts that are lost due to late payments by isolating them in the Purchase Discounts Lost account. This method doesn't accumulate information about the amount of purchase discounts the company *did* take advantage of, but information as to the dollars lost by paying after the discount period is tracked.

The net method has some distinct advantages. However, it may be these advantages that make the method less popular than the gross method. For instance, management's reluctance to disclose the dollars lost by missing discounts may be one reason the net method is not chosen.

PURCHASE RETURNS AND ALLOWANCES

When the perpetual inventory system is used, the return of merchandise to the supplier is simply recorded as a reversal of the purchase entry. For example, assume that Speace Electrical Supply returns merchandise which cost $500 to its supplier. The **purchase return** is recorded as shown below:

```
Accounts Payable          500
        Inventory                 500
```

The effect of the above entry is a reduction in Inventory caused by the return and also a reduction in the amount owed to the supplier. The *amount* for which a purchase return is recorded is dependent upon whether the company uses the gross or net method of recording purchases. That is, if the gross method is being used to record purchases, the gross amount of the merchandise returned would be recorded; if the net method is being used, the purchase return would be recorded at the net amount of the merchandise returned.

Merchandise may be returned for a variety of reasons. Often, when a buyer wishes to return merchandise because it is not of the quality expected, or the buyer is in some other way dissatisfied, the seller may offer a price reduction and allow the buyer to keep the merchandise. This approach may allow the seller to avoid taking the product back while, hopefully, satisfying the buyer. From the buyer's point of view, this type of cost reduction which does not require the return of the product is called a **purchase allowance**.

When the perpetual inventory system is used, the entry to record a purchase allowance is exactly the same as the entry to record a purchase return. Even though no merchandise is being returned to the supplier, the *cost* of the merchandise is reduced and this cost reduction should be reflected in the Inventory account. If Speace were granted a $200 purchase allowance from a supplier, the entry made would be:

```
Accounts Payable          200
        Inventory                 200
```

As was the case with purchase returns, the *amount* recorded for a purchase allowance should coincide with the method used to record purchases — net or gross.

NOTE: When invoices are paid after a purchase return or a purchase allowance, it is important to consider that any discount terms (e.g., 2%) apply only to the balance still owed to the supplier.

FREIGHT COSTS RELATED TO MERCHANDISE

In some operations, freight costs associated with transporting merchandise are significant amounts. Proper recording of these costs is important. From the buyer's point of view, the cost of having the merchandise purchased transported to the company is referred to as **freight-in** or **transportation-in**. Getting the merchandise in stock and available for customers is an integral part of the cost of the inventory itself. In a perpetual inventory system, freight-in costs are considered additions to the Inventory balance. For example, if Speace Electrical Supply receives a $100 freight bill for the cost of transporting merchandise from its supplier, the entry to record the freight bill would be:

```
Inventory                   100
        Accounts Payable            100
```

Generally, discounts are not offered on freight costs, so there is no issue as to whether to record these costs at their net or gross amounts.

Another type of freight charge which companies may encounter is the cost of shipping goods to customers. Even if the same carrier (e.g., a trucking company) is used for both types of shipping, the costs must be tracked separately. The cost of having merchandise shipped to customers is often referred to as **freight-out** (or **transportation-out**), and although this cost may seem very similar to freight-in, it is quite different. Freight-out is NOT a part of inventory costs and should not be recorded as an increase in Inventory. It is simply a selling expense, the cost of completing a sale by delivering the goods to the customer. Thus, if Speace pays ACME Trucking $75 to ship goods to a customer, the transaction would be recorded as:

```
Freight-Out                 75
        Cash                        75
```

The Freight-Out account is an expense account with a normal debit balance.

RECORDING SALES

When product is sold to a customer, Cash or Accounts Receivable is increased with a debit and Sales is increased with a credit to reflect that the company has earned revenue. Also, when the perpetual inventory system is used, because inventory is being removed, the **Inventory** account should be decreased by the *cost* of the merchandise sold. Under a perpetual system, the cost of inventory that has been sold is recorded in an account called **Cost of Goods Sold**. This account, an expense account, should be increased by the *cost* of the merchandise sold to the customer.

Let's take another look at our example for Speace Electrical Supply and this time assume that merchandise which cost $1,900 is sold on account to a customer for $2,300. An entry to increase Accounts Receivable and increase revenue (Sales) is necessary. In addition, when the perpetual inventory system is used, an entry is made to reduce Inventory and increase Cost of Goods Sold for the *cost* of merchandise sold. Accordingly, the perpetual system requires two entries to record a sale. One entry records the sale itself; the other records the cost of the sale. The entries to record the sale made by Speace Electrical Supply appear below:

```
Accounts Receivable         2,300
        Sales                       2,300

Cost of Goods Sold          1,900
        Inventory                   1,900
```

Again, the first entry records the actual sale, and therefore, uses the sale price. The second entry removes the cost of the inventory sold from the balance in Inventory and increases the expense account Cost of Goods Sold by that amount. Under a perpetual inventory system, after sales are recorded and the entries are posted to the general ledger, the cost of merchandise sold to customers and the cost of merchandise still on hand are easily determined by looking at the Cost of Goods Sold and Inventory accounts respectively. The fact that the Cost of Goods Sold and Inventory balances are kept up-to-date as transactions occur is a distinct advantage of the perpetual inventory system.

SALES DISCOUNTS

As we have seen, companies often offer discounts to their customers for the prompt payment of invoices. The sales terms used to indicate when the seller expects payment and if any prompt-payment discounts are offered are the same as those described during the discussion of purchase discounts. In fact, the topic we will explore now covers the same type of transactions as those described earlier — we are simply viewing the transactions from a different point of view. From the seller's point of view, discounts offered to customers for the prompt payment of invoices are called **sales discounts**. As with purchase discounts, there are two methods to account for sales discounts. Again, they are the gross method and the net method. Because of these two different approaches to tracking information about sales discounts, there are two different approaches to the *amount* for which a sale on account may be recorded.

GROSS METHOD

When the gross method is used, sales are originally recorded at the gross invoice amount. That is, sales are recorded at the full invoice price, without deducting the discount. As an example, assume that Speace Electrical Supply sells merchandise costing $700 for $1,000 with terms of 3 10, N 30. The sales invoice would be recorded at its gross amount ($1,000) as shown below:

```
Accounts Receivable          1,000
     Sales                            1,000

Cost of Goods Sold             700
     Inventory                         700
```

If the invoice is paid within the discount period, the customer pays the invoice amount, less the discount. In our example, the customer would pay $970, as calculated below:

```
Gross invoice amount      $1,000
Less the 3% discount        − 30
Amount paid               $   970
```

Although only $970 is received in payment of the invoice, the payment would fully settle the $1,000 receivable shown on Speace's books. The difference between the amount received and the invoice amount is the sales discount. An entry to record the receipt of the $970 payment is shown below:

```
Cash                           970
Sales Discounts                 30
     Accounts Receivable              1,000
```

Notice that Cash is increased with a debit for the $970 received and that a credit of $1,000 appropriately reduces Accounts Receivable for this sale to zero. The difference ($30) is debited to **Sales Discounts**. The Sales Discounts account is a contra-sales account. That is, it is classified or grouped with Sales but works to reduce Sales. Sales Discounts has a normal debit balance — just the opposite of Sales.

If the invoice is not paid within the discount period, the customer must pay the entire invoice amount. In this case, under the gross method, the amount of cash received equals the amount originally recorded in Accounts Receivable. Accordingly, the entry is a simple matter of debiting Cash for the $1,000 received and crediting Accounts Receivable for the same amount, as shown in the entry below:

```
Cash                        1,000
        Accounts Receivable          1,000
```

Under the gross method, the original sale was recorded ignoring any possible discount, so when the customer misses the discount, the entry to record the collection simply increases Cash and decreases Accounts Receivable.

NET METHOD

The net method is far less popular than the gross method for recording sales. When the net method is used, the sale is recorded at the net amount. That is, the sale is recorded at the amount of the invoice less the discount. Using the example for Speace, the sale would be recorded as shown below, using the perpetual inventory system and the net method for recording sales.

```
Accounts Receivable          970
        Sales                            970

Cost of Goods Sold           700
        Inventory                        700
```

Notice that the entry to record the sale itself, the first entry above, is different from the entry made to record the sale under the gross method. However, the second entry, to record the removal of the *cost* of the merchandise sold from Inventory and add it to Cost of Goods Sold is the same as it was under the gross method. The way in which the *cost* of the inventory is recorded is not impacted by the method chosen to record sales.

Under the net method, the receivable is recorded at the amount the customer will pay *IF* the invoice is paid within the discount period. So, recording the receipt of payment from a customer within the discount period is a simple matter of increasing Cash and decreasing Accounts Receivable by the amount collected. In our example of Speace Electrical Supply, if the customer pays within the discount period, Speace will receive $970, the invoice amount less the discount. In this case, recording the receipt of payment from the customer is a simple matter of increasing Cash with a $970 debit and eliminating the receivable for this invoice by crediting Accounts Receivable for $970, as shown below:

```
Cash                          970
    Accounts Receivable              970
```

If Speace's customer does not pay within the discount period, no discount is allowed. Accordingly, the customer should pay the entire $1,000 invoice amount. In this case, under the net method, the entry should increase Cash by the $1,000 received and eliminate the $970 accounts receivable recorded at the time of the sale. The $30 difference between the cash received of $1,000 and the $970 in Accounts Receivable is the amount of sales discount forfeited by the customer for not paying within the discount period. This amount is credited to an account called **Sales Discounts Forfeited** to balance the entry, as shown below:

```
Cash                          1,000
    Accounts Receivable              970
    Sales Discounts Forfeited   30
```

Under the net method, sales and the associated receivables are recorded at the amount the customer will pay if the invoice *is* paid within the discount period. If the customer forfeits the discount and pays a greater amount, the difference is credited to Sales Discounts Forfeited. In a sense, Sales Discounts Forfeited, which has a normal credit balance, represents interest earned by the seller in addition to the sales recorded at the net invoice amount. When financial statements are prepared, the balance in this account is shown as a miscellaneous revenue, generated from allowing customers to defer payment.

The net method of recording sales is not widely used. There are two major drawbacks which have caused the limited use of this method. First, when sales are recorded under the net method, the invoice amount is not used. Instead, additional calculations are required to determine the net amount. Second, when the net method is used, each time financial statements are prepared an adjusting entry is required to increase Accounts Receivable and Sales Discounts Forfeited for the amount of discounts applicable to all uncollected accounts receivable which are beyond the discount period.

A summary of the entries to record sales on account and the subsequent collection of receivables using the gross and net method under the perpetual inventory system is offered below:

Entries Related to a $1,000 Sale — Terms 3 10, N 30 When the Perpetual Inventory System is Used		
	GROSS METHOD	NET METHOD

Invoice Date 2-1-95	Accounts Receivable 1,000
	  Sales 1,000
	
	Cost Goods Sold 700
	  Inventory 700
		Accounts Receivable 970
		  Sales 970
		
		Cost Goods Sold 700
		  Inventory 700

IF Payment Is Made 2-10-95	Cash 970
	Sales Discounts 30
	  Accounts Receivable 1,000
		Cash 970
		  Accounts Receivable 970

IF Payment Is Made 2-30-95	Cash 1,000
	  Accounts Receivable 1,000
		Cash 1,000
		  Accounts Receivable 970
		  Sales Disc. Forfeited 30

As you examine the table above, notice that some accounts are different under the two methods, while others are the same. The cash amounts collected *cannot* be affected by a choice between recording methods, so the debits to Cash are the same for each method. The choice between the gross and net methods of recording sales also has no impact on the entries to remove the *cost* of the inventory sold from Inventory and record it in the expense account Cost of Goods Sold. However, other accounts *are* affected by the choice.

Under the gross method, Accounts Receivable is increased by the gross amount, $1,000, but the net method only records the receivable as $970. If all collections were made by the end of the period, no difference between the methods would be seen in Accounts Receivable. However, any uncollected receivables would be shown at a higher amount under the gross method than under the net method.

The Sales account is affected in a similar fashion. Sales are recorded at a higher amount under the gross method than under the net method. If, however, all receivables were collected within the discount period, the two methods would provide the same figure for what is called **net sales** — that is, Sales less all contra-sales account balances. In our example, net sales for this one transaction would be:

$$
\begin{array}{lr}
\text{Sales} & \$1{,}000 \\
-\text{ Sales Discounts} & \underline{30} \\
\text{Net Sales} & \underline{\$970} \\
\end{array}
$$

Since the net method uses no contra-sales accounts, the $970 balance in Sales would also be net sales. Realistically, it is unlikely that all receivables will be collected within the discount period, and there are distinct differences between the methods when customers miss the discount. In the example above, under the gross method, if the customer paid on 2-30-95, there is no additional information gathered — the $1,000 sale remains. Under the net method, if the customer missed the discount, a sale of only $970 is recorded, but an additional revenue of $30 is also recorded. In total, the revenues recorded in this situation are the same under the two methods. However, the $30 in Sales Discounts Forfeited is reported as a miscellaneous revenue — not an addition to Sales — so the information presented on the income statement is different.

Notice the information made available in the accounting records as a result of the use of the two methods. Under the gross method, Sales Discounts tracks the amount of prompt-payment discounts earned by customers. However, no information is kept to indicate the amount collected by the company as a result of customers paying after the discount period. In contrast, the net method of recording sales highlights the magnitude of sales discounts missed by customers by isolating them in the Sales Discounts Forfeited account. This method doesn't accumulate information about the amount of sales discounts customers *did* take advantage of, but information as to the additional dollars collected as a result of payments being received after the discount period is tracked.

Either method of recording sales may be chosen, but the drawbacks of the net method described in the previous section have limited its use; the gross method remains the more popular approach.

RETURNED MERCHANDISE AND SALES ALLOWANCES

When a customer returns goods to the merchandiser, it might seem appropriate for the seller to simply reverse the entry used to record the sale. However, if that were done, information would be lost. When merchandise is returned, an account called **Sales Returns** is debited and Cash or Accounts Receivable is credited. The benefit of using a separate account to record returns of merchandise by customers is that the company can track the level of sales returns in relation to the amount of sales.

Now let's assume that a customer returns merchandise to Speace Electrical Supply. The merchandise was purchased on account for $900, and the merchandise cost Speace $750. The entries to record this transaction are shown below:

```
Sales Returns                    900
      Accounts Receivable               900

Inventory                        750
      Cost of Goods Sold                750
```

Notice that the entries are the opposite of the entries to record a sale except that, instead of debiting Sales, a debit is made to Sales Returns. Sales Returns is a contra-sales account, which means its balance will be reported as a reduction of Sales. Sales Returns has a normal debit balance — just the opposite of Sales. As was the case with purchase returns, the *amount* for which a sales return is recorded is dependent upon whether the company uses the gross or net method of recording sales. That is, if the gross method is being used to record sales, the gross amount of the merchandise returned would be recorded; if the net method is being used, the sales return would be recorded at the net amount of the merchandise returned.

As you know, sales returns occur when a customer is unhappy with a purchase for one reason or another. Sometimes a merchandiser will satisfy a customer's complaint by refunding a portion of the selling price without taking back any of the merchandise. This type of transaction has already been explored from the buyer's point of view in our discussion of purchase allowances. From the seller's point of view, a refund of part of the selling price not requiring the customer to return any of the merchandise is known as a **sales allowance**. As with the recording of sales returns, a special account is used to track sales allowances. However, because no merchandise is received back from the customer, no entry is made to change Cost of Goods Sold or Inventory.

If Speace, in an attempt to avoid bringing merchandise back while at the same time making a customer happy, granted the buyer a sales allowance of $200, the necessary entry would be:

```
Sales Allowances              200
        Accounts Receivable           200
```

Again, because no merchandise was returned by the customer, the entry has no effect on Cost of Goods Sold or Inventory. **Sales Allowances** is a contra-sales account — its balance will be reported as a reduction of sales. Sales Allowances has a normal debit balance — just the opposite of Sales. Again, the purpose of keeping the allowances in a separate account is to provide information helpful in the evaluation of the company's performance. Management should investigate the reason for customer dissatisfaction if the level of sales allowances climbs.

If management decides there is no reason to keep separate information about the levels of sales returns and sales allowances, results of these transactions may be recorded in the same account. It is not unusual for companies to use a single account called **Sales Returns and Allowances** to record results of both types of transactions. Sales Returns and Allowances would, of course, be a contra-sales account with a normal debit balance.

PHYSICAL INVENTORY VERSUS BOOK INVENTORY

Under a perpetual inventory system, the Inventory account is changed each time a transaction involving inventory is recorded. The balance in the Inventory account *should* reflect the cost of the actual amount of inventory owned by the company. However, for a variety of reasons, the balance in Inventory (referred to as "book inventory") may not be exactly the same as the inventory on hand. For instance, during the period inventory items may have been dropped and broken. If the items were discarded without any change being recorded in the Inventory account, a difference between the book inventory and the actual inventory on hand would exist. Also, employees or customers may have stolen inventory items. With the numerous entries required by the perpetual inventory system, mistakes in the recording of transactions could also cause book inventory to be different than the amount of inventory actually owned by the company.

In any case, it is likely that the accounting records do not reflect the exact amount of inventory in the warehouse. Accordingly, a physical count of merchandise inventory is made at least annually and the Inventory balance shown in the accounting records is adjusted to reflect the cost of the inventory actually on hand. Often, this physical count of the inventory is completed as part of the adjustment process. Reconciling the physical inventory count with the balance in the Inventory account assures that an appropriate asset figure will be used in the preparation of financial statements.

Unless the difference between book inventory and the physical count is a material amount or is the result of a specific loss, a basic adjusting entry is made. The Cost of Goods Sold account absorbs any adjustments to the Inventory account deemed necessary as a result of the physical count.

For example, assume that the physical inventory count indicates that actual inventory on hand is $20,000 and the accounting records reflect an Inventory balance of only $19,800. The Inventory account should be increased with a debit of $200, and the Cost of Goods Sold account should be credited for the same amount. The entry is shown below:

```
Inventory                       200
        Cost of Goods Sold              200
```

The effect of this entry is to increase the balance in the Inventory account from $19,800 to the correct amount of $20,000. This entry also decreases Cost of Goods Sold by $200. Indeed, if the physical count suggests $200 more inventory is still on hand than the records indicated, $200 less inventory should have been converted from an asset to an expense.

A similar approach is taken if the physical inventory indicates an amount less than is reflected in the accounting records. For example, if the physical inventory suggests the company has $12,500 of inventory, but the balance in Inventory is $12,850, an adjusting entry to bring the Inventory account to its proper balance is needed.

```
Cost of Goods Sold              350
        Inventory                      350
```

The entry above brings the Inventory account down to its correct amount, $12,500, as indicated by the physical inventory count. If $350 less inventory is on hand than the records had indicated, $350 more of the inventory's cost should be converted from an asset to an expense (Cost of Goods Sold).

ACCOUNTS USED IN THE PERPETUAL INVENTORY SYSTEM

We have explored the transactions of a merchandiser using the perpetual inventory system. The transactions illustrated thus far are those that would not have existed for a service company. Because a merchandiser has inventory which is bought and resold, several new accounts and procedures have been introduced in this module. As we said earlier, many of the basics you learned in Modules 1 through 6 will hold true for a merchandiser as well as a service firm. To illustrate the aspects unique to a merchandising company, and to further explore the perpetual inventory system, we present a chart of accounts for Speace Electrical Supply. The accounts which were introduced in this module are presented in **bold**.

```
Speace Electrical Supply
   Chart of Accounts
Account
Number         Account Name

110            Cash
130            Accounts Receivable
190            Inventory
210            Office Equipment
215            Accumulated Depreciation
310            Accounts Payable
510            Common Stock
520            Retained Earnings
525            Income Summary
530            Dividends
610            Sales
615            Sales Discounts
620            Sales Returns
625            Sales Allowances
640            Interest Revenue
705            Cost of Goods Sold
740            Wage Expense
750            Rent Expense
760            Freight-Out
770            Depreciation Expense
```

Recall that companies may choose from two methods for recording purchases and sales. The gross method may be chosen for one and the net method for the other, or the same method may be used for both purchases and sales. The method chosen may affect the accounts a company uses.

In the case of recording purchases of merchandise on account under a perpetual inventory system, the gross method uses no accounts other than Inventory and Accounts Payable, whether payment is made within the discount period or not. In the chart of accounts above and in the illustrations that follow, it is assumed that Speace Electrical Supply uses the gross method for recording purchases of inventory. *If* Speace had used the net method for recording purchases and had paid invoices after the discount period, the company would use a Purchase Discounts Lost account.

In the case of recording sales on account under a perpetual inventory system, the gross method keeps track of the discounts given to customers for paying within the discount period. The balance in Sales Discounts reflects these amounts, and the fact that the chart of accounts above shows Sales Discounts indicates that Speace uses the gross method of recording its sales on account. *If* Speace had used the net method, no information about the discounts taken by customers would be kept. However, if customers paid after the discount period, the additional amount collected would be reflected in Sales Discounts Forfeited.

Throughout this module, we have explored *some* of the transactions from Speace's 1995 fiscal year. The company ends its business year on June 30, and has already completed the adjustment process for the 1995 fiscal year. The adjusted trial balance below reflects the account balances which are ready for use in financial statement preparation. Again, the accounts in **bold** are those introduced in this module.

Speace Electrical Supply
Adjusted Trial Balance
As of June 30, 1995

Cash	$ 7,400	
Accounts Receivable	4,100	
Inventory	**6,300**	
Office Equipment	27,500	
Accumulated Depreciation		$ 6,000
Accounts Payable		4,200
Common Stock		13,000
Retained Earnings		8,550
Dividends	700	
Sales		**87,000**
Sales Discounts	**1,150**	
Sales Returns	**1,250**	
Sales Allowances	**400**	
Interest Revenue		250
Cost of Goods Sold	**51,000**	
Wage Expense	11,100	
Rent Expense	5,500	
Freight-Out	**600**	
Depreciation Expense	2,000	
	$119,000	$119,000

FINANCIAL STATEMENTS UNDER A PERPETUAL INVENTORY SYSTEM

The financial statements explored in earlier modules are appropriate for service companies. As we have said, the biggest difference in the recording process for a merchandiser is the addition of inventory and the information requirements that accompany it. Thus far we have examined the recording of transactions dealing with inventory and we have seen the use of accounts not necessary in a service company. The financial statements of a merchandising company are also a bit different from those of a service company.

The basic difference between the balance sheet of a merchandiser and that of a service company is the existence of inventory. Inventory (sometimes called merchandise inventory) is shown on the balance sheet as a current asset. This figure should reflect the amount of inventory the company owns as of the balance sheet date. As we said earlier, companies generally take a physical count of inventory at least annually, and, if necessary, adjust the perpetual inventory records to reflect the actual amount of inventory owned by the business.

The bridge statement (e.g., the statement of retained earnings or statement of capital) is no different for a merchandiser than for a service business. This statement shows changes in retained earnings (or capital) as a result of net income and dividends (or drawings).

The most significant differences in the financial statements of a merchandiser are found on the income statement. Indeed, most of the accounts introduced in this module are found on the income statement. Based on the adjusted trial balance presented earlier, the following income statement for Speace Electrical Supply can be drawn:

```
                    Speace Electrical Supply
                        Income Statement
              For the Fiscal Year Ended June 30, 1995

    Sales                                    $87,000
       Less: Sales Discounts    $1,150
             Sales Returns       1,250
             Sales Allowances      400        2,800
    Net Sales                                            $84,200
    Cost of Goods Sold                                    51,000
    Gross Margin                                         $33,200
    Operating Expenses:
             Wage Expense       $11,100
             Rent Expense         5,500
             Depreciation Expense 2,000
             Freight-Out           600
       Total Operating Expenses                          19,200
    Operating Income                                    $14,000
    Other Revenue:
          Interest Revenue                                 250
    Net Income                                          $14,250
```

As you examine the income statement above, notice that all contra-sales accounts are deducted from Sales to arrive at Net Sales. In this context, the Sales figure ($87,000) may be referred to as **gross sales**.

From Net Sales, Cost of Goods Sold is deducted to arrive at **Gross Margin**. Presentation of gross margin is one of the features of the **multistep income statement**. In this format, even if a company has other sources of revenue, only sales information is presented at the beginning of the income statement. The relationship between Net Sales and Cost of Goods Sold, the expense related to the inventory sold to produce those sales dollars, is highlighted.

$$\text{Net Sales} - \text{Cost of Goods Sold} = \text{Gross Margin}$$

Gross margin is also called gross profit. From this figure, operating expenses, the expenses incurred to support the primary business activity of the company, are deducted. **Operating Income** (also called Income from Operations) is the result. Presentation of this figure is the other feature unique to the multistep income statement format.

Below the presentation of Operating Income, any other revenues or expenses are reported. In the case of Speace Electrical Supply, Interest Revenue is the only non-operating item reported. The basic format of a multistep income statement is:

```
         Net Sales              $X,XXX
       - Cost of Goods Sold        XXX
         Gross Margin           $  XXX
       - Operating Expenses         XX
         Operating Income       $   XX
       + Other Revenues              X
       - Other Expenses             X
         Net Income            $     X
```

The multistep income statement, featuring gross margin and operating income is not the only acceptable format for a merchandising company. The single-step income statement format is also acceptable. For Speace Electrical Supply, the following income statement could be presented instead:

```
                Speace Electrical Supply
                    Income Statement
            For the Fiscal Year Ended June 30, 1995

    Sales                                        $87,000
       Less: Sales Discounts      $1,150
             Sales Returns         1,250
             Sales Allowances        400          2,800
    Net Sales                                              $84,200
    Interest Revenue                                           250
    Total Revenue                                          $84,450
         Expenses:
             Cost of Goods Sold    $51,000
             Wage Expense           11,100
             Rent Expense            5,500
             Depreciation Expense    2,000
             Freight-Out              600
    Total Expenses                                          70,200
    Net Income                                             $14,250
```

Notice that the net income figures for the two income statements are the same. Indeed, choice of income statement format cannot affect the final net income figure. What *is* affected is the information presented. In a single-step income statement, all revenues are gathered together at the beginning. In our example, we see the contra-sales accounts deducted from Sales to provide the net sales figure as before, but then Interest Revenue is added to Net Sales to present Total Revenue. The single-step income statement does not show gross margin. In fact, cost of goods sold is given no special treatment in this format. It is included in the list of *all* expenses, which is totalled to provide Total Expenses. Cost of goods sold is often listed first because of its size, but it is not separated from the other expenses. In the single-step income statement format, no distinction is made between operating and non-operating revenues and expenses. The basic format of a single-step income statement is:

```
        Total Revenues        $X,XXX
      - Total Expenses            XXX
        Net Income            $     X
```

Again, whether a company chooses the multistep or single-step income statement format, net income will be the same.

NOTE: In the examples, we assumed Speace used the gross method for recording purchases and sales. If the net method had been used, and the company had balances in Purchase Discounts Lost or Sales Discounts Forfeited, these amounts would have been presented as an "other expense" and "other revenue", respectively. The exact placement of these items on the income statement would depend on the format (multistep or single-step) chosen.

THE CLOSING PROCESS UNDER A PERPETUAL INVENTORY SYSTEM

The basic closing process was described in detail in Module 5. Recall that in that module, the entire closing process was summed up in four simple steps:

1. Close all revenue accounts to Income Summary.
2. Close all expense accounts to Income Summary.
3. Close Income Summary to Retained Earnings.
4. Close the Dividends account to Retained Earnings.

The purpose of closing entries and the basic approach to the process are the same for a merchandiser using a perpetual inventory system. However, as you might expect, we now have some additional accounts with which to contend. Building on the basics presented above, we can describe the closing process under a perpetual inventory system as:

1. Close all revenue accounts to Income Summary.

This step remains the same, but the primary revenue is now Sales and a new revenue (Sales Discounts Forfeited) *may* exist.

2. Close all expense accounts and contra-sales accounts to Income Summary.

Closing expense accounts is not new, but three new expenses were introduced in this module: Cost of Goods Sold, Freight-out, and Purchase Discounts Lost. The contra-sales accounts, having normal debit balances, will be closed at the same time as expenses.

3. Close Income Summary to Retained Earnings.

This step is exactly the same as it is in the closing process for a service company — nothing new. In the case of a proprietorship or partnership, Capital accounts replace Retained Earnings.

4. Close the Dividends account to Retained Earnings.

Nothing new here, either. *IF* a balance exists in Dividends, it is closed as the final step of the closing process. In the case of a proprietorship or partnership, Drawings accounts replace Dividends and Capital accounts replace Retained Earnings.

As you can see, the closing process for a merchandiser using a perpetual inventory system is not too different from what you have seen before. To complete the illustration of Speace Electrical Supply, the company's adjusted trial balance is repeated below, and the necessary closing entries follow:

Speace Electrical Supply
Adjusted Trial Balance
As of June 30, 1995

Cash	$ 7,400	
Accounts Receivable	4,100	
Inventory	6,300	
Office Equipment	27,500	
Accumulated Depreciation		$ 6,000
Accounts Payable		4,200
Common Stock		13,000
Retained Earnings		8,550
Dividends	700	
Sales		87,000
Sales Discounts	1,150	
Sales Returns	1,250	
Sales Allowances	400	
Interest Revenue		250
Cost of Goods Sold	51,000	
Wage Expense	11,100	
Rent Expense	5,500	
Freight-Out	600	
Depreciation Expense	2,000	
	$119,000	$119,000

Step 1.

Sales	87,000	
Interest Revenue	250	
Income Summary		87,250

Step 2.

Income Summary	73,000	
Cost of Goods Sold		51,000
Wage Expense		11,100
Rent Expense		5,500
Freight-Out		600
Depreciation Expense		2,000
Sales Discounts		1,150
Sales Returns		1,250
Sales Allowances		400

Step 3.

Income Summary	14,250	
Retained Earnings		14,250

Step 4.

Retained Earnings	700	
Dividends		700

You have now seen the recording process for a merchandising operation using a perpetual inventory system. The only other part of the process that would be any different for this type of business than what you learned about in other modules is the worksheet. Again, use of this tool is optional, but a worksheet for Speace Electrical Supply based on the example used thus far is illustrated in the final section at the end of this module.

PERIODIC INVENTORY SYSTEM

When the periodic inventory system is used, the Inventory account is not changed each time merchandise is purchased or sold to customers. Rather, the Inventory account is updated only when a physical count of the inventory on hand is made, and the cost of the inventory is determined. The entries to update the Inventory account are discussed later in this module as part of the closing process.

BUYING MERCHANDISE

Under the periodic inventory system, as merchandise is purchased from suppliers, its cost is accumulated in an account called **Purchases**. As an example, assume that Speace Electrical Supply purchases $4,500 worth of merchandise on account. The entry to record this purchase would increase both the Purchases account and Accounts Payable as shown below:

```
Purchases                    4,500
       Accounts Payable              4,500
```

The Purchases account has a normal debit balance and is a component of cost of goods sold.

PURCHASE DISCOUNTS

Suppliers commonly offer a discount for the prompt payment of invoices. **Sales terms**, also called **terms of sale** are indicated on each invoice to inform the customer when the supplier expects payment and if any prompt-payment discounts are applicable to the transaction. Sales terms are generally stated in an abbreviated fashion. For example, terms of "2 10, N 30" are common. In words, these terms are described as "2 percent, 10 days, net 30 days." *In this context*, the term *net* refers to the full invoice amount, ignoring any discount. Thus, 2 10, N 30 means a 2% discount is allowed if the buyer pays the invoice within 10 days; otherwise, the entire amount of the invoice is due within 30 days. Unless otherwise indicated, the days start counting at the invoice date. If the abbreviation "EOM" is included in the sales terms, the days start counting at the End Of the Month of the sale. Although sales terms vary, the following key is useful for most popular sales terms.

```
                          1 15, N 45

Discount Percentage ─────────────┘    │    │    │

Discount Period in Days ──────────────┘    │    │

Net, which means the invoice amount────────┘    │

Days within which invoice amount is due─────────┘
```

NOTE: It is common business practice to use the postmark on the envelope to prove the date payment was made. That is, in order to earn the discount, the buyer must *send* payment by the end of the discount period.

The table below includes a sample of the multitude of sales terms available.

TERMS	Discount	Discount Allowed If Paid Within	Invoice Amount Is Due Within	When Days Start Counting
2 10, N 30	2%	10 Days	30 Days	Invoice Date
1 10, N 45	1%	10 Days	45 Days	Invoice Date
2 10 EOM, N 30 EOM	2%	10 Days	30 Days	End of Month of Sale
3% 15, Net 30 Days	3%	15 Days	30 Days	Invoice Date
Net 10 Days	None		10 Days	Invoice Date
Net 30	None		30 Days	Invoice Date
N 30	None		30 Days	Invoice Date
Net 10 EOM	None		10 Days	End of Month of Sale
N 30 EOM	None		30 Days	End of Month of Sale

From the buyer's point of view, discounts offered for the prompt payment of invoices are called **purchase discounts**. There are two methods used to account for purchase discounts — the gross method and the net method. We have already seen how purchases of merchandise on account are recorded under the perpetual inventory system — the Inventory account and Accounts Payable are both increased. However, the *amount* for which a purchase of merchandise is recorded depends on the method used to deal with purchase discounts.

GROSS METHOD

When the gross method is used, the purchase is originally recorded at the **gross invoice amount**. In this context, recording a purchase at the gross amount means recording the full invoice price without deducting the discount. As an example, assume that Speace Electrical Supply purchased $10,000 of merchandise from its supplier with terms of 2 10, N 30. If the gross method (under a periodic inventory system) is used, the purchase would be recorded as shown below:

```
Purchases                      10,000
       Accounts Payable                10,000
```

If the invoice is paid within the discount period, Speace would not pay the supplier $10,000.

Rather, the company would pay the invoice amount, less the discount. In our example, Speace Electrical Supply would pay $9,800 as calculated below:

```
Gross invoice amount        $10,000
Less the 2% discount         - 200
Amount paid                 $ 9,800
```

Although only $9,800 would be remitted to the supplier, the payment would fully settle the $10,000 debt owed by Speace. The original purchase of this merchandise was recorded as an increase in Purchases of $10,000. The fact is that if Speace pays the invoice within the discount period, those purchases will end up costing the company $9,800. However, payment of the invoice *does not* affect the Purchases account. The difference between the amount paid and the invoice amount is the amount of the purchase discount. Companies using the periodic inventory system and the gross method of recording purchases, keep track of the amount of purchase discounts in a separate account called **Purchase Discounts**.

The entry to record Speace's payment of the invoice within the discount period is shown below:

```
Accounts Payable            10,000
     Cash                             9,800
     Purchase Discounts               200
```

Notice that Cash is decreased with a credit for the $9,800 paid and Accounts Payable for this purchase is appropriately reduced to zero with a debit of $10,000. The difference ($200) is credited to Purchase Discounts. The Purchase Discounts account is a contra-purchases account. That is, its balance will be reported as a reduction of purchases. Purchase Discounts has a normal credit balance — just the opposite of Purchases.

If the purchaser fails to pay the invoice within the discount period, the entire invoice amount must be paid. If the purchase was recorded using the gross method, the amount of cash paid will equal the amount recorded in Accounts Payable for the purchase. In the case of Speace Electrical Supply, if the purchase of $10,000 of merchandise on account had been recorded using the gross method, payment of the invoice if the discount period had passed would require a debit to Accounts Payable for $10,000 and a credit to Cash for the same amount, as shown in the entry below:

```
Accounts Payable            10,000
     Cash                             10,000
```

Under the gross method, the original purchase was recorded ignoring any possible discount, so when the discount is missed, the entry simply reduces Accounts Payable and Cash.

NET METHOD

When the net method is used, purchases of inventory on account are recorded at the **net invoice amount**. *In this context*, the net amount refers to the gross invoice amount less any discount offered for prompt payment. In the example of Speace Electrical Supply, the purchase of $10,000 of merchandise on account with terms of 2 10, N 30 would be recorded as follows using the net method of recording purchases of merchandise under a periodic inventory system:

```
Purchases                      9,800
     Accounts Payable                   9,800
```

The entry to record the purchase under the net method increases Accounts Payable by the net invoice amount. That is, the amount owed is recorded as the amount which is due *IF* the discount is taken.

Then if the purchaser pays within the discount period, recording payment under the net method is a simple matter of reducing Cash by the amount paid and reducing Accounts Payable by an equal amount. In the example of Speace, the $10,000 invoice can be settled by a payment of $9,800 within the discount period. Recording payment of the invoice within the discount period is a simple matter of eliminating the Accounts Payable for this invoice with a $9,800 debit and decreasing Cash with a credit of $9,800. The entry is shown below:

```
Accounts Payable               9,800
     Cash                              9,800
```

If, however, Speace pays this invoice after the discount period has expired, the amount owed is not the amount originally recorded in Accounts Payable under the net method. If a buyer does not pay within the discount period, no discount is allowed, and the supplier expects payment of the full invoice amount. If Speace makes payment after the discount period has expired, the company must pay the entire $10,000 invoice amount. In this case, the entry should decrease Cash by the $10,000 paid and eliminate the $9,800 Accounts Payable for this invoice. The $200 difference between the cash paid of $10,000 and the $9,800 originally recorded in Accounts Payable is the amount of the purchase discount forfeited by Speace for not paying within the discount period. This amount is debited to an account called **Purchase Discounts Lost**, as seen in the entry below:

```
Accounts Payable               9,800
Purchase Discounts Lost                  200
     Cash                             10,000
```

Lost discounts are commonly thought of as part of the cost of financing the company's operations. The balance in Purchase Discounts Lost is generally classified as a type of interest expense and may be included in the "other expense" section of an income statement.

GROSS METHOD VS. NET METHOD — A COMPARISON

A summary of the entries to record purchases on account and subsequent payment of the invoices using the gross and net method under the periodic inventory system is offered below:

Entries Related to a $10,000 Purchase — Terms 2 10, N 30 When the Periodic Inventory System is Used		
	GROSS METHOD	NET METHOD

Invoice
Date
2-1-95
	Purchases 10,000
	    Accounts Payable 10,000
		Purchases 9,800
		    Accounts Payable 9,800

IF
Payment
Is Made
2-10-95
	Accounts Payable 10,000
	    Cash 9,800
	    Purchase Discounts 200
		Accounts Payable 9,800
		    Cash 9,800

IF
Payment
Is Made
2-30-95
	Accounts Payable 10,000
	    Cash 10,000
		Accounts Payable 9,800
		Purch. Disc. Lost 200
		    Cash 10,000

As you examine the table above, notice that not all accounts are affected by the choice of recording method. The credits to Cash are the same under the two methods. A choice between the gross and net methods of recording purchases *cannot* impact the amount that must be paid for the items, but it can affect the balances of accounts other than Cash.

Under the gross method, Purchases is increased by the gross amount, $10,000, but the net method only records the increase as $9,800. If, however, all payables related to purchases of inventory were paid within the discount period, the two methods would provide the same figure for what is called **net purchases** — that is, Purchases less all contra-purchases account balances. In our example, net purchases for this one transaction would be:

Purchases	$10,000
− Purchase Discounts	200
Net Purchases	$ 9,800

Since the net method uses no contra-purchases accounts, the $9,800 balance in Purchases would also be net purchases. Realistically, it is unlikely that a company will make every payment related to the purchase of inventory within the discount period, and there are distinct differences between the methods when payments are made after the discount period has expired. In the example above, under the gross method, if the invoice is paid on 2-30-95, there is no additional information gathered — the $10,000 increase in Purchases remains. Under the net method, if the invoice is paid after the discount period, the $9,800 increase in Purchases remains, and a $200 increase in Purchase Discounts Lost is recorded. Since the balance in Purchase Discounts Lost is reported as a type of interest expense and is not part of the cost of inventory, the two methods of recording purchases result in different information on a company's income statement when invoices are paid after the discount period.

Notice the information made available in the accounting records as a result of the use of the two methods. Under the gross method, Purchase Discounts tracks the amount of prompt-payment discounts earned by the company. However, no information is kept to indicate the amount of discounts missed by not paying invoices within the discount period. In contrast, the net method of recording purchases highlights the magnitude of purchase discounts missed by isolating them in the Purchase Discounts Lost account. This method doesn't accumulate information about the amount of purchase discounts the company *did* take advantage of, but information as to the additional dollars spent as a result of invoices being paid after the discount period is tracked.

The net method has some distinct advantages. Some would argue the lower amount recorded in Purchases under this method more accurately reflects the cost of the inventory, because the company *could* buy it for the net amount. Also, the amount of purchase discounts missed rather than the amount earned is more useful information in helping a company improve its performance. However, it may be this advantage that makes the method less popular than the gross method. Management's reluctance to disclose the dollars lost by missing discounts may be one reason the net method is not chosen.

PURCHASE RETURNS AND ALLOWANCES

You might think that the entry to record the return of merchandise to the supplier is simply a reversal of the purchase entry. However, when the periodic inventory system is used, this is not the case. Instead of reducing the Purchases account, a separate account called **Purchase Returns** is used to accumulate the cost of merchandise returned to suppliers. For example, if Speace Electrical Supply returns merchandise which cost $500 to its supplier, the transaction would be recorded as:

```
Accounts Payable          500
     Purchase Returns            500
```

The *amount* for which a purchase return is recorded is dependent upon whether the company uses the gross or net method of recording purchases. That is, if the gross method is being used to record purchases, the gross amount of the merchandise returned would be recorded; if the net method is being used, the purchase return would be recorded at the net amount of the merchandise returned. Accumulating the cost of returned merchandise in the Purchase Returns account allows management to monitor the amount of returns made by the company. Purchase Returns is a contra-purchases account and, accordingly, has a normal credit balance — just the opposite of the Purchases account.

Merchandise may be returned for a variety of reasons. Often, when a buyer wishes to return merchandise because it is not of the quality expected, or the buyer is in some other way dissatisfied, the seller may offer a price reduction and allow the buyer to keep the merchandise. This approach may allow the seller to avoid taking the product back while, hopefully, satisfying the buyer. From the buyer's point of view, this type of cost reduction which does not require the return of the product is called a purchase allowance. When the periodic inventory system is used, such a cost reduction is recorded in the **Purchase Allowances** account. The entry to record a $200 purchase allowance when the periodic inventory system is used is shown below:

```
Accounts Payable          200
     Purchase Allowances          200
```

As was the case with purchase returns, the *amount* recorded for a purchase allowance should coincide with the method used to record purchases — net or gross. The Purchase Allowances account is a contra-purchases account and has a normal credit balance.

Some companies record results of both purchase returns and purchase allowances in a single account called Purchase Returns and Allowances — another contra-purchases account with a normal credit balance.

NOTE: When invoices are paid after a purchase return or a purchase allowance, it is important to consider that any discount terms (e.g., 2%) apply only to the balance still owed to the supplier.

FREIGHT COSTS RELATED TO MERCHANDISE

In some operations, freight costs associated with transporting merchandise are significant amounts. Proper recording of these costs is important. From the buyer's point of view, the cost of having the merchandise purchased transported to the company is recorded in an account called **Freight-In** or **Transportation-In**. For example, if Speace Electrical Supply receives a $100 freight bill for the cost of transporting merchandise from its supplier, the entry to record the freight bill would be:

```
Freight-In              100
     Accounts Payable          100
```

Getting the merchandise in stock and available for customers is an integral part of the cost of the inventory itself. For that reason, as we will see when the income statement is prepared, the balance in Freight-In is an addition to the cost of purchases. Under a periodic inventory system, Freight-In is a component in the calculation of cost of goods sold. Generally, discounts are not offered on freight costs, so there is no issue as to whether to record these costs at their net or gross amounts.

Another type of freight charge which companies may encounter is the cost of shipping goods to customers. Even if the same carrier (e.g., a trucking company) is used for both types of shipping, the costs must be tracked separately. The cost of having merchandise shipped to customers is often recorded as **Freight-Out** (or **Transportation-Out**), and although the account titles are similar, treatment of this cost is very different from that of Freight-In. Freight-Out is NOT a part of inventory costs and has no relation to Purchases. It is simply a selling expense, the cost of completing a sale by delivering the goods to the customer. Thus, if Speace pays ACME Trucking $75 to ship goods to a customer, the transaction would be recorded as:

```
Freight-Out             75
     Cash                      75
```

The Freight-Out account is an expense account with a normal debit balance.

RECORDING SALES

When the periodic inventory system is used, sales to customers are recorded by an entry increasing either Cash or Accounts Receivable with a debit and increasing the revenue account, Sales, with a credit.

As an example, assume that Speace Electrical Supply sold merchandise which cost $1,900 to a customer for $2,300 on account. The entry to record the sale appears below:

```
Accounts Receivable      2,300
        Sales                        2,300
```

NOTE: The *cost* of the inventory sold was provided in the information above, but this information has no impact on the recording of sales under a periodic system.

SALES DISCOUNTS

As we have seen, companies often offer discounts to their customers for the prompt payment of invoices. The sales terms used to indicate when the seller expects payment and if any prompt-payment discounts are offered are the same as those described during the discussion of purchase discounts. In fact, the topic we will explore now covers the same type of transactions as those described earlier — we are simply viewing the transactions from a different point of view. From the seller's point of view, discounts offered to customers for the prompt payment of invoices are called **sales discounts**. As with purchase discounts, there are two methods to account for sales discounts. Again, they are the gross method and the net method. Because of these two different approaches to tracking information about sales discounts, there are two different approaches to the *amount* for which a sale on account may be recorded.

GROSS METHOD

When the gross method is used, sales are originally recorded at the gross invoice amount. That is, sales are recorded at the full invoice price, without deducting the discount. As an example, assume that Speace Electrical Supply sells merchandise costing $700 for $1,000 with terms of 3 10, N 30. The sales invoice would be recorded at its gross amount ($1,000) as shown below:

```
Accounts Receivable      1,000
        Sales                        1,000
```

If the invoice is paid within the discount period, the customer pays the invoice amount, less the discount. In our example, the customer would pay $970, as calculated below:

```
Gross invoice amount     $1,000
Less the 3% discount      - 30
Amount paid              $  970
```

Although only $970 is received in payment of the invoice, the payment would fully settle the $1,000 receivable shown on Speace's books. The difference between the amount received and the invoice amount is the sales discount. An entry to record the receipt of the $970 payment is shown below:

```
Cash                        970
Sales Discounts              30
        Accounts Receivable       1,000
```

Notice that Cash is increased with a debit for the $970 received and that a credit of $1,000 appropriately reduces Accounts Receivable for this sale to zero. The difference ($30) is debited to **Sales Discounts**. The Sales Discounts account is a contra-sales account. That is, it is classified or grouped with Sales but works to reduce Sales. Sales Discounts has a normal debit balance — just the opposite of Sales.

If the invoice is not paid within the discount period, the customer must pay the entire invoice amount. In this case, under the gross method, the amount of cash received equals the amount originally recorded in Accounts Receivable. Accordingly, the entry is a simple matter of debiting Cash for the $1,000 received and crediting Accounts Receivable for the same amount, as shown in the entry below:

```
Cash                      1,000
        Accounts Receivable       1,000
```

Under the gross method, the original sale was recorded ignoring any possible discount, so when the customer misses the discount, the entry to record the collection simply increases Cash and decreases Accounts Receivable.

NET METHOD

The net method is far less popular than the gross method for recording sales. When the net method is used, the sale is recorded at the net amount. That is, the sale is recorded at the amount of the invoice less the discount. Using the example for Speace, the sale would be recorded as shown below, using the periodic inventory system and the net method for recording sales.

```
Accounts Receivable         970
        Sales                      970
```

Under the net method, the receivable is recorded at the amount the customer will pay *IF* the invoice is paid within the discount period. So, recording the receipt of payment from a customer within the discount period is a simple matter of increasing Cash and decreasing Accounts Receivable by the amount collected. In our example of Speace Electrical Supply, if the customer pays within the discount period, Speace will receive $970, the invoice amount less the discount. In this case, recording the receipt of payment from the customer is a simple matter of increasing Cash with a $970 debit and eliminating the receivable for this invoice by crediting Accounts Receivable for $970, as shown below:

```
Cash                        970
        Accounts Receivable       970
```

If Speace's customer does not pay within the discount period, no discount is allowed.

Accordingly, the customer should pay the entire $1,000 invoice amount. In this case, under the net method, the entry should increase Cash by the $1,000 received and eliminate the $970 accounts receivable recorded at the time of the sale. The $30 difference between the cash received of $1,000 and the $970 in accounts receivable is the amount of sales discount forfeited by the customer for not paying within the discount period. This amount is credited to an account called **Sales Discounts Forfeited** to balance the entry, as shown below:

```
Cash                                  1,000
        Accounts Receivable                 970
        Sales Discounts Forfeited            30
```

Under the net method, sales and the associated receivables are recorded at the amount the customer will pay if the invoice is paid within the discount period. If the customer forfeits the discount and pays a greater amount, the difference is credited to Sales Discounts Forfeited. In a sense, Sales Discounts Forfeited, which has a normal credit balance, represents interest earned by the seller in addition to the sales recorded at the net invoice amount. When financial statements are prepared, the balance in this account is shown as a miscellaneous revenue, generated from allowing customers to defer payment.

The net method of recording sales is not widely used. There are two major drawbacks which have caused the limited use of this method. First, when sales are recorded under the net method, the invoice amount is not used. Instead, additional calculations are required to determine the net amount. Second, when the net method is used, each time financial statements are prepared an adjusting entry is required to increase Accounts Receivable and Sales Discounts Forfeited for the amount of discounts applicable to all uncollected accounts receivable which are beyond the discount period.

GROSS METHOD VS. NET METHOD — A COMPARISON

A summary of the entries to record sales on account and the subsequent collection of receivables using the gross and net method under the periodic inventory system is offered below:

Entries Related to a $1,000 Sale — Terms 3 10, N 30 When the Periodic Inventory System is Used		
	GROSS METHOD	NET METHOD

Invoice Date 2-1-95	Accounts Receivable 1,000
	    Sales 1,000
		Accounts Receivable 970
		    Sales 970

IF Payment Is Made 2-10-95	Cash 970
	Sales Discounts 30
	    Accounts Receivable 1,000
		Cash 970
		    Accounts Receivable 970

IF Payment Is Made 2-30-95	Cash 1,000
	    Accounts Receivable 1,000
		Cash 1,000
		    Accounts Receivable 970
		    Sales Disc. Forfeited 30

As you examine the table above, notice that not all accounts are different under the two methods. The cash amounts collected *cannot* be affected by a choice between recording methods, so the debits to Cash are the same for each method.

Under the gross method, Accounts Receivable is increased by the gross amount, $1,000, but the net method only records the receivable as $970. If all collections were made by the end of the period, no difference between the methods would be seen in Accounts Receivable. However, any uncollected receivables would be shown at a higher amount under the gross method than under the net method.

The Sales account is affected in a similar fashion. Sales are recorded at a higher amount under the gross method than under the net method. If, however, all receivables were collected within the discount period, the two methods would provide the same figure for what is called **net sales** — that is, Sales less all contra-sales account balances. In our example, net sales for this one transaction would be:

```
    Sales                 $1,000
  - Sales Discounts            30
    Net Sales             $   970
```

Since the net method uses no contra-sales accounts, the $970 balance in Sales would also be net sales. Realistically, it is unlikely that all receivables will be collected within the discount period, and there are distinct differences between the methods when customers miss the discount. In the example above, under the gross method, if the customer paid on 2-30-95, there is no additional information gathered — the $1,000 sale remains. Under the net method, if the customer missed the discount, a sale of only $970 is recorded, but an additional revenue of $30 is also recorded. In total, the revenues recorded in this situation are the same under the two methods. However, the $30 in Sales Discounts Forfeited is reported as a miscellaneous revenue — not an addition to Sales — so the information presented on the income statement is different.

Notice the information made available in the accounting records as a result of the use of the two methods. Under the gross method, Sales Discounts tracks the amount of prompt-payment discounts earned by customers. However, no information is kept to indicate the amount collected by the company as a result of customers paying after the discount period. In contrast, the net method of recording sales highlights the magnitude of sales discounts missed by customers by isolating them in the Sales Discounts Forfeited account. This method doesn't accumulate information about the amount of sales discounts customers *did* take advantage of, but information as to the additional dollars collected as a result of payments being received after the discount period is tracked.

Either method of recording sales may be chosen, but the drawbacks of the net method described in the previous section have limited its use; the gross method remains the more popular approach.

RETURNED MERCHANDISE AND SALES ALLOWANCES

When a customer returns goods to the merchandiser, it might seem appropriate for the seller to simply reverse the entry used to record the sale. However, if that were done, information would be lost. When merchandise is returned, an account called **Sales Returns** is debited and Cash or Accounts Receivable is credited. The benefit of using a separate account to record returns of merchandise by customers is that the company can track the level of sales returns in relation to the amount of sales.

Now let's assume that a customer returns merchandise to Speace Electrical Supply. The merchandise was purchased on account for $900, and the merchandise cost Speace $750. The entry to record this transaction is shown below:

```
Sales Returns                     900
        Accounts Receivable              900
```

As with the entries to record sales, when the periodic inventory system is used, the *cost* of the merchandise has no impact on the recording of returns by customers. Sales Returns is a contra-sales account, which means its balance will be reported as a reduction of Sales. Sales Returns has a normal debit balance — just the opposite of Sales. As was the case with purchase returns, the *amount* for which a sales return is recorded is dependent upon whether the company uses the gross or net method of recording sales. That is, if the gross method is being used to record sales, the gross amount of the merchandise returned would be recorded; if the net method is being used, the sales return would be recorded at the net amount of the merchandise returned.

As you know, sales returns occur when a customer is unhappy with a purchase for one reason or another. Sometimes a merchandiser will satisfy a customer's complaint by refunding a portion of the selling price without taking back any of the merchandise. This type of transaction has already been explored from the buyer's point of view in our discussion of purchase allowances. From the seller's point of view, a refund of part of the selling price not requiring the customer to return any of the merchandise is known as a **sales allowance**. As with the recording of sales returns, a special account is used to track sales allowances.

If Speace, in an attempt to avoid bringing merchandise back while at the same time making a customer happy, granted the buyer a sales allowance of $200, the necessary entry would be:

```
Sales Allowances                  200
        Accounts Receivable              200
```

Sales Allowances is a contra-sales account — its balance will be reported as a reduction of sales. Sales Allowances has a normal debit balance — just the opposite of Sales. Again, the purpose of keeping the allowances in a separate account is to provide information helpful in the evaluation of the company's performance. Management should investigate the reason for customer dissatisfaction if the level of sales allowances climbs.

If management decides there is no reason to keep separate information about the levels of sales returns and sales allowances, results of these transactions may be recorded in the same account. It is not unusual for companies to use a single account called **Sales Returns and**

Allowances to record results of both types of transactions. Sales Returns and Allowances would, of course, be a contra-sales account with a normal debit balance.

ACCOUNTS USED IN THE PERIODIC INVENTORY SYSTEM

We have explored the transactions of a merchandiser using the periodic inventory system. The transactions illustrated thus far are those that would not have existed for a service company. Because a merchandiser has inventory which is bought and resold, several new accounts and procedures have been introduced in this module. As we said earlier, many of the basics you learned in Modules 1 through 6 will hold true for a merchandiser as well as a service firm. To illustrate the aspects unique to a merchandising company, and to further explore the periodic inventory system, we present a chart of accounts for Speace Electrical Supply. The accounts which were introduced in this module are presented in **bold**.

```
        Speace Electrical Supply
          Chart of Accounts

    Account
    Number      Account Name

    110         Cash
    130         Accounts Receivable
    190         Inventory
    210         Office Equipment
    215         Accumulated Depreciation
    310         Accounts Payable
    510         Common Stock
    520         Retained Earnings
    525         Income Summary
    530         Dividends
    610         Sales
    615         Sales Discounts
    620         Sales Returns
    625         Sales Allowances
    640         Interest Revenue
    705         Purchases
    710         Purchase Discounts
    715         Purchase Returns
    720         Purchase Allowances
    730         Freight-In
    740         Wage Expense
    750         Rent Expense
    760         Freight-Out
    770         Depreciation Expense
```

Recall that companies may choose from two methods for recording purchases and sales. The gross method may be chosen for one and the net method for the other, or the same method may be used for both purchases and sales. The method chosen may affect the accounts a company uses.

In the case of recording purchases of merchandise on account under a periodic inventory system, the gross method keeps track of discounts the company *did* take advantage of, and the net method tracks discounts missed. As the chart of accounts above indicates, Speace Electrical Supply has a Purchase Discounts account. Existence of this account suggests that the company uses the gross method for recording purchases of inventory. *If* Speace had used the net method for recording purchases and had paid invoices after the discount period, the company would use a Purchase Discounts Lost account.

In the case of recording sales on account under a periodic inventory system, the gross method keeps track of the discounts given to customers for paying within the discount period. The balance in Sales Discounts reflects these amounts, and the fact that the chart of accounts above shows Sales Discounts indicates that Speace uses the gross method of recording its sales on account. *If* Speace had used the net method, no information about the discounts taken by customers would be kept. However, if customers paid after the discount period, the additional amount collected would be reflected in Sales Discounts Forfeited.

Throughout this module, we have explored *some* of the transactions from Speace's 1995 fiscal year. The company ends its business year on June 30, and has already completed the adjustment process for the 1995 fiscal year. The adjusted trial balance below reflects the account balances which are ready for use in financial statement preparation. Again, the accounts in **bold** are those introduced in this module.

Speace Electrical Supply
Adjusted Trial Balance
As of June 30, 1995

Cash	$ 7,400	
Accounts Receivable	4,100	
Inventory	**9,000**	
Office Equipment	27,500	
Accumulated Depreciation		$ 6,000
Accounts Payable		4,200
Common Stock		13,000
Retained Earnings		8,550
Dividends	700	
Sales		**87,000**
Sales Discounts	**1,150**	
Sales Returns	**1,250**	
Sales Allowances	**400**	
Interest Revenue		250
Purchases	**49,500**	
Purchase Discounts		**750**
Purchase Returns		**550**
Purchase Allowances		**350**
Freight-In	**450**	
Wage Expense	11,100	
Rent Expense	5,500	
Freight-Out	**600**	
Depreciation Expense	2,000	
	$120,650	$120,650

FINANCIAL STATEMENTS UNDER A PERIODIC INVENTORY SYSTEM

The financial statements explored in earlier modules are appropriate for service companies. As we have said, the biggest difference in the recording process for a merchandiser is the addition of inventory and the information requirements that accompany it. Thus far we have examined the recording of transactions dealing with inventory and we have seen the use of accounts not necessary in a service company. The financial statements of a merchandising company are also a bit different from those of a service company.

The basic difference between the balance sheet of a merchandiser and that of a service company is the existence of inventory. Inventory (sometimes called merchandise inventory) is shown on the balance sheet as a current asset. This figure should reflect the amount of inventory the company owns as of the balance sheet date. Under a periodic inventory system, the Inventory account is not changed during the period to reflect amounts of merchandise bought or sold. Therefore, the amount shown as the balance in the Inventory account in the adjusted trial balance is *not* the company's ending inventory. Rather, it reflects the amount of inventory the company had at the beginning of the period. A physical count of inventory is taken at the end of the period to determine the actual amount of inventory owned by the business. This figure (ending inventory) is reported as the asset amount on the company's balance sheet. When we examine the closing process under a periodic inventory system, *how* the Inventory account is changed will become clear.

The bridge statement (e.g., the statement of retained earnings or statement of capital) is no different for a merchandiser than for a service business. This statement reflects changes in retained earnings or capital as a result of net income and dividends (or drawings).

The most significant differences in the financial statements of a merchandiser are found on the income statement. Indeed, under a periodic inventory system, all of the accounts introduced in this module impact the income statement.

In most cases, the largest expense for a merchandising company is the cost related to the merchandise that is sold during the period. This expense is very appropriately called Cost of Goods Sold. In a periodic inventory system, no single account exists to accumulate the costs associated with this expense. Rather, at the end of the period, the amount of cost of goods sold for the period can be calculated.

The logic for determining the cost of goods sold under the periodic inventory system is really quite simple. At the end of the period, we have several pieces of key information: (1) Since the Inventory account balance is not changed during the period, the balance shown on the adjusted trial balance tells us how much inventory we started with (beginning inventory). (2) We also know how much inventory we bought during the period. To get an accurate count, we will use information from Purchases and several other accounts to determine this figure. (3) Cost of the inventory left on hand at the end of the period (ending inventory) is determined by a physical count.

Cost of the inventory we started with (beginning inventory) plus cost of the inventory we bought (delivered cost of purchases) gives the cost of the goods we *could have sold*. This amount is referred to as cost of goods available for sale. Subtracting the cost of what we still have on hand at the end of the period (ending inventory) from what was available to sell gives us the cost of the goods we *did* sell — cost of goods sold.

```
  Beginning Inventory
+ Delivered Cost of Purchases
  Cost of Goods Available for Sale
- Ending Inventory
  Cost of Goods Sold
```

Now we can calculate cost of goods sold for Space Electrical Supply. Beginning Inventory is the figure shown on the adjusted trial balance, $9,000.

Delivered cost of purchases begins with the balance in Purchases. All contra-purchases account balances are deducted from this figure to determine net purchases. The cost of getting the inventory items to us, Freight-in, is added to net purchases, resulting in Delivered Cost of Purchases. This calculation is illustrated below:

```
Purchases                            $49,500
Less:
   Purchase Discounts    $750
   Purchase Returns       550
   Purchase Allowances    350          1,650
Net Purchases                        $47,850
Add: Freight-In                         450
Delivered Cost of Purchases          $48,300
```

Under a periodic inventory system, the ending inventory figure is determined from a physical count of the merchandise owned at the end of the period. In our example, a physical count revealed that Space owned $6,300 of inventory as of June 30, 1995.

With these figures, we can calculate Space's cost of goods sold for the year:

```
  Beginning Inventory               $ 9,000
+ Delivered Cost of Purchases         48,300
  Cost of Goods Available for Sale  $57,300
- Ending Inventory                     6,300
  Cost of Goods Sold                $51,000
```

In the preparation of an income statement, cost of goods sold may be presented as the single amount (in this case, $51,000), or a detailed calculation showing how the figure was determined may be presented. If Space chose to offer a detailed presentation on its income statement, the cost of goods sold section would appear as:

```
Beginning Inventory                                     $ 9,000
Purchases                               $49,500
Less:
    Purchase Discounts      $750
    Purchase Returns         550
    Purchase Allowances      350     1,650
Net Purchases                           $47,850
Add: Freight-In                            450
Delivered Cost of Purchases              48,300
Cost of Goods Available for Sale        $57,300
Less: Ending Inventory                    6,300
Cost of Goods Sold                                      $51,000
```

In the following illustrations of Speace's income statements, the detailed schedule above could be substituted for the single line identifying cost of goods sold. Even though the periodic inventory system, by its very nature, requires a calculation to determine cost of goods sold for a given period, details of the calculation are not part of the required disclosures for a company using this system.

Based on the adjusted trial balance presented earlier, the following income statement for Speace Electrical Supply can be drawn:

```
                    Speace Electrical Supply
                       Income Statement
             For the Fiscal Year Ended June 30, 1995

    Sales                                      $87,000
       Less: Sales Discounts     $1,150
             Sales Returns        1,250
             Sales Allowances       400          2,800
    Net Sales                                           $84,200
    Cost of Goods Sold                                   51,000
    Gross Margin                                        $33,200
    Operating Expenses:
                Wage Expense      $11,100
                Rent Expense        5,500
                Depreciation Expense 2,000
                Freight-Out           600
          Total Operating Expenses                       19,200
    Operating Income                                    $14,000
    Other Revenue:
          Interest Revenue                                  250
    Net Income                                          $14,250
```

As you examine the income statement above, notice that all contra-sales accounts are deducted from Sales to arrive at Net Sales. In this context, the Sales figure ($87,000) may be referred to as **gross sales**.

From Net Sales, Cost of Goods Sold is deducted to arrive at **Gross Margin**. Presentation of gross margin is one of the features of the **multistep income statement**. In this format, even if a company has other sources of revenue, only sales information is presented at the beginning of the income statement. The relationship between Net Sales and Cost of Goods Sold, the expense related to the inventory sold to produce those sales dollars, is highlighted.

Gross margin is also called gross profit. From this figure, operating expenses, the expenses incurred to support the primary business activity of the company, are deducted. **Operating Income** (also called Income from Operations) is the result. Presentation of this figure is the other feature unique to the multistep income statement format.

Below the presentation of Operating Income, any other revenues or expenses are reported. In the case of Speace Electrical Supply, Interest Revenue is the only non-operating item reported. The basic format of a multistep income statement is:

```
    Net Sales               $X,XXX
  — Cost of Goods Sold          XXX
    Gross Margin            $    XX
  — Operating Expenses           XX
    Operating Income        $    XX
  + Other Revenues                X
  - Other Expenses                X
    Net Income              $       X
```

The presentation of gross margin and operating income are the key features of the multistep income statement. Under a periodic inventory system, a company's multistep income statement may present cost of goods sold in a single line as shown above, or it may include a detailed schedule calculating the cost of goods sold figure.

The multistep income statement is not the only acceptable format for a merchandising company. The single-step income statement format is also acceptable. For Speace Electrical Supply, the following income statement could be presented instead:

```
                    Speace Electrical Supply
                        Income Statement
              For the Fiscal Year Ended June 30, 1995

Sales                                    $87,000
   Less: Sales Discounts    $1,150
         Sales Returns       1,250
         Sales Allowances      400         2,800
Net Sales                                           $84,200
Interest Revenue                                        250
Total Revenue                                       $84,450
      Expenses:
            Cost of Goods Sold    $51,000
            Wage Expense           11,100
            Rent Expense            5,500
            Depreciation Expense    2,000
            Freight-Out               600
Total Expenses                                       70,200
Net Income                                          $14,250
```

Notice that the net income figures for the two income statements are the same. Indeed, choice of income statement format cannot affect the final net income figure. What *is* affected is the information presented. In a single-step income statement, all revenues are gathered together at the beginning. In our example, we see the contra-sales accounts deducted from Sales to provide the net sales figure as before, but then Interest Revenue is added to Net Sales to present Total Revenue. The single-step income statement does not show gross margin. In fact, cost of goods sold is given no special treatment in this format. It is included in the list of *all* expenses, which is totalled to provide Total Expenses. Cost of goods sold is often listed first because of its size, but it is not separated from the other expenses. Even if a company chooses to include the detailed calculation of cost of goods sold, the figure is added to all the other expenses. In the single-step income statement format, no distinction is made between operating and non-operating revenues and expenses. The basic format of a single-step income statement is:

```
    Total Revenues      $X,XXX
  − Total Expenses         XXX
    Net Income          $    X
```

Again, whether a company chooses the multistep or single-step income statement format, net income will be the same.

NOTE: In the examples, we assumed Speace used the gross method for recording purchases and sales. If the net method had been used, and the company had balances in Purchase Discounts Lost or Sales Discounts Forfeited, these amounts would have been presented as an "other expense" and "other revenue", respectively. The exact placement of these items on the income statement would depend on the format (multistep or single-step) chosen.

THE CLOSING PROCESS UNDER A PERIODIC INVENTORY SYSTEM

The basic closing process was described in detail in Module 5. Recall that in that module, the entire closing process was summed up in four simple steps:

1. Close all revenue accounts to Income Summary.
2. Close all expense accounts to Income Summary.
3. Close Income Summary to Retained Earnings.
4. Close the Dividends account to Retained Earnings.

The purpose of closing entries and the basic approach to the process are the same for a merchandiser using a periodic inventory system. However, as you might expect, we now have some additional accounts with which to contend. Steps 1. and 2. of the process now have to accomplish three tasks instead of one. Building on the basics presented above, we can describe the closing process under a periodic inventory system as:

1.   Close all revenue accounts to Income Summary.
Close all other nominal accounts with credit balances.
Record the ending inventory amount in the Inventory account.

Closing the revenue accounts is the same, but the primary revenue is now Sales and a new revenue (Sales Discounts Forfeited) *may* exist. At the same time, close any other nominal (temporary) accounts that have credit balances. For a merchandiser using a periodic inventory system, contra-purchases accounts are the most common. The ending inventory figure determined from the physical count must be recorded in the Inventory account with a debit.

2.   Close all expense accounts to Income Summary.
Close all other nominal accounts with debit balances.
Remove the beginning inventory figure from the Inventory account.

Closing expense accounts is not new, but two new expenses were introduced: Freight-out and Purchase Discounts Lost. At the same time, close any other nominal (temporary) accounts that have debit balances. For a merchandiser using a periodic inventory system, this group includes contra-sales accounts, Purchases, and Freight-in. The beginning inventory figure, which has been in the Inventory account since the last closing process must be removed with a credit.

3.   Close Income Summary to Retained Earnings.

This step is exactly the same as it is in the closing process for a service company — nothing new. Even with the added complexity of Steps 1. and 2., this step still adds net income to owners' equity. In the case of a proprietorship or partnership, Capital accounts replace Retained Earnings.

4.   Close the Dividends account to Retained Earnings.

Nothing new here, either. *IF* a balance exists in Dividends, it is closed as the final step of the closing process. In the case of a proprietorship or partnership, Drawings accounts replace

Dividends and Capital accounts replace Retained Earnings.

As you can see, the closing process for a merchandiser using a periodic inventory system is not too different from what you have seen before. To complete the illustration of Speace Electrical Supply, the company's adjusted trial balance is repeated below, and the necessary closing entries follow:

Speace Electrical Supply
Adjusted Trial Balance
As of June 30, 1995

Cash	$ 7,400	
Accounts Receivable	4,100	
Inventory	9,000	
Office Equipment	27,500	
Accumulated Depreciation		$ 6,000
Accounts Payable		4,200
Common Stock		13,000
Retained Earnings		8,550
Dividends	700	
Sales		87,000
Sales Discounts	1,150	
Sales Returns	1,250	
Sales Allowances	400	
Interest Revenue		250
Purchases	49,500	
Purchase Discounts		750
Purchase Returns		550
Purchase Allowances		350
Freight-In	450	
Wage Expense	11,100	
Rent Expense	5,500	
Freight-Out	600	
Depreciation Expense	2,000	
	$120,650	$120,650

```
Step 1.   Sales                              87,000
          Interest Revenue                      250
          Purchase Discounts                    750
          Purchase Returns                      550
          Purchase Allowances                   350
          Inventory                           6,300
                Income Summary                          95,200


Step 2.   Income Summary                      80,950
                Wage Expense                            11,100
                Rent Expense                             5,500
                Freight-Out                                600
                Depreciation Expense                     2,000
                Sales Discounts                          1,150
                Sales Returns                            1,250
                Sales Allowances                           400
                Purchases                               49,500
                Freight-In                                 450
                Inventory                                9,000


Step 3.   Income Summary                      14,250
                Retained Earnings                       14,250


Step 4.   Retained Earnings                      700
                Dividends                                  700
```

You have now seen the recording process for a merchandising operation using a periodic inventory system. The only other part of the process that would be any different for this type of business than what you learned about in other modules is the worksheet. Again, use of this tool is optional, but a worksheet for Speace Electrical Supply based on the example used thus far is illustrated in the final section of this module.

WORKSHEETS FOR MERCHANDISING COMPANIES

As was the case with the worksheets for service companies introduced in Module 4, worksheets for merchandisers are optional tools. They are, however, even more useful in this setting because of the added complexities brought on by the addition of inventory.

The inventory system being used (perpetual or periodic) impacts many of the entries for day-to-day transactions and the entries for the closing process. The two inventory systems also require slightly different worksheets. A brief description and illustration of the worksheet for each inventory system follows.

WORKSHEET USING A PERPETUAL INVENTORY SYSTEM

The illustration of Speace Electrical Supply's worksheet on the next page assumes the company uses a perpetual inventory system. Under this system, the worksheet is very similar to the one prepared for the service company in Module 4. The first two columns are balances drawn from the company's general ledger accounts before any adjustments have been made. For clarity, only one adjusting entry is illustrated, but any necessary adjustments would be shown in the adjustment columns. The adjusted trial balance columns show figures that were previously presented as part of the example earlier in this module.

The accounts in **bold** are those that were introduced in this module. Only one of these new accounts, Inventory, affects the balance sheet. The others are all components of the income statement and are moved from the adjusted trial balance columns to the income statement columns.

As was the case with worksheets for service companies, the items in the income statement columns of the worksheet are all that should be necessary for preparation of the company's income statement. When the income statement columns and balance sheet columns are first totalled, they don't balance. However, the net income figure ($14,250) is used to bring them into balance.

Except for the addition of the new accounts, preparation of a worksheet for a merchandiser using a perpetual inventory system is no different than for a service company.

Speace Electrical Supply (Perpetual Inventory System)

ACCOUNT TITLES	Trial Balance DEBIT	Trial Balance CREDIT	Adjustments DEBIT	Adjustments CREDIT	Adj. Trial Balance DEBIT	Adj. Trial Balance CREDIT	Income Statement DEBIT	Income Statement CREDIT	Balance Sheet DEBIT	Balance Sheet CREDIT
Cash	7,400				7,400				7,400	
Accounts Rec.	4,100				4,100				4,100	
Inventory	6,300				6,300				6,300	
Office Equipment	27,500				27,500				27,500	
Accumulated Dep.		4,000		2,000		6,000				6,000
Accounts Payable		4,200				4,200				4,200
Common Stock		13,000				13,000				13,000
Retained Earnings		8,550				8,550				8,550
Dividends	700				700				700	
Sales		87,000				87,000		87,000		
Sales Discounts	1,150				1,150		1,150			
Sales Returns	1,250				1,250		1,250			
Sales Allowances	400				400		400			
Interest Revenue		250				250		250		
Cost of Goods Sold	51,000				51,000		51,000			
Wage Expense	11,100				11,100		11,100			
Rent Expense	5,500				5,500		5,500			
Freight-Out	600				600		600			
Depreciation Exp.			2,000		2,000		2,000			
	117,000	117,000	2,000	2,000	119,000	119,000	73,000	87,250	46,000	31,750
							14,250			14,250
							87,250	87,250	46,000	46,000

WORKSHEET USING A PERIODIC INVENTORY SYSTEM

The illustration of Speace Electrical Supply's worksheet on the next page assumes the company uses a periodic inventory system. Under this system, the worksheet shows some basic similarities to the one prepared for the service company in Module 4. The first two columns are balances drawn from the company's general ledger accounts before any adjustments have been made. For clarity, only one adjusting entry is illustrated, but any necessary adjustments would be shown in the adjustment columns. The adjusted trial balance columns show figures that were previously presented as part of the example earlier in this module.

The accounts in **bold** are those that were introduced in this module. Look closely at how each one is treated on the worksheet. All of these new accounts (except Inventory) are simply brought from the adjusted trial balance to the income statement columns. Each of the new accounts impacts the income statement. Even if the detailed calculation of cost of goods sold is not presented, Purchases, all the contra-purchases accounts, and Freight-In are used to determine the figure reported as cost of goods sold.

Inventory figures are also needed in the calculation of cost of goods sold. As you recall, both beginning inventory and ending inventory figures are used. For this reason, both beginning and ending inventory figures are included in the income statement columns of the worksheet. In fact, as you look at the income statement and balance sheet columns, you will see that Inventory shows three figures. The figure that was in the trial balance at the beginning of the worksheet ($9,000) is beginning inventory. From a physical count, the ending inventory figure ($6,300) was determined. Since both beginning and ending inventory amounts are used to determine cost of goods sold, both of these amounts are shown in the income statement columns. Ending inventory is the appropriate figure to report as the asset amount on the company's balance sheet. Thus, Inventory is recorded in the financial statement columns as beginning, ending, ending — three amounts in a row.

The unique presentation of inventory figures within a worksheet for a company using a periodic inventory system is the only significant difference from the service company worksheet. As was the case with worksheets for service companies, the items in the income statement columns of the worksheet are all that should be necessary for preparation of the company's income statement. When the income statement columns and balance sheet columns are first totalled, they don't balance. However, the net income figure ($14,250) is used to bring them into balance.

Speace Electrical Supply (Periodic Inventory System)

ACCOUNT TITLES	Trial Balance DEBIT	Trial Balance CREDIT	Adjustments DEBIT	Adjustments CREDIT	Adj. Trial Balance DEBIT	Adj. Trial Balance CREDIT	Income Statement DEBIT	Income Statement CREDIT	Balance Sheet DEBIT	Balance Sheet CREDIT
Cash	7,400				7,400				7,400	
Accounts Rec.	4,100				4,100				4,100	
Inventory	9,000				9,000		9,000	6,300	6,300	
Office Equipment	27,500				27,500				27,500	
Accumulated Dep.		4,000		2,000		6,000				6,000
Accounts Payable		4,200				4,200				4,200
Common Stock		13,000				13,000				13,000
Retained Earnings		8,550				8,550				8,550
Dividends	700				700				700	
Sales		87,000				87,000		87,000		
Sales Discounts	1,150				1,150		1,150			
Sales Returns	1,250				1,250		1,250			
Sales Allowances	400				400		400			
Interest Revenue		250				250		250		
Purchases	49,500				49,500		49,500			
Purchase Allow.		350				350		350		
Purchase Returns		550				550		550		
Purchase Disc.		750				750		750		
Freight-In	450				450		450			
Wage Expense	11,100				11,100		11,100			
Rent Expense	5,500				5,500		5,500			
Freight-Out	600				600		600			
Depreciation Exp.			2,000		2,000		2,000			
	118,650	118,650	2,000	2,000	120,650	120,650	80,950	95,200	46,000	31,750
							14,250			14,250
							95,200	95,200	46,000	46,000

APPLY WHAT YOU HAVE LEARNED

"A." HOMEWORK PROBLEMS FOR PERPETUAL INVENTORY SYSTEM

7-1A. (PERPETUAL — Merchandising Accounts)

For each of the following accounts, indicate whether it is an income statement account or a balance sheet account, and what the normal balance of the account is.

Account	I=Income Statement B=Balance Sheet	Normal Balance (Debit or Credit)
Accounts Payable		
Accumulated Depreciation		
Cash		
Common Stock		
Cost of Goods Sold		
Depreciation Expense		
Dividends		
Equipment		
Expired Insurance		
Freight-Out		
Inventory		
Prepaid Insurance		
Purchase Discounts Lost		
Retained Earnings		
Sales Discounts		
Sales Returns		
Sales Discounts Forfeited		
Sales Allowances		
Sales		
Unearned Revenue		
Unexpired Insurance		

7-2A. (PERPETUAL — Computing Cash Discounts)

For each of the following, compute the amount of the cash discount and the net amount.

TERMS	GROSS INVOICE AMOUNT	CASH DISCOUNT	NET AMOUNT
2 10, N 30	$1,000		
1 10, N 45	$1,000		
2 10 EOM, N 30 EOM	$4,000		
3% 15, Net 30 Days	$2,500		
Net 10 Days	$3,000		
2 10, N 30	$3,000		
N 30 EOM	$5,000		
1 10 EOM, N 40 EOM	$5,000		
3 10, N 40	$6,000		

7-3A. (PERPETUAL — Gross and Net Methods of Recording Purchases)

Reimer Products, Inc. completed the following transactions:

July 1   Purchased $10,000 merchandise from Peters Company, terms 2 10, N 30.

July 3   Purchased $5,000 merchandise from Joseph Enterprises, terms 1 10, N 30.

July 7   Paid the Peters invoice.

August 3   Paid the Joseph invoice.

Required:

Assuming Reimer Products uses the *perpetual* inventory method, prepare journal entries for each of the transactions using:

    a.   The Gross Method

    b.   The Net Method

7-3A. a. Reimer Products, *Perpetual*, Gross Method

Date	Description	Debit	Credit
July 1			
July 3			
July 7			
August 3			

7-3A. b. Reimer Products, *Perpetual*, Net Method

Date	Description	Debit	Credit
July 1			
July 3			
July 7			
August 3			

7-4A. (PERPETUAL — Gross and Net Methods of Recording Purchases)

Buffalo Tobacco Products completed the following transactions:

June 22	Purchased $1,000 merchandise from Hershey's, terms 1 10 EOM, N 30 EOM.
June 25	Purchased $4,000 merchandise from American Tobacco Company, terms 2 10, N 30.
July 8	Paid the Hershey's invoice.
July 25	Paid the American Tobacco Company invoice.

Required:

Assuming Buffalo Tobacco Products uses the *perpetual* inventory method, prepare journal entries for each of the transactions using:

    a.   The Gross Method

    b.   The Net Method

	a. Gross Method	b. Net Method
Jun 22		
Jun 25		
Jul 8		
Jul 25		

7-5A. (PERPETUAL — Purchase Returns and Allowances)

Carrie's Cooperatives engaged in the following transactions:

August 2   Purchased $7,000 merchandise from Karen's Krafts, terms 2 10, N 30.

August 6   Returned $2,000 of the merchandise for credit.

August 8   Carrie was granted an allowance of $500 for some of the merchandise which was slightly damaged.

August 11   Paid the amount due to Karen's Krafts.

Required:

Assuming Carrie's Cooperatives uses the *Perpetual* Inventory Method, record the transactions under the:

    a.   Gross Method

    b.   Net Method

	a. Gross Method	b. Net Method
Aug 2		
Aug 6		
Aug 8		
Aug 11		

7-6A. (PERPETUAL — Freight Costs)

Cybill Enterprises purchased merchandise on account for $1,000 plus freight charges of $100. Cybill then sold the merchandise on account for $1,500, and paid cash of $85 to ship the goods to the customer.

Required: a.   Prepare journal entries for the above transactions.

              b.   What is the total cost of the inventory? $_____

              c.   What kind of account is Freight-Out? _____
                     What is its normal balance? _____
                     Where is it shown in the financial statements? _____

7-7A. (PERPETUAL — Recording Purchases and Sales)

Kumen's Kernels purchased inventory on account at a cost of $12,000, and sold half of the inventory on account for $9,000.

Required: a.   Prepare journal entries for the above transactions.

              b.   What is the cost of inventory on hand after the sale? $_____
                     Where is it shown in the financial statements? _____

              c.   What is the gross profit on the sale? $_____

7-8A. (PERPETUAL — Purchases, Sales, and Freight)

Delectables By Decastro purchased inventory on account at a cost of $25,000, and sold $10,000 of the inventory on account for $16,000. Freight costs of $600 were paid in cash to ship the goods to the customer.

Required: a.   Prepare journal entries for the above transactions.

              b.   What is the cost of inventory on hand after the sale? $_____
                     Where is it shown in the financial statements? _____

              c.   What is the gross profit on the sale? $_____
                     How should the freight costs be accounted for in the financial
                     statements? _____

7-9A. (PERPETUAL — Gross and Net Methods of Recording Sales)

Bonnie's Bouquets purchased inventory on account at a cost of $2,000, and sold the inventory on October 1 for $3,000, terms 2 10, N 30. Bonnie uses the perpetual inventory system.

Required:

Prepare journal entries for the following transactions using: (a.) the *Gross* method, and (b.) the *Net* method.

(a.) Bonnie's Bouquets, *Gross Method*

Oct 1   To record the sale of inventory.

Oct 11   If the discount is taken, give the entry to record the receipt of cash.

Oct 31   If the discount is not taken, give the entry to record the receipt of cash.

(b.) Bonnie's Bouquets, *Net* Method

Oct 1   To record the sale of inventory.

Oct 11   If the discount is taken, give the entry to record the receipt of cash.

Oct 31   If the discount is not taken, give the entry to record the receipt of cash.

7-10A. (PERPETUAL — Gross and Net Methods of Recording Sales)

Frank's Security Systems purchased inventory at a cost of $5,000, and sold the inventory on April 20 for $7,500, terms 1 10 EOM, N 30 EOM. Frank uses the perpetual inventory system.

Required:

Prepare journal entries for the following transactions using: (a.) the *Gross* method, and (b.) the *Net* method.

(a.) Frank's Security Systems, *Gross Method*

Apr 20   To record the sale of inventory.

May 10   If the discount is taken, give the entry to record the receipt of cash.

May 30   If the discount is not taken, give the entry to record the receipt of cash.

(b.) Frank's Security Systems, *Net* Method

Apr 20   To record the sale of inventory.

May 10   If the discount is taken, give the entry to record the receipt of cash.

May 30   If the discount is not taken, give the entry to record the receipt of cash.

7-11A. (PERPETUAL — Sales Returns and Allowances)

Beth's Baby World sold several items of nursery furniture and baby supplies to a customer on account for a total sales price of $1,200. The merchandise had cost Beth $750. Later, the customer returned $100 of the merchandise for credit (Beth's cost $65), and Beth granted an allowance of $50 on some of the merchandise due to minor imperfections in workmanship.

Required: Prepare journal entries for each of the above transactions.

7-12A. (PERPETUAL — Sales Returns and Allowances)

Sam's Custom Auto installed a new convertible top and some sound equipment in a customer's vehicle. The total sales price was $3,500 on account, and the inventory had cost Sam $2,100. When the customer picked up her car, she noticed a small flaw in the convertible top, and Sam graciously granted an allowance of $100. Later, the customer returned $250 of the sound equipment for credit (Sam's cost was $150).

Required: Prepare journal entries for each of the above transactions.

7-13A. (PERPETUAL — Income Statement Formats)

The Adjusted Trial Balance for Braun Wholesale is:

Braun Wholesale
Adjusted Trial Balance
September 30, 1995

	Debit	Credit
Cash	$ 9,000	
Accounts Receivable	12,000	
Inventory	9,600	
Office Equipment	28,500	
Accumulated Depreciation		$ 3,600
Accounts Payable		14,000
Common Stock		30,000
Retained Earnings		5,000
Dividends	3,500	
Sales		75,000
Sales Discounts	2,000	
Sales Returns	1,400	
Sales Allowances	1,100	
Interest Revenue		3,200
Cost of Goods Sold	40,000	
Wages Expense	12,500	
Rent Expense	6,800	
Freight-Out	2,600	
Depreciation Expense	1,800	1,800
Totals	$130,800	$130,800

Required: Prepare an income statement using the:
a. Multistep format
b. Single-step format

7-14A. (PERPETUAL — Financial Statement Preparation)

Using the trial balance information in Problem 7-13A, prepare a multistep income statement, a statement of retained earnings, and a balance sheet. Use arrows to indicate the articulation of the financial statements.

7-15A. (PERPETUAL — Closing Entries)

Using the information from Problem 7-13A, prepare closing entries for Braun Wholesale.

7-16A. (PERPETUAL — Worksheet and Financial Statements)

A partially completed worksheet for Braun Wholesale at September 30, 1995 is included on the next page.

Required: a. Complete the worksheet.

b. Prepare a multistep income statement, a statement of retained earnings, and a balance sheet for the company's fiscal year ending September 30, 1995.

Homework Problem A   Braun Wholesale, September 30, 1995 (Perpetual)

ACCOUNT TITLES	Trial Balance DEBIT	Trial Balance CREDIT	Adjustments DEBIT	Adjustments CREDIT	Adj. Trial Balance DEBIT	Adj. Trial Balance CREDIT	Income Statement DEBIT	Income Statement CREDIT	Balance Sheet DEBIT	Balance Sheet CREDIT
Cash	9,000				9,000					
Accounts Rec.	12,000				12,000					
Inventory	9,600				9,600					
Office Equipment	28,500				28,500					
Accumulated Dep.		1,800		1,800		3,600				
Accounts Payable		14,000				14,000				
Common Stock		30,000				30,000				
Retained Earnings		5,000				5,000				
Dividends	3,500				3,500					
Sales		75,000				75,000				
Sales Discounts	2,000				2,000					
Sales Returns	1,400				1,400					
Sales Allowances	1,100				1,100					
Interest Revenue		3,200				3,200				
Cost of Goods Sold	40,000				40,000					
Wage Expense	12,500				12,500					
Rent Expense	6,800				6,800					
Freight-Out	2,600				2,600					
Depreciation Exp.			1,800		1,800					
Totals	129,000	129,000	1,800	1,800	130,800	130,800				

7-17A. (PERPETUAL — Book and Physical Inventory)

Marianne's Music-Video uses a perpetual inventory system which keeps an up-to-date record of inventory purchases, sales, and the balance of inventory on hand. At the end of December, the Inventory account shows a balance on hand (book inventory) of $175,000. Marianne periodically counts the inventory on hand and compares the physical inventory count with the book inventory.

Required:

Give the journal entry to adjust the inventory account if the physical inventory at the end of December is:

a. $174,000.

b. $175,600.

The preliminary adjusted trial balance for Niagara Sales as of September 25, 1995 is:

```
                      Niagara Sales
                      Trial Balance
                   September 25, 1995

                                   Debit           Credit
Cash                             $ 18,000
Accounts Receivable                24,000
Inventory                          19,200
Supplies                            4,800
Prepaid Insurance                   3,000
Equipment                          57,000
Accumulated Depreciation                          $   7,200
Accounts Payable                                     28,000
Wages Payable                                         3,200
Long-Term Notes Payable                               8,000
Common Stock                                         60,000
Retained Earnings                                    10,000
Dividends                           7,000
Sales                                               150,000
Sales Discounts                     4,000
Sales Returns                       2,800
Sales Allowances                    2,200
Interest Revenue                                      6,600
Cost of Goods Sold                 80,000
Wages Expense                      25,000
Rent Expense                       13,600
Insurance Expense                   2,400
Supplies Expense                    1,000
Depreciation Expense                3,600
Freight-Out                         5,400
Totals                           $273,000          $273,000
```

During the last five days of September, Niagara Sales completed the following additional transactions. Niagara Sales uses the gross method to record purchases and sales.

Sep 26   Purchased $1,000 of merchandise on account from VanDeWater Auto, plus freight charges of $100.

Sep 26   Returned $300 of merchandise purchased earlier in the month from Davies Industrial.

Sep 27   Sold merchandise on account to Remack for $5,000. The cost of the inventory was $3,600.

Sep 27   Received payment on account from a customer, Wright Stuff, for an invoice amount of $2,000 less a sales discount of 1.5%.

Sep 28   Paid freight charges of $1,300 on merchandise shipped to customers.

| Sep 28 | A customer, Picky Picky, returned $400 of merchandise for credit (cost of the merchandise was $300), and was also granted an additional allowance of $50 for inventory that was slightly damaged in transit. |

| Sep 29 | Paid for merchandise purchased earlier in the month from Lane Autobody. The invoice price was $4,000, and a 2% purchase discount was taken. |

| Sep 30 | A physical count of inventory on hand shows an actual inventory of $16,000. Compute book inventory, and make the necessary entry to adjust the inventory account. |

Required:

a. Prepare journal entries to record the transactions for the last five days of September.

b. Prepare an updated trial balance to include the above transactions.

c. Calculate:
net sales $_____ gross margin $_____

d. Prepare closing entries.

e. Prepare a multistep income statement, a statement of retained earnings, and a balance sheet.

7-1B. (PERIODIC — Merchandising Accounts)

For each of the following accounts, indicate whether it is an income statement account or a balance sheet account, and what the normal balance of the account is.

Account	I=Income Statement B=Balance Sheet	Normal Balance (Debit or Credit)
Accounts Payable		
Accumulated Depreciation		
Common Stock		
Depreciation Expense		
Freight-In		
Freight-Out		
Inventory		
Purchase Discounts Lost		
Purchase Discounts		
Purchase Allowances		
Purchase Returns		
Purchases		
Retained Earnings		
Sales		
Sales Returns		
Sales Discounts		
Sales Discounts Forfeited		
Sales Allowances		

7-2B. (PERIODIC — Computing Cash Discounts)

For each of the following, compute the amount of the cash discount and the net amount.

TERMS	GROSS INVOICE AMOUNT	CASH DISCOUNT	NET AMOUNT
2 10, N 30	$1,000		
1 10, N 45	$1,000		
2 10 EOM, N 30 EOM	$4,000		
3% 15, Net 30 Days	$2,500		
Net 10 Days	$3,000		
2 10, N 30	$3,000		
N 30 EOM	$5,000		
1 10 EOM, N 40 EOM	$5,000		
3 10, N 40	$6,000		

7-3B. (PERIODIC — Gross and Net Methods of Recording Purchases)

Reimer Products, Inc. completed the following transactions:

July 1   Purchased $10,000 merchandise from Peters Company, terms 2 10, N 30.

July 3   Purchased $5,000 merchandise from Joseph Enterprises, terms 1 10, N 30.

July 7   Paid the Peters invoice.

August 3   Paid the Joseph invoice.

Required:

Assuming Reimer Products uses the *periodic* inventory method, prepare journal entries for each of the transactions using:

   a.   The Gross Method

   b.   The Net Method

7-3B. a. Reimer Products, *Periodic*, Gross Method

Date	Description	Debit	Credit
July 1			
July 3			
July 7			
August 3			

7-3B. b. Reimer Products, *Periodic*, Net Method

Date	Description	Debit	Credit
July 1			
July 3			
July 7			
August 3			

7-4B. (PERIODIC — Gross and Net Methods of Recording Purchases)

Buffalo Tobacco Products completed the following transactions:

June 22   Purchased $1,000 merchandise from Hershey's, terms 1 10 EOM, N 30 EOM.

June 25   Purchased $4,000 merchandise from American Tobacco Company, terms 2 10, N 30.

July 8   Paid the Hershey's invoice.

July 25   Paid the American Tobacco Company invoice.

Required:

Assuming Buffalo Tobacco Products uses the *periodic* inventory method, prepare journal entries for each of the transactions using:

   a.   The Gross Method

   b.   The Net Method

	a. Gross Method	b. Net Method
Jun 22		
Jun 25		
Jul 8		
Jul 25		

7-5B. (PERIODIC — Purchase Returns and Allowances)

Carrie's Cooperatives engaged in the following transactions:

August 2   Purchased $7,000 merchandise from Karen's Krafts, terms 2 10, N 30.

August 6   Returned $2,000 of the merchandise for credit.

August 8   Carrie was granted an allowance of $500 for some of the merchandise which was slightly damaged.

August 11 Paid the amount due to Karen's Krafts.

Required:

Assuming Carrie's Cooperatives uses the *Periodic* Inventory Method, record the transactions under the:

    a.   Gross Method

    b.   Net Method

	a. Gross Method	b. Net Method
Aug 2		
Aug 6		
Aug 8		
Aug 11		

7-6B. (PERIODIC — Freight Costs)

Cybill Enterprises purchased merchandise on account for $1,000 plus freight charges of $100. Cybill then sold the merchandise on account for $1,500, and paid cash of $85 to ship the goods to the customer.

Required: a.   Prepare journal entries for the above transactions.

          b.   What is the delivered cost of purchases? $_____

          c.   What kind of account is Freight-Out? _____
              What is its normal balance? _____
              Where is it shown in the financial statements? _____

7-7B. (PERIODIC — Recording Purchases and Sales)

Kumen's Kernels purchased inventory on account at a cost of $12,000, and sold half of the inventory on account for $9,000.

Required: a.   Prepare journal entries for the above transactions.

          b.   What is the cost of inventory on hand after the sale? $_____
              Where is it shown in the financial statements? _____

          c.   What is the gross profit on the sale? $_____

7-8B. (PERIODIC — Purchases, Sales, and Freight)

Delectables By Decastro purchased inventory on account at a cost of $25,000, and sold $10,000 of the inventory on account for $16,000. Freight costs of $600 were paid in cash to ship the goods to the customer.

Required: a.   Prepare journal entries for the above transactions.

          b.   What is the cost of inventory on hand after the sale?
              $_____
              Where is it shown in the financial statements? _____

          c.   What is the gross profit on the sale? $_____
               How should the freight costs be accounted for in the financial
              statements? _____

7-9B. (PERIODIC — Gross and Net Methods of Recording Sales)

Bonnie's Bouquets purchased inventory on account at a cost of $2,000, and sold the inventory on October 1 for $3,000, terms 2 10, N 30. Bonnie uses the periodic inventory system.

Required:

Prepare journal entries for the following transactions using: (a.) the *Gross* method, and (b.) the *Net* method.

(a.) Bonnie's Bouquets, *Gross Method*

Oct 1   To record the sale of inventory.

Oct 11   If the discount is taken, give the entry to record the receipt of cash.

Oct 31   If the discount is not taken, give the entry to record the receipt of cash.

(b.) Bonnie's Bouquets, *Net* Method

Oct 1   To record the sale of inventory.

Oct 11   If the discount is taken, give the entry to record the receipt of cash.

Oct 31   If the discount is not taken, give the entry to record the receipt of cash.

7-10B. (PERIODIC — Gross and Net Methods of Recording Sales)

Frank's Security Systems purchased inventory at a cost of $5,000, and sold the inventory on April 20 for $7,500, terms 1 10 EOM, N 30 EOM. Frank uses the periodic inventory system.

Required:

Prepare journal entries for the following transactions using: (a.) the *Gross* method, and (b.) the *Net* method.

(a.) Frank's Security Systems, *Gross Method*

Apr 20   To record the sale of inventory.

May 10   If the discount is taken, give the entry to record the receipt of cash.

May 30   If the discount is not taken, give the entry to record the receipt of cash.

(b.) Frank's Security Systems, *Net* Method

Apr 20   To record the sale of inventory.

May 10   If the discount is taken, give the entry to record the receipt of cash.

May 30   If the discount is not taken, give the entry to record the receipt of cash.

7-11B. (PERIODIC — Sales Returns and Allowances)

Beth's Baby World sold several items of nursery furniture and baby supplies to a customer on account for a total sales price of $1,200. The merchandise had cost Beth $750. Later, the customer returned $100 of the merchandise for credit (Beth's cost $65), and Beth granted an allowance of $50 on some of the merchandise due to minor imperfections in workmanship.

Required: Prepare journal entries for each of the above transactions.

7-12B. (PERIODIC — Sales Returns and Allowances)

Sam's Custom Auto installed a new convertible top and some sound equipment in a customer's vehicle. The total sales price was $3,500 on account, and the inventory had cost Sam $2,100. When the customer picked up her car, she noticed a small flaw in the convertible top, and Sam graciously granted an allowance of $100. Later, the customer returned $250 of the sound equipment for credit (Sam's cost was $150).

Required: Prepare journal entries for each of the above transactions.

7-13B. (PERIODIC — Income Statement Formats)

The Adjusted Trial Balance for Braun Wholesale is:

```
                    Braun Wholesale
                  Adjusted Trial Balance
                   September 30, 1995
```

	Debit	Credit
Cash	$ 9,000	
Accounts Receivable	12,000	
Inventory	11,000	
Office Equipment	28,500	
Accumulated Depreciation		$ 3,600
Accounts Payable		14,000
Common Stock		30,000
Retained Earnings		5,000
Dividends	3,500	
Sales		75,000
Sales Discounts	2,000	
Sales Returns	1,400	
Sales Allowances	1,100	
Interest Revenue		3,200
Purchases	41,100	
Purchase Discounts		1,600
Purchase Returns		1,200
Purchase Allowances		1,000
Freight-In	1,300	
Wages Expense	12,500	
Rent Expense	6,800	
Freight-Out	2,600	
Depreciation Expense	1,800	
Totals	$134,600	$134,600

A physical count of inventory at the end of the period revealed that inventory costing $9,600 was on hand.

Required: Prepare an income statement for Braun's fiscal year ending September 30, 1995 using the:
a.   Multistep format
b.   Single-step format

7-14B. (PERIODIC — Financial Statement Preparation)

Using the information in Problem 7-13B, prepare a multistep income statement, a statement of retained earnings, and a balance sheet for Braun's Wholesale. Use arrows to indicate the articulation of the financial statements.

7-15B. (PERIODIC — Closing Entries)

Using the information from Problem 7-13B, prepare closing entries for Braun Wholesale.

7-16B. (PERIODIC — Worksheet and Financial Statements)

A partially completed worksheet for Braun Wholesale at September 30, 1995 is provided on the next page. Ending inventory is $9,600.

Required:

a.   Complete the worksheet.

b.   Prepare a multistep income statement, a statement of retained earnings, and a balance sheet for Braun Wholesale.

Homework Problem B   Braun Wholesale, September 30, 1995 (Periodic)

ACCOUNT TITLES	Trial Balance DEBIT	Trial Balance CREDIT	Adjustments DEBIT	Adjustments CREDIT	Adj. Trial Balance DEBIT	Adj. Trial Balance CREDIT	Income Statement DEBIT	Income Statement CREDIT	Balance Sheet DEBIT	Balance Sheet CREDIT
Cash	9,000				9,000					
Accounts Rec.	12,000				12,000					
Inventory	11,000				11,000					
Office Equipment	28,500				28,500					
Accumulated Dep.		1,800		1,800		3,600				
Accounts Payable		14,000				14,000				
Common Stock		30,000				30,000				
Retained Earnings		5,000				5,000				
Dividends	3,500				3,500					
Sales		75,000				75,000				
Sales Discounts	2,000				2,000					
Sales Returns	1,400				1,400					
Sales Allowances	1,100				1,100					
Interest Revenue		3,200				3,200				
Purchases	41,100				41,100					
Purchase Discounts		1,600				1,600				
Purchase Returns		1,200				1,200				
Purchase Allow.		1,000				1,000				
Freight-In	1,300				1,300					
Wage Expense	12,500				12,500					
Rent Expense	6,800				6,800					
Freight-Out	2,600				2,600					
Depreciation Exp.			1,800		1,800					
Totals	132,800	132,800	1,800	1,800	134,600	134,600				

The preliminary adjusted trial balance for Niagara Sales as of September 25, 1995 is:

```
                    Niagara Sales
                    Trial Balance
                  September 25, 1995

                               Debit          Credit
Cash                        $ 18,000
Accounts Receivable           24,000
Inventory                     22,000
Supplies                       4,800
Prepaid Insurance              3,000
Equipment                     57,000
Accumulated Depreciation                     $  7,200
Accounts Payable                               28,000
Wages Payable                                   3,200
Long-Term Notes Payable                         8,000
Common Stock                                   60,000
Retained Earnings                              10,000
Dividends                      7,000
Sales                                         150,000
Sales Discounts                4,000
Sales Returns                  2,800
Sales Allowances               2,200
Interest Revenue                                6,600
Purchases                     82,200
Purchase Discounts                              3,200
Purchase Returns                                2,400
Purchase Allowances                             2,000
Freight-In                     2,600
Wages Expense                 25,000
Rent Expense                  13,600
Insurance Expense              2,400
Supplies Expense               1,000
Depreciation Expense           3,600
Freight-Out                    5,400
Totals                      $280,600          $280,600
```

During the last five days of September, Niagara Sales completed the following additional transactions. Niagara Sales uses the gross method to record purchases and sales.

Sep 26   Purchased $1,000 of merchandise on account from VanDeWater Auto, plus freight charges of $100.

Sep 26   Returned $300 of merchandise purchased earlier in the month from Davies Industrial.

Sep 27   Sold merchandise on account to Remack for $5,000. The cost of the inventory was $3,600.

Sep 27   Received payment on account from a customer, Wright Stuff, for an invoice amount of $2,000 less a sales discount of 1.5%.

Sep 28   Paid freight charges of $1,300 on merchandise shipped to customers.

Sep 28   A customer, Picky Picky, returned $400 of merchandise for credit (cost of the merchandise was $300), and was also granted an additional allowance of $50 for inventory that was slightly damaged in transit.

Sep 29   Paid for merchandise purchased earlier in the month from Lane Autobody. The invoice price was $4,000, and a 2% purchase discount was taken.

Sep 30   A physical count of inventory on hand shows an ending inventory of $16,000.

Required:

a.   Prepare journal entries to record the transactions for the last five days of September.

b.   Prepare an updated trial balance to include the above transactions.

c.   Calculate:

net sales $_____

cost of goods sold $_____

gross margin $_____

d.   Prepare closing entries.

e.   Prepare a multistep income statement, a statement of retained earnings, and a balance sheet.

MODULE 8

SUBSIDIARY LEDGERS AND SPECIAL JOURNALS

In prior modules we discussed the recording process and how accounting information is prepared for financial reporting. The system we described, although adequate for some small businesses, does not provide detailed information about the items represented in general ledger account balances and is somewhat inefficient.

In this module, we will describe two important accounting tools: subsidiary ledgers and special journals. These tools are used to provide valuable details related to the accounting information we have been gathering and to streamline the recording process.

As you explore subsidiary ledgers and special journals, keep in mind that accountants typically design accounting systems but seldom become involved in the process of making routine accounting entries. The work of making routine accounting entries is typically done by a bookkeeper or accounting clerk. Accordingly, bookkeepers and accounting clerks *use* subsidiary ledgers and special journals extensively, but these accounting systems are usually *designed* by accountants. Therefore, an understanding of subsidiary ledgers and special journals is of benefit to both bookkeepers and accountants.

SUBSIDIARY LEDGERS

In almost all cases, the general ledger provides inadequate information regarding the detail of what makes up the account balance. When detailed information is needed, a separate ledger system called a subsidiary ledger is often created.

Webster's Dictionary defines subsidiary as: "serving to assist or supplement; auxiliary; supplementary". A **subsidiary ledger** is a ledger system that supplements the general ledger system by providing additional detail regarding the individual components that make up the account balance. A subsidiary ledger system is made up of a set of subsidiary ledger accounts. For example, an Accounts Receivable subsidiary ledger system consists of a set of separate ledger accounts — one for each customer. The total of all of the customer Accounts Receivable subsidiary ledger accounts equals the balance of the general ledger account, Accounts Receivable.

When a subsidiary ledger is established, the general ledger account to which it relates is called the **control account**. And, as stated earlier, the total balance in all of the subsidiary ledger accounts should equal the balance in the corresponding control account.

In this module, we will discuss two common subsidiary ledgers — the Accounts Receivable subsidiary ledger and the Accounts Payable subsidiary ledger.

ACCOUNTS RECEIVABLE SUBSIDIARY LEDGER

By now, you know that Accounts Receivable represents the amount owed to the company by its charge account customers. But when the general ledger is examined, it reveals no information regarding the amounts owed by individual customers. Take a moment to review the illustration of the Accounts Receivable general ledger account of Frank's Marine, in which the beginning balance for the new accounting period (1996) is shown.

Accounts Receivable				No. 130
Date 1996	Ref	Debit	Credit	Balance
Balance				2,100

The fact that Accounts Receivable has a balance of $2,100 does not provide any information regarding the amounts owed by individual customers. A detailed listing of the amounts owed by individual customers is essential. In essence, a ledger account is needed for each charge account customer. But, if a general ledger account were established for each charge customer, the general ledger would be a huge, overly-detailed document. To avoid this problem, a subsidiary ledger system is often created for Accounts Receivable. The Accounts Receivable subsidiary ledger consists of a subsidiary ledger account for each charge account customer.

The Accounts Receivable subsidiary ledger and general ledger below show the beginning 1996 balances for the books of Frank's Marine. A quick review of the subsidiary ledger reveals that F. Dunn owes Frank's Marine $1,000 and V. Kundrat owes $1,100.

Accounts Receivable Subsidiary Ledger

F. Dunn				
Date 1996	Ref	Debit	Credit	Balance
Bal.				1,000

V. Kundrat				
Date 1996	Ref	Debit	Credit	Balance
Bal.				1,100

General Ledger

Accounts Receivable				No. 130
Date 1996	Ref	Debit	Credit	Balance
Bal.				2,100

To determine the balance of the entire Accounts Receivable subsidiary ledger, the balances of the individual customer accounts are totaled. This balance should equal the Accounts Receivable control account in the general ledger. In the example above, the $2,100 total of the balances of the subsidiary ledger accounts ($1,000 + $1,100 = $2,100) equals the balance of the Accounts Receivable general ledger account.

As with the general ledger, the information found in subsidiary ledgers originates in journals. Journal entries are posted to subsidiary ledgers more frequently than to the general ledger. In fact, most companies post to the Accounts Receivable subsidiary ledger daily. Keeping subsidiary ledger account information up-to-date is crucial for providing valuable information. It is the subsidiary ledger accounts rather than the general ledger accounts that provide information such as the amount an individual customer owes.

Posting to subsidiary ledgers is a process similar to posting to the general ledger. The steps for posting to a subsidiary ledger are:

1. Identify and locate the correct subsidiary ledger account.

2. Enter the transaction date in the subsidiary ledger.

3. Enter an explanation in the subsidiary ledger if appropriate. (For simplicity, we are not including explanations in our illustrations.)

4. Enter the dollar amount of the entry in the appropriate debit or credit column of the subsidiary ledger.

5. Enter an abbreviation for the journal name and the page number in the posting reference column of the subsidiary ledger.

6. Lastly, enter the subsidiary ledger account number, or a check mark if subsidiary account numbers are not used, in the posting reference column back on the *journal*.

The general journal entries shown below were posted to the general ledger using the steps outlined in Module 3, and to the Accounts Receivable subsidiary ledger using the six steps described above.

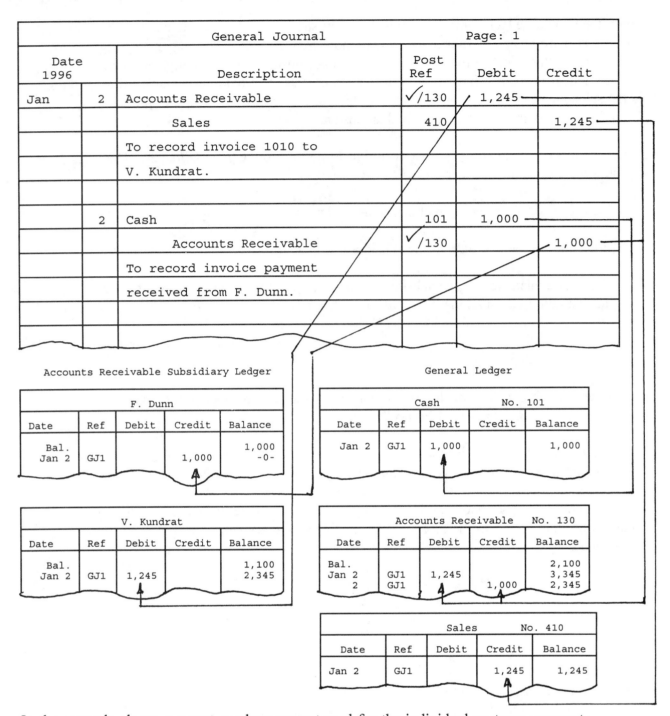

In the example above, account numbers are not used for the individual customer accounts. Therefore, the posting reference entered on the general journal to indicate that the entry was posted to the subsidiary account is a check mark. The check mark is entered along side the posting reference indicating that the entry was posted to the general ledger. It is customary to separate the two posting references with a slash ("/") mark. For example, "√/130" means that the transaction was posted to the subsidiary ledger and to general ledger account 130.

As the illustration shows, using the information provided in the Accounts Receivable subsidiary ledger, the amount owed by individual customers can be readily determined. The Accounts Payable subsidiary ledger provides similarly useful information.

ACCOUNTS PAYABLE SUBSIDIARY LEDGER

Accounts Payable represents the amount owed on account. However, the balance of the Accounts Payable general ledger account provides little information regarding the amounts owed to individual suppliers. Accordingly, when it comes time to pay bills, the information provided by the general ledger reveals little insight regarding where to send the checks. As with Accounts Receivable, a subsidiary ledger system is often established for Accounts Payable to provide valuable details which are unavailable in the general ledger. The Accounts Payable subsidiary ledger consists of separate ledger accounts for each vendor. Once a subsidiary ledger system is established for Accounts Payable, the general ledger account becomes the control account. The total of all the individual subsidiary ledger accounts should equal the balance of the control account.

The Accounts Payable subsidiary ledger and its general ledger account illustrated below show the beginning 1996 balances for Frank's Marine. A quick review of the subsidiary ledger reveals that Frank's Marine owes CMC Distributors $700 and Eroa Engines $500.

Accounts Payable Subsidiary Ledger

General Ledger

CMC Distributors				
Date 1996	Ref	Debit	Credit	Balance
Bal.				700

		Accounts Payable		No. 210
Date 1996	Ref	Debit	Credit	Balance
Bal.				1,200

Eroa Engines				
Date 1996	Ref	Debit	Credit	Balance
Bal.				500

To determine the balance of the Accounts Payable subsidiary ledger, the balances of the individual customer accounts are totaled. This amount should equal the balance of the control account in the general ledger. In the example above, the $1,200 total of the balances of the subsidiary ledger accounts ($700 + $500 = $1,200) equals the balance of the Accounts Payable general ledger account.

The principles of posting to the Accounts Payable subsidiary ledger are the same as those of posting to the Accounts Receivable subsidiary ledger. Therefore, there is nothing to be gained by restating the posting procedure step-by-step. An illustration of the results of posting from the general journal to the Accounts Payable subsidiary ledger and the general ledger are shown below.

General Journal			Post Ref	Debit	Credit
Date 1996		Description			
Jan	1	Purchases	510	2,235	
		Accounts Payable	✓/210		2,235
		To record purchase from			
		Mercury Marine.			
	10	Accounts Payable	✓/210	1,200	
		Cash	101		1,200
		To record payment on account			
		to CMC Distributors.			

Accounts Payable Subsidiary Ledger

CMC Distributors

Date	Ref	Debit	Credit	Balance
Bal. Jan 10	GJ1	1,200		1,200 -0-

Eroa Engines

Date	Ref	Debit	Credit	Balance
Bal.				500

Mercury Marine

Date	Ref	Debit	Credit	Balance
Jan 1	GJ1		2,235	2,235

General Ledger

Cash   No. 101

Date	Ref	Debit	Credit	Balance
Bal. Jan 10	GJ1		1,200	2,500 1,300

Accounts Payable   No. 210

Date	Ref	Debit	Credit	Balance
Bal. Jan 1	GJ1		2,235	1,700 3,935
10	GJ1	1,200		2,735

Purchases   No. 510

Date	Ref	Debit	Credit	Balance
Jan 1	GJ1	2,235		2,235

In this example, vendor account numbers are not used for the individual suppliers. Therefore, the posting reference entered on the general journal when the entry is posted to the subsidiary account is a check mark which is entered along side the posting reference for the posting to the general ledger account.

Now that a subsidiary ledger has been established for each vendor, the amount owed to individual suppliers can be readily determined.

BALANCE SHEET ACCOUNTS AND THE NEED FOR DETAILED RECORDS

Accounts Receivable and Accounts Payable are not the only accounts that benefit from detailed records such as subsidiary ledgers.

When you think about it, each balance sheet account represents an amount of "something" as of a particular point in time. For assets, the "something" may be a store of supplies, an amount of money in the bank, a stock of inventory on hand, or a variety of equipment used by the company. For liabilities, the "something" may be an amount owed to the bank, or services owed to customers who have paid in advance.

Because balance sheet accounts represent an amount of "something" as of a particular point in time, they typically require auxiliary records which detail the items making up the general ledger account's balance. These auxiliary records may consist of a formal subsidiary ledger system, or less formal work papers. For example, the records relating to the physical count of inventory detail the balance of the Inventory general ledger account. Even if a formal subsidiary ledger system is not used for a particular account, some form of detailed records may be maintained. The dollar total of these records should equal the balance in the corresponding general ledger account.

SPECIAL JOURNALS - STREAMLINING THE RECORDING PROCESS

In prior modules we explained how business transactions are recorded using the general journal. The general journal works well, but it is not known for its efficiency. You may have noticed the repetitive, time-consuming writing requirements of journalizing each individual transaction when the general journal is used. In addition, each general journal transaction requires at least two separate posting entries. With thousands of business transactions to record each year, you may have wondered how real companies cope with the inefficiencies of the general journal. There must be a better way. Well, there is! The recording process is greatly streamlined through the use of special journals.

In any business there are types of transactions that occur again and again. For example, sales transactions may happen every day. Because of the similarities of the recurring sale transactions, a custom-made journal is often created to record them. A journal that is tailor-made to record a specific type of transaction is called a **special journal**. It is common for businesses to use special journals to record repetitive transactions like sales on account, purchases of merchandise on account, the receipt of cash, and cash payments. Each of these transaction types use a special journal designed specifically to do the job as efficiently as possible.

The following table shows transaction types and the special journals used to record them.

TYPICAL SPECIAL JOURNALS	
Transaction Type	Special Journal
Sales of Merchandise on Account	Sales Journal
Purchases of Merchandise on Account	Purchases Journal
Payments of Cash	Cash Payments Journal
Receipts of Cash	Cash Receipts Journal

In this section we will explore the most popular special journals — those listed above. In order to better understand special journals, you should try to draw upon your current accounting and business knowledge. Steer clear of memorization. Instead, try to understand the need for each special journal, the accounts that might be affected when making entries in it, and the information that should be provided by the journal.

As you know, no two companies are exactly alike. Although there are similarities, each one is unique. Accounting systems must be designed to suit the unique characteristics of each company. Special journals are almost always a key element of this design. Because special journals are custom-made to suit the needs of each particular company, their design and use varies somewhat from one company to the next. It would be impossible to show all the different combinations of special journals in this, or any other text. Rather, we will explore some basic special journals so that you will be able to create similar journals to suit the unique characteristics that you encounter in business.

The special journals appearing in this module assume a periodic inventory system is used. Certainly, companies using a perpetual inventory system are just as likely to use special journals. Although the accounts may vary, the basics involved in using the special journals illustrated in this text apply to journals used in a perpetual system as well. The first journal we will explore is the sales journal.

SALES JOURNAL

The **sales journal** is used to record a very specific type of transaction — sales on account. As you will see later in this module, *cash* sales are recorded in a different special journal.

In order to understand the design of the sales journal, it is helpful to review what happens when sales on account are recorded in the general journal. As an example, assume that on January 2, 1996, Frank's Marine sells marine parts on account to V. Kundrat on invoice number 1010 for $1,245. Assume further that Frank's makes similar sales to G. Steinmann on invoice number 1018 dated January 2 for $1,900 and F. Dunn on invoice 1022 dated January 5 for $258. The general journal entries to record these transactions appear below:

General Journal					Page: 1
Date 1996		Description	Post Ref	Debit	Credit
Jan	2	Accounts Receivable		1,245	
		Sales			1,245
		To record invoice 1010 to			
		V. Kundrat.			
	2	Accounts Receivable		1,900	
		Sales			1,900
		To record invoice 1018 to			
		G. Steinmann.			
	5	Accounts Receivable		258	
		Sales			258
		To record invoice 1022 to			
		F. Dunn.			

It is helpful to study general journal entries reflecting sales on account to help determine what information should be included in the sales journal we are about to create. When our sales journal is completed, it should provide all the information included in the general journal.

The general journal includes the following information for each transaction:

> The sale date
> The debit account (Accounts Receivable)
> The debit amount
> The credit account (Sales)
> The credit amount
> The customer name
> The posting references

The sales journal must provide a space to enter each item of information listed above. But, in designing the sales journal, we must keep in mind that we are trying to reduce the amount of writing required for each entry. This reduction is accomplished in part by, whenever possible, using a single column to provide more than one item of information.

As shown below, four columns are used for Frank's Marine's sales journal. A detailed description of each column follows the presentation of the sales journal.

Sales Journal				Page: 1
Date 1996		Customer	Ref	Amount
Jan	2	V. Kundrat		1,245
	2	G. Steinmann		1,900
	5	F. Dunn		258
	12	V. Kundrat		894
	24	M. Tailor		2,487
	25	F. Dunn		488

Column 1:   The sale date column:

As with the general journal, the first column on the sales journal (and other special journals) is used to indicate the date.

Column 2:   An information column for the customer name:

In order to keep track of which customer has charged on account, a column identifying the customer is needed. This information is crucial to determine the amount owed by each individual customer.

Column 3:   Posting reference column:

As with the general journal, special journals typically have a column to enter a posting reference. As we will see later in this module, the posting reference column works a bit differently for special journals than it does for the general journal.

Column 4:   The dollar amount column:

On the illustrated sales journal we use a single column for the dollar amount. It may seem nearly impossible, but the amount column on our sales journal is used to indicate the debit account, debit amount, credit account and credit amount. To help understand how it is possible that a single column provides so much information, let's look back at the general journal and make some observations. First, Accounts Receivable is debited and Sales is credited for each and every sales entry. Secondly, for our example company, the dollar amount of both the Accounts Receivable and the Sales entry are the same. Because the sales journal is used exclusively to record sales on account, and accountants and bookkeepers know that the same two accounts are affected in the same way each time a sale is made, it is unnecessary to spell out the account name on each entry. Also, because, for our example company, the dollar amount of the Accounts Receivable and Sales entries are the same, the amount need only be indicated once. Accountants and bookkeepers know that the dollar amount applies to both general ledger accounts. Because the same two general ledger accounts are affected by every transaction and because the amount of the debit and credit are the same, only a single dollar amount column is needed on our sales journal.

You may have noticed that the order of the original list of information items we wanted to include in the sales journal differs from the columns described above. Although there are no hard and fast rules with regard to the order of the columns, in all journals, the date usually comes first. After the date, the next column provides information about the entry — in the sales journal, the customer name is recorded. Then, the posting reference followed by the dollar amount columns appear.

Just as recording in a special journal is a bit different from recording in the general journal, the posting process for special journals is also a bit different. However, the process still involves transferring information from the journal to the subsidiary ledger and the general ledger.

POSTING TO A SUBSIDIARY LEDGER FROM A SPECIAL JOURNAL

As was the case with the general journal, postings from a special journal to individual subsidiary ledger accounts are generally made on a daily basis. In fact, the process of posting to a subsidiary ledger from a special journal is nearly identical to posting from the general journal.

Because the subsidiary ledger posting steps are the same for special journals as they are for posting from the general journal, we will not list them again. When all six transactions have been posted to the subsidiary ledger, the sales journal would appear as shown below:

	Sales Journal		Page: 1
Date 1996	Customer	Ref	Amount
Jan 2	V. Kundrat	✓	1,245
2	G. Steinmann	✓	1,900
5	F. Dunn	✓	258
12	V. Kundrat	✓	894
24	M. Tailor	✓	2,487
25	F. Dunn	✓	488

You should note that the sales journal shown above has twice as many entries as the previously shown general journal. Notice how much less writing is required to record sales on account in the sales journal compared to the general journal.

POSTING TO THE GENERAL LEDGER FROM A SPECIAL JOURNAL

Postings to the general ledger are made periodically (most often monthly) regardless of whether the entries were originally journalized in the general journal or a special journal.

A major distinction between posting from the general journal and posting from special journals is that many of the entries posted to the general ledger from special journals are summarized and only the totals for each journal are posted. The time savings from not having to post each entry individually far outweighs the time and effort required to total the dollar amounts in the special journals.

In order to post from the sales journal to the general ledger, the amount column must be totaled. In the case of our example, the total of the amount column on the sales journal is $7,272.

	Sales Journal		Page: 1
Date 1996	**Customer**	**Ref**	**Amount**
Jan 2	V. Kundrat	✓	1,245
2	G. Steinmann	✓	1,900
5	F. Dunn	✓	258
12	V. Kundrat	✓	894
24	M. Tailor	✓	2,487
25	F. Dunn	✓	488
			7,272

The next step is to determine which account or accounts should be affected by the entries appearing in the special journal. In the case of the sales journal, each entry represents a sale on account. When a sale on account is recorded, both Accounts Receivable and Sales should be increased.

Once we have determined which accounts should be affected, the next step is to determine whether the accounts should be debited or credited. Special journals sometimes lack an indication as to whether accounts should be debited or credited. These indications may be absent because accounting personnel rely on their experience and knowledge to determine how each account should be affected by the entries on various special journals.

As stated earlier, the sales transactions recorded in the sales journal increase both Accounts Receivable and Sales. To achieve an increase in these accounts, we must debit Accounts Receivable and credit Sales. Posting a $7,272 debit to Accounts Receivable and a $7,272 credit to Sales will have the same impact on the general ledger accounts as if we had posted six separate general journal entries for the six sale transactions.

Now that we know how the general ledger accounts are to be affected, all that remains is to post the amounts using steps similar to the ones for posting from the general journal. The posting steps listed below have been tailored to accommodate the special characteristics of posting from special journals.

1. Identify and locate the appropriate general ledger account.

2. Enter the date in the general ledger. Because the amount being posted from a special journal often reflects a summary of many entries, transaction dates are not used for posting. Rather, the date used for posting from a special journal is the last day of the accounting period (month) being posted.

3. Enter an explanation in the general ledger if appropriate. (For simplicity, we are not including explanations in the general ledgers accounts used in our example.)

4. Enter the dollar amount of the posting in the appropriate debit or credit column of the general ledger account.

5. Enter an abbreviation for the journal name and the page number in the posting reference column of the general ledger account. For example, the first page of the sales journal might be called "S1", and the 31st page of the sales journal might be called "S31".

6. Lastly, enter the posting reference back on the *special journal*. The posting reference consists of the general ledger account number(s) or check mark(s) if account numbers are not used. The posting reference should be entered on the journal below or to the side of the amount posted. When posting to the general ledger, the posting reference is not always entered in the posting reference column on the special journal. This is because columnar totals are being posted instead of the amounts from individual transactions. Accordingly, the posting reference should be placed in close proximity to the dollar amount posted rather than in the posting reference column.

The following figure depicts how the sales journal, the Accounts Receivable subsidiary ledger, and the general ledger would look after posting has been completed.

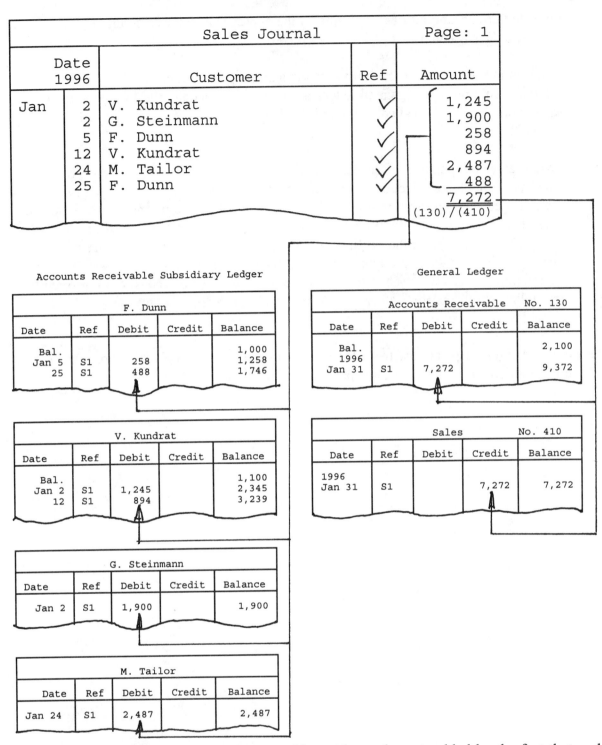

Sales Journal — Page: 1

Date 1996		Customer	Ref	Amount
Jan	2	V. Kundrat	✓	1,245
	2	G. Steinmann	✓	1,900
	5	F. Dunn	✓	258
	12	V. Kundrat	✓	894
	24	M. Tailor	✓	2,487
	25	F. Dunn	✓	488
				7,272
				(130)/(410)

Accounts Receivable Subsidiary Ledger

F. Dunn

Date	Ref	Debit	Credit	Balance
Bal.				1,000
Jan 5	S1	258		1,258
25	S1	488		1,746

V. Kundrat

Date	Ref	Debit	Credit	Balance
Bal.				1,100
Jan 2	S1	1,245		2,345
12	S1	894		3,239

G. Steinmann

Date	Ref	Debit	Credit	Balance
Jan 2	S1	1,900		1,900

M. Tailor

Date	Ref	Debit	Credit	Balance
Jan 24	S1	2,487		2,487

General Ledger

Accounts Receivable — No. 130

Date	Ref	Debit	Credit	Balance
Bal. 1996				2,100
Jan 31	S1	7,272		9,372

Sales — No. 410

Date	Ref	Debit	Credit	Balance
1996 Jan 31	S1		7,272	7,272

As you might imagine, accounting personnel have always been troubled by the fact that each sales transaction must be individually posted to the Accounts Receivable subsidiary ledger. This led to the development of several systems that enabled bookkeepers to journalize a transaction in the sales journal and simultaneously post it to the Accounts Receivable subsidiary ledger.

One of these systems, called the peg-board system uses registration pins to align the ledger page precisely over the appropriate line on the journal so that (through the use of carbon paper) a bookkeeper's single entry would record the information in both the sales journal and the subsidiary ledger account. This system is still used today and works well for very small companies.

Another system used a large machine called a bookkeeping machine. Both Burrows and National Cash Register Company manufactured several popular bookkeeping machines. These machines required the operator to insert a customer's ledger card into the machine. The bookkeeping machine would then precisely align the customer's ledger card so that a single recording would both journalize the transaction in the sales journal and post the transaction to the customer's Accounts Receivable ledger card. During the 1960's and 1970's bookkeeping machines completely disappeared from use in the United States because companies large enough to use a bookkeeping machine switched to computers for recording sales and keeping track of customers' accounts receivable.

Computerized systems reduce much of the duplication of effort required to journalize and post transactions in a manual system. However, even for users of the most technologically advanced system, an understanding of the relationships among various journals, general ledgers, and subsidiary ledgers is valuable.

PURCHASES JOURNAL

Like the sales journal, the purchases journal is used to record a single type of transaction. The **purchases journal** is used exclusively to record the purchase of merchandise on account.

The purchases journal mirrors the sales journal in design, use, and efficiency. The journals are so similar that there is little to be gained by a separate, step-by-step presentation of the design and use of the purchases journal. Accordingly, our discussion of the purchases journal will be brief.

Our presentation assumes the periodic inventory system is being used. When the periodic inventory system is used, the two accounts that are affected each and every time merchandise is purchased on account are Purchases, which is debited, and Accounts Payable, which is credited.

In addition to a column for recording the *amount* of each transaction, most purchases journals also provide columns for the date, the supplier's name, the supplier's invoice number, and a posting reference.

The purchases journal for Frank's Marine appears below:

Purchases Journal					Page: 1
Date		Supplier	Invoice Number	Ref	Amount
Jan	1	Mercury Marine	127831		2,235
	5	Eroa Engines	7282		1,500
	9	CMC Distributors	88658		2,580

In the purchases journal above, each figure placed in the "amount" column represents a debit to Purchases and a credit to Accounts Payable. The idea of having one amount represent both the debit amount and the credit amount of a transaction is a familiar concept — we saw it used in the sales journal.

POSTING FROM THE PURCHASES JOURNAL

The principles of posting from the purchases journal are identical to those of posting from the sales journal. Of course the journal name and accounts affected are different, but the basic principles are the same. Amounts are posted daily to the subsidiary ledgers, and periodically (usually monthly) to the general ledger accounts.

The purchases journal of Frank's Marine is presented below along with the Accounts Payable subsidiary ledger and affected general ledger accounts. The arrows illustrate how amounts were posted from the journal. Also, the posting references can be used to cross reference journal entries to the subsidiary and general ledgers, or from the subsidiary and general ledgers back to the journal.

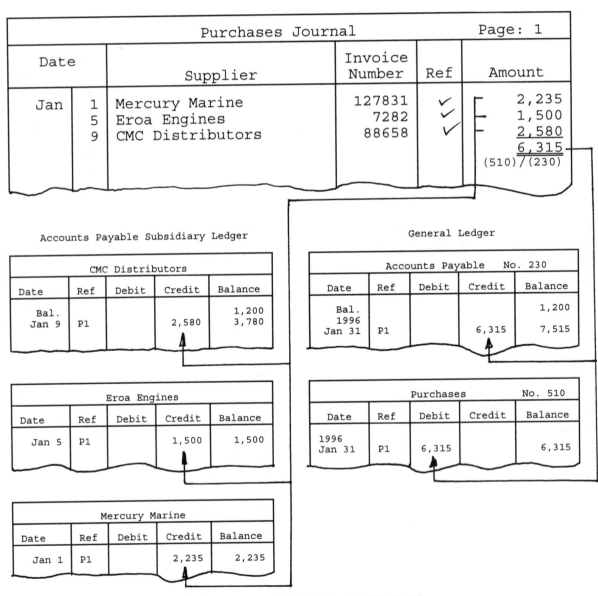

THE CASH RECEIPTS JOURNAL

The **cash receipts** journal is used to record all cash received by the company. The "cash" received may be in the form of currency or a check, but for accounting purposes, it is all simply considered cash.

The main sources of cash for many companies are cash sales and cash payments on account received from charge account customers. There may, however, be other sources of cash as well. For example, the company may receive checks for interest, dividends, or for purchase returns.

Designing the cash receipts journal is somewhat more involved than designing the sales or purchases journal. The reason for this is that entries to record the receipt of cash affect a variety of accounts. Because of the added complexity, we will explore the design of the cash receipts journal in detail. Let's start by examining how cash receipt transactions are depicted in the general journal.

The following general journal shows the entries to record various cash receipt transactions:

Date 1996		Description	Post Ref	Debit	Credit
Jan	5	Cash		1,862	
		Sales Discounts		38	
		Accounts Receivable			1,900
		To record payment on account			
		from G. Steinmann.			
	6	Cash		350	
		Sales			350
		To record cash sales.			
	8	Cash		105	
		Interest Revenue			105
		To record interest received.			

General Journal — Page

These transactions all have one thing in common — each includes a debit to Cash. Therefore, a special journal designed to accommodate these transactions will certainly have a column for debits to Cash. As indicated in the first entry recorded in the general journal above, Cash is not the only account expected to be debited when cash receipts are recorded. If a company uses the gross method of recording sales, Sales Discounts will be debited when customers pay within the discount period. Therefore, a cash receipts journal for a company using the gross method for recording sales will include a column to record debits to Sales Discounts.

Entries representing the receipt of cash all have a common debit, but the credits for these transactions vary. Recording cash received for a cash sale requires a credit to Sales, whereas recording cash received as payment on account from a charge account customer requires a credit to Accounts Receivable. Recording cash received for other reasons would require credits to still other accounts. The journal must provide a mechanism to accommodate the various accounts that should be credited when recording cash receipts. This is accomplished by establishing a dedicated column on the cash receipts journal for each account that is likely to be affected by the receipt of cash.

It is unlikely that a dedicated column can be established for every single account that might be affected when cash receipts are recorded. This is because, at the time the cash receipts journal is being designed, it may be impossible to anticipate all the accounts that will be affected by the receipt of cash. Also, if an account is expected to be affected only rarely, it may be decided that a column dedicated to that account is not necessary. In addition, there may be so many accounts that might be credited as cash receipts are recorded that there may not be enough columns on the journal paper to accommodate them all. To solve this problem, special journals often provide an "other account" section.

The **other account** section, which is sometimes called the **miscellaneous account** or **sundry account** section, is used to record entries to accounts which have no dedicated column on the special journal. Any special journal may include an other account section. The other account section includes a column to identify the account name and a column for the dollar amount. Often, the column used to identify subsidiary account information such as the customer name doubles as the column used to indicate the other general ledger account. This is possible because accounts which are used so seldom that they are identified in the other account section typically do not have subsidiary ledgers.

Although it depends on the journal, for the cash receipts journal, the other account dollar amount column is generally for credit entries. This is because the receipt of cash increases Cash, requiring a debit, while the other side of the entry, in this case the "other" account, requires a credit.

As we prepare to create the cash receipts journal, we must determine the information that the journal should provide. Using the information provided by the general journal entries involving the receipt of cash as a guide, we can determine the information that the cash receipts journal should provide. The following list contains items of information that should be included in the cash receipts journal:

The cash receipt date
The debit account (Cash and Sales Discounts)
The debit amount
The credit account (Sales, Accounts Receivable,
      Interest Revenue, etc.)
The credit amount
Information such as customer name
Posting references

The cash receipts journal must provide a space to enter each item of information listed above. But, in designing the cash receipts journal, we must continue to keep in mind that we are trying to reduce the amount of writing required for each entry to a minimum.

Compare the cash receipts journal shown below to the cash receipts entries recorded in the general journal shown previously. The general journal illustration included only three transactions. Note that the cash receipts journal has almost three times as many entries, but about the same amount of writing.

	Cash Receipts Journal				Page 1			
Date 1996	Account	Ref	Cash Dr.	Sales Discounts Dr.	Accts. Rec. Cr.	Sales Cr.	Other Account Cr.
Jan 5	G. Steinmann	✓	1,862	38	1,900		
6			350			350	
8	Interest Revenue		105				105
12			500			500	
18	V. Kundrat	✓	882	18	900		
25			1,800			1,800	
30	F. Dunn	✓	980	20	1,000		
30	Notes Payable		3,000				3,000

As shown above, eight columns are used for Frank's Marine's cash receipts journal. A detailed description of each column follows:

Column 1:   The cash receipt date column:

As with other journals, the first column on the cash receipts journal is for the date.

Column 2:   A column for the account:

In this case, the word "account" refers to the name or number of the charge *account* customer who is remitting cash or the other *account*.

Column 3:   Posting reference column:

In this case, the posting reference column is used to indicate individual postings to subsidiary ledger accounts as well as postings to general ledger accounts affected by amounts in the "other account" column. Since postings to subsidiary ledgers are done on a daily basis, the transactions shown in the cash receipts journal above have already been posted to the Accounts Receivable subsidiary ledger accounts, as indicated by the check marks in the posting reference column.

Column 4: The first dollar amount column — for entries that affect the Cash account:

A column is established on the cash receipts journal for each general ledger account that is likely to be affected by a cash receipts transaction. The ledger account that is likely to be used most often occupies the first amount column. Because *every* cash receipt entry includes a debit to Cash, the Cash account is used most often and, accordingly, occupies the first column after the posting reference.

Column 5: The second dollar amount column — for entries that affect the Sales Discounts account:

Charge customers who pay invoices within the discount period will deduct the discount amount from the invoice amount to determine the amount they must remit. If sales are recorded using the gross method, an entry to record such a receipt from a customer would require a debit not only to Cash, but also to the Sales Discounts account. Generally, the columns representing debits are grouped together, so next to the column for debits to Cash is one for debits to Sales Discounts.

Column 6: The third dollar amount column — for entries that affect the Accounts Receivable account:

The Accounts Receivable account is always credited when cash is received as payment on account from customers, so a column on the cash receipts journal is dedicated to credits to Accounts Receivable.

Column 7: The fourth dollar amount column — for entries that affect the Sales account:

If cash sales are a common source of cash receipts, a column is dedicated to the Sales account.

Column 8: The last amount column — for entries that affect other accounts:

The other account column on the cash receipts journal is generally used to enter credit amounts. Note that the amount is placed in this last column, but the account title is recorded on the left side of the journal, in the "account" column.

As with other special journals, although there are no hard and fast rules with regard to the order of the columns, the date usually comes first. After the date, the next columns provide information about the entry. Then the posting reference followed by the dollar amount columns appear. The dollar amount columns in special journals are generally in order of frequency of use. Therefore, for special journals, the rule that debits come first followed by credits often does not hold true. The miscellaneous account section generally comprises the later column or columns on a special journal because, by their nature, they are used less than other columns. Because they are more seldom used, miscellaneous account columns are placed on the far right side of the journal.

POSTING FROM THE CASH RECEIPTS JOURNAL

As with other journals, when posting from the cash receipts journal to the Accounts Receivable subsidiary ledger, entries are posted individually on a daily basis. In our example, customer account numbers are not used for individual customers. Therefore, the posting reference entered on the cash receipts journal when the entry is posted to the subsidiary account is a check mark. This check mark is entered in the posting reference column on the cash receipts journal.

In order to post from the cash receipts journal to the general ledger accounts, the amount columns are totaled. These amounts are then posted using steps similar to the ones described previously. The process of preparing the column totals on this type of special journal for posting involves three steps. The cash receipts journal below shows the results of this process.

Cash Receipts Journal					Page 1			
Date 1996		Account	Ref	Cash Dr.	Sales Discounts Dr.	Accts. Rec. Cr.	Sales Cr.	Other Account Cr.
Jan	5	G. Steinmann	✓	1,862	38	1,900		
	6			350			350	
	8	Interest Revenue		105				105
	12			500			500	
	18	V. Kundrat	✓	882	18	900		
	25			1,800			1,800	
	30	F. Dunn	✓	980	20	1,000		
	30	Notes Payable		3,000				3,000
				9,479	76	3,800	2,650	3,105

Step 1.
The first step entails totaling each amount column in the special journal. As seen in the cash receipts journal that follows, the total of the Cash column is $9,479. Other totals in the cash receipts journal are: Sales Discounts $76, Accounts Receivable $3,800, Sales $2,650, and other accounts $3,105.

Step 2.
The next step is to determine whether each account total should be a debit or a credit. In some journals, care is taken to indicate whether the column is for debits or credits. The abbreviations Dr. and Cr. are used in the column headings. These indications are not always used however, because experienced accounting personnel know how each account is affected by entries on the various special journals. Although you may not realize it yet, you too can easily determine whether an account is debited or credited depending on the account and the journal. For example, the Cash column in the Cash receipts journal is used to record additions to the Cash account. Because an increase to cash requires a debit, the Cash column must be a debit column. In the case of the cash receipts journal, both the Cash column total and the Sales Discounts column total are debits, while the Accounts Receivable, Sales and other accounts column totals are credits.

Step 3.

Once all the totals are available and each is identified as a debit or a credit, a check should be made to assure that debits and credits equal. If they do not, an error has been made in the journalizing or in the summation process. In the case of our cash receipts journal, the $9,555 ($9,479 + $76) total of the debit columns equals the $9,555 ($3,800 + $2,650 + $3,105) total of the credit columns.

When posting from the cash receipts journal, the columnar totals for Cash, Sales Discounts, Accounts Receivable, and Sales are posted to their respective general ledger accounts. As was the case with the sales journal and the purchases journal, the posting reference for these entries is placed in the journal below the columnar total being posted. Again, the impact of posting a column total to a general ledger account is the same as if each individual amount in that column had been posted separately.

The only columnar total that is *not* posted is the total of the other accounts column. (The illustration below shows an (X) instead of an account number below this column total.) Totalling this column is necessary in order to confirm that debits and credits are equal. However, the column total is comprised of amounts which must be posted to a variety of accounts, so each amount must be posted individually. The posting references for the other account entries are entered in the cash receipts journal's posting reference column.

The cash receipts journal for Frank's Marine is presented below along with the Accounts Receivable subsidiary ledger and affected general ledger accounts. The arrows indicate where amounts were posted from the journal. Also, the posting references can be used to cross reference journal entries to the subsidiary and general ledgers, or from the subsidiary and general ledgers back to the journal.

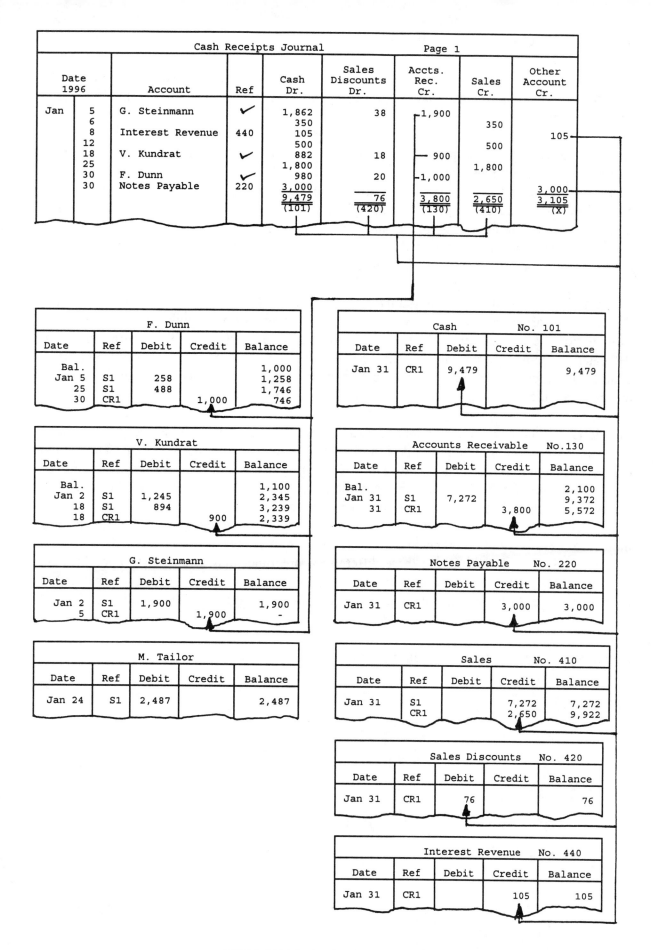

Cash Receipts Journal   Page 1

Date 1996		Account	Ref	Cash Dr.	Sales Discounts Dr.	Accts. Rec. Cr.	Sales Cr.	Other Account Cr.
Jan	5	G. Steinmann	✔	1,862	38	1,900		
	6			350			350	
	8	Interest Revenue	440	105				105
	12			500			500	
	18	V. Kundrat	✔	882	18	900		
	25			1,800			1,800	
	30	F. Dunn	✔	980	20	1,000		
	30	Notes Payable	220	3,000				3,000
				9,479	76	3,800	2,650	3,105
				(101)	(420)	(130)	(410)	(X)

F. Dunn

Date	Ref	Debit	Credit	Balance
Bal.				1,000
Jan 5	S1	258		1,258
25	S1	488		1,746
30	CR1		1,000	746

V. Kundrat

Date	Ref	Debit	Credit	Balance
Bal.				1,100
Jan 2	S1	1,245		2,345
18	S1	894		3,239
18	CR1		900	2,339

G. Steinmann

Date	Ref	Debit	Credit	Balance
Jan 2	S1	1,900		1,900
5	CR1		1,900	-

M. Tailor

Date	Ref	Debit	Credit	Balance
Jan 24	S1	2,487		2,487

Cash   No. 101

Date	Ref	Debit	Credit	Balance
Jan 31	CR1	9,479		9,479

Accounts Receivable   No. 130

Date	Ref	Debit	Credit	Balance
Bal.				2,100
Jan 31	S1	7,272		9,372
31	CR1		3,800	5,572

Notes Payable   No. 220

Date	Ref	Debit	Credit	Balance
Jan 31	CR1		3,000	3,000

Sales   No. 410

Date	Ref	Debit	Credit	Balance
Jan 31	S1		7,272	7,272
	CR1		2,650	9,922

Sales Discounts   No. 420

Date	Ref	Debit	Credit	Balance
Jan 31	CR1	76		76

Interest Revenue   No. 440

Date	Ref	Debit	Credit	Balance
Jan 31	CR1		105	105

THE CASH PAYMENTS JOURNAL

The **cash payments journal**, which is sometimes called the **cash disbursements journal** is used to record cash payments made by the company. An entry is made for each check the company writes.

As you might imagine, companies write checks for a wide variety of reasons. Checks are written to pay for utilities, supplies, maintenance, payroll, taxes, accounts payable and a variety of other things. Although the Cash account is credited for each payment, which account is debited depends upon the reason for the payment. Accordingly, the cash payment journal must be able to accommodate entries to a large number of accounts. As with the cash receipts journal, this is accomplished by establishing a dedicated column for the most often used ledger accounts and the use of an other section for the lesser used accounts.

When designing a cash payments journal, the accountant must try to determine the accounts that might be affected by a cash payment. Then, depending on the number of columns available on the journal paper, the accountant must choose the accounts that warrant their own dedicated columns. As you might imagine, within reason, the more columns available, the better. Often, companies have very wide cash payments journals which use both the right and left pages of the open ledger book to form a single journal page!

The design of the cash payments journal is quite similar to that of the cash receipts journal. Therefore, we will not explore the design of the cash payments journal in detail. There are a couple of noteworthy differences, however. One difference is that the cash payments journal requires columns for the check number and the payee (the person to whom the check is written). Another difference is that a dedicated column is used to identify the account for other account entries. Still another difference is that the cash payments journal generally has more dedicated account columns because of the multitude of accounts that are often affected by cash payments. In addition to these differences, one other may be of most importance as you begin to review the process of recording transactions in the cash payments journal and posting from it. Columns indicating credits to accounts are presented *before* columns for debits.

An example of a cash payments journal is shown on the following page.

Cash Payments Journal Page 1

Date 1996	Check No.	Payee	Cash Cr.	Ref	Purch. Discount Cr.	Accts. Payable Dr.	Purch. Dr.	Supplies Expense Dr.	Other Accounts	Amount Dr.
Jan 2	211	Art's Office Supplies	165					165		
5	212	Van Kirk Marine	450				450			
10	213	CMC Distributors	1,176	✓	24	1,200				
11	214	Strickland Marine	375				375			
15	215	Eroa Engines	1,470	✓	30	1,500				
20	216	Florida Power	250						Utility Expense	250
22	217	David's Supply Co.	55					55		
25	218	Ace Maintenance Co.	75						Maintenance Exp.	75

POSTING FROM THE CASH PAYMENTS JOURNAL

The principles of posting from the cash payments journal are identical to those of posting from the cash receipts journal. Of course the journal name, and accounts affected are different, but the basic principles are the same.

Our example of the cash payments journal is presented on the following page along with the Accounts Payable subsidiary ledger and affected general ledger accounts. The arrows indicate where amounts were posted from the journal to the various ledgers. Also, the posting references can be used to cross reference journal entries to the subsidiary and general ledgers, or from the subsidiary and general ledgers back to the journal.

Cash Payments Journal — Page 1

Date 1996	Check No.	Payee	Cash Cr.	Ref	Purch. Discount Cr.	Accts. Payable Dr.	Purch. Dr.	Supplies Expense Dr.	Other Accounts	Amount Dr.
Jan 2	211	Art's Office Supplies	165					165		
5	212	Van Kirk Marine	450				450			
10	213	CMC Distributors	1,176		24	1,200				
11	214	Strickland Marine	375				375			
15	215	Eroa Engines	1,470		30	1,500				
20	216	Florida Power	250	620					Utility Expense	250
22	217	David's Supply Co.	55					55		
25	218	Ace Maintenance Co.	75	630					Maintenance Exp.	75
			4,016		54	2,700	825	220		325
			(101)		(520)	(230)	(510)	(610)		(X)

General Ledger

Supplies Expense — No. 610

Date	Ref	Debit	Credit	Balance
Jan 31	CP1	220		220

Utilities Expense — No. 620

Date	Ref	Debit	Credit	Balance
Jan 31	CP1	250		250

Maintenance Expense — No. 630

Date	Ref	Debit	Credit	Balance
Jan 31	CP1	75		75

Cash — No. 101

Date	Ref	Debit	Credit	Balance
Jan 31	CR1	9,479		9,479
31	CP1		4,016	5,463

Accounts Payable — No. 230

Date	Ref	Debit	Credit	Balance
Bal				1,200
Jan 31	P1		6,315	7,515
31	CP1	2,700		4,815

Purchases — No. 510

Date	Ref	Debit	Credit	Balance
Jan 31	P1	6,315		6,315
31	CP1	825		7,140

Purchase Discounts — No. 520

Date	Ref	Debit	Credit	Balance
Jan 31	CP1		54	54

Accounts Payable Subsidiary Ledger

CMC Distributors

Date	Ref	Debit	Credit	Balance
Bal				1,200
Jan 9	P1		2,580	3,780
10	CP1	1,200		2,580

Eroa Engines

Date	Ref	Debit	Credit	Balance
Jan 5	P1		1,500	1,500
15	CP1	1,500		-0-

Mercury Marine

Date	Ref	Debit	Credit	Balance
Jan 1	P1		2,235	2,235

SUBSIDIARY LEDGERS AND SPECIAL JOURNALS

The wonderful thing about special journals is that they limit the amount of writing required to make a complete accounting entry and they greatly streamline the posting process. This streamlining of work required to process accounting entries is a key factor in designing a successful accounting system. Without special journals, the work to record the thousands of business transactions would be so burdensome that the cost of the resulting accounting information would be enormous.

Now, this is not to say that the general journal has no place in a well-designed accounting system. Rather, it plays a key role by providing a place to record transactions that are not accommodated by the special journals. Often, the general journal is referred to as the journal of last resort. If a transaction can't be entered in any of the special journals, record it in the general journal.

Even if a business operates all special journals possible, the general journal is still needed. Not only do unusual transactions requiring odd entries occur occasionally, but some recurring entries must be entered in the general journal. Adjusting entries, closing entries, and reversing entries are all recorded in the general journal. Also, any necessary correcting entries are most often recorded in the general journal.

By now, you have probably learned more than you ever wanted to know about the recording process. The accounting procedures included in this book provide a solid foundation for future accounting study. Additionally, the concepts presented are crucial for designing and using both manual and computerized accounting systems.

APPLY WHAT YOU HAVE LEARNED

8-1. (Which Journal To Use)

Required: For each of the following transactions, indicate which journal should be used.

S = Sales Journal   CR = Cash Receipts Journal
P = Purchases Journal   CP = Cash Payments Journal   G = General Journal

Transaction	Journal
Adjusting entry for depreciation	
Cash sales	
Closing entries	
Collection of accounts receivable	
Payment of interest expense	
Purchase of equipment on account	
Purchase returns for cash	
Purchase returns for credit	
Purchases of merchandise on account	

8-2. (Which Journal To Use)

Required:

For each of the following transactions, indicate which journal should be used.

S = Sales Journal   CR = Cash Receipts Journal
P = Purchases Journal   CP = Cash Payments Journal
G = General Journal

Transaction	Journal
Adjusting entry for accrued wages	
Cash sales	
Collection of accounts receivable	
Payment of wages	
Payment of utilities expense	
Payment of accounts payable	
Purchase of supplies on account	
Purchases of merchandise on account	
Reversing entries	
Sales on account	
Sales returns for credit	
Sales returns for cash	

8-3. (Recording in the Sales Journal)

Selected sales on account for Bart's Bikes during the month of May, 1995 are shown below. All credit sales are made on terms of 2 10, N 30.

May   3   Sold touring bicycles to Ray's Sports for $1,350, invoice number 5003.

      10   Sold Mopeds to Land Rover, Inc. for $3,775, invoice number 5010.

      26   Sold ten-speed racing bikes to Fleet Feet for $2,465, invoice number 5026.

      30   Sold helmets and other safety equipment to Adventure Incorporated for $1,800, invoice number 5030.

Required:

a.   Record the above transactions in the Sales Journal.

b.   Total the *Amount* column of the Sales Journal. To which general ledger accounts should this total be posted?

	Sales Journal	Page: 5		
Date		Customer	Ref	Amount

8-4. (Recording in the Sales Journal)

Dorin Company made the following sales on account during the month of March, 1995. All credit sales are made on terms of 1 10, N 30.

Mar 4   Sold merchandise to Philbin, Inc. for $2,700, invoice number 3004.

12   Sold merchandise to Karen's Cousins for $3,600, invoice number 3012.

22   Sold merchandise to Casper's Corners for $1,300, invoice number 3022.

30   Sold merchandise to Patrick & Deal for $1,100, invoice number 3030.

Required:

a.   Record the above transactions in the Sales Journal.

b.   Total the *Amount* column of the Sales Journal.

c.   What additional accounts would be included in the Sales Journal if the *perpetual* inventory system were used?

Sales Journal		Page: 5		
Date		Customer	Ref	Amount

8-5. (Posting from the Sales Journal)

Required:

Using the information from Problem 8-4:

a.   How is the *total* of the *Amount* column of the Sales Journal posted?

     DEBIT to _____

     CREDIT to _____

b.   How are the *individual* customer accounts posted?

c.   Post from the Sales Journal to the General Ledger and to the Accounts Receivable Subsidiary Ledger.

d.   How many credit sales transactions occurred during the month? How many postings to the general ledger are needed? If there were a million credit sales transactions during the month, how many general ledger postings would be needed?

e.   Explain in your own words the advantages of special journals.

Accounts Receivable Subsidiary Ledger

General Ledger

Philbin, Inc.

Date	Ref	Debit	Credit	Balance

Accounts Receivable   No. 130

Date	Ref	Debit	Credit	Balance

Karen's Cousins

Date	Ref	Debit	Credit	Balance

Sales   No. 410

Date	Ref	Debit	Credit	Balance

Casper's Corners

Date	Ref	Debit	Credit	Balance

Patrick & Deal

Date	Ref	Debit	Credit	Balance

8-6. (Recording in the Purchases Journal)

During the month of September, 1995, Golden's Nursery made the following purchases of merchandise on account:

Sep 10   From Mueller Gardens, invoice number M1217, $1,950, terms 2 10 EOM, N 30 EOM.

    17   From Salmeri Sunflower, invoice number S3345, $2,100, terms N 30.

    24   From Filadora's Flowers, invoice number F1234, $2,300, terms 1 10, N 30.

    30   From McGrath Farms, invoice number MC1011, $4,100, terms 2 15, N 30.

Required:

a.   Record the above transactions in the Purchases Journal.

b.   Total the *Amount* column of the Purchases Journal. To which general ledger accounts should this total be posted?

Purchases Journal		Page: 9		
Date	Supplier	Invoice Number	Ref	Amount

8-7. (Recording in the Purchases Journal)

During the month of November, 1995, Rosa & Company made the following purchases of merchandise on account:

Nov 13   From Maria, Inc., invoice number M233, $3,200, terms 1
          10 EOM, N 30 EOM.

16   From Stevens Limited, invoice number S327, $1,575,
          terms N 30.

26   From Floria General, invoice number F409, $1,600, terms
          2 10, N 30.

29   From Computer City, invoice number C289, $4,600, terms
          2 15, N 30.

Required:

a.   Record the above transactions in the Purchases Journal.

b.   Total the *Amount* column of the Purchases Journal.

c.   What accounts would be included in the Purchases Journal if the *perpetual* inventory system were used?

Purchases Journal		Page: 9		
Date	Supplier	Invoice Number	Ref	Amount

8-8. (Posting from the Purchases Journal)

Required:

Using the information from Problem 8-7:

a.   How is the *total* of the *Amount* column of the Purchases Journal posted?

     DEBIT to _____

     CREDIT to _____

b.   How are the *individual* supplier accounts posted?

c.   Post from the Purchases Journal to the General Ledger and to the Accounts Payable Subsidiary Ledger.

d.   How many credit purchase transactions occurred during the month? How many postings to the general ledger are needed? If there were a million credit purchase transactions during the month, how many general ledger postings would be needed?

e.   Explain in your own words the advantages of special journals.

Accounts Payable Subsidiary Ledger

General Ledger

Maria, Inc.

Date	Ref	Debit	Credit	Balance

Accounts Payable   No. 230

Date	Ref	Debit	Credit	Balance

Stevens Limited

Date	Ref	Debit	Credit	Balance

Purchases   No. 510

Date	Ref	Debit	Credit	Balance

Floria General

Date	Ref	Debit	Credit	Balance

Computer City

Date	Ref	Debit	Credit	Balance

8-9. (Recording in the Cash Receipts Journal)

Selected cash receipts for Bart's Bikes are shown below. All credit sales of Bart's Bikes are made on terms of 2 10, N 30.

May 13   Received cash from Ray's Sports in payment of invoice number 5003 dated May 3 for $1,350, less the cash discount.

15   Made cash sales of $2,554.

Jun 9   Received cash from Adventure Incorporated in payment of invoice number 5030 dated May 30 for $1,800, less the cash discount.

10   Received cash from Land Rover, Inc. in payment of invoice number 5010 dated May 10 for $3,775.

15   Made cash sales of $5,296.

26   Received cash from Fleet Feet in payment of invoice number 5026 dated May 26 for $2,465.

30   Received cash of $4,400 for a note receivable of $4,000 plus interest of $400.

Required:

a.   Record the above transactions in the Cash Receipts Journal.

b.   Total the amount columns of the Cash Receipts Journal. Prove that total debits equal total credits by completing the following table:

Column	Debit	Credit
Cash		
Sales Discounts		
Accounts Receivable		
Sales		
Other Accounts	_____	_____
Totals	_____	_____

c.   What additional accounts would be included in the Cash Receipts Journal if the *perpetual* inventory system were used?

Cash Receipts Journal							Page 6
Date 1995		Account	Ref	Cash Dr.	Sales Discounts Dr.	Accts. Rec. Cr.	Sales Cr.	Other Accounts Cr.

8-10. (Recording in the Cash Receipts Journal)

Selected cash receipts for Dorin Company are shown below. All credit sales of Dorin Company are made on terms of 1 10, N 30.

Mar 14   Received cash from Philbin, Inc. in payment of invoice number 3004 dated March 4 for $2,700, less the cash discount.

15   Made cash sales of $3,666.

22   Received cash from Karen's Cousins in payment of invoice number 3012 dated March 12 for $3,600, less the cash discount.

Apr 9   Received cash from Patrick & Deal in payment of invoice number 3030 dated March 30 for $1,100, less the cash discount.

15   Made cash sales of $4,123.

22   Received cash from Casper's Corners in payment of invoice number 3022 dated March 22 for $1,300.

30   Received cash of $3,360 for a note receivable of $3,000 plus interest of $360.

Required:

a.   Record the above transactions in the Cash Receipts Journal.

b.   Total the amount columns of the Cash Receipts Journal. Prove that total debits equal total credits by completing the following table:

Column	Debit	Credit
Cash		
Sales Discounts		
Accounts Receivable		
Sales		
Other Accounts	____	____
Totals	════	════

			Cash Receipts Journal		Page 6		
Date 1995	Account	Ref	Cash Dr.	Sales Discounts Dr.	Accts. Rec. Cr.	Sales Cr.	Other Accounts Cr.

8-11. (Posting from the Cash Receipts Journal)

Required:

Using the information from Problem 8-10:

a.   Indicate how each of the column *totals* of the Cash Receipts Journal should be posted.

Column Total	How Posted D = DEBIT C = CREDIT N = NOT POSTED
Cash	
Sales Discounts	
Accounts Receivable	
Sales	
Other Accounts	

b.   How are the *individual* Accounts Receivable entries posted? How are the *individual* Other Accounts posted?

c.   Post from the Cash Receipts Journal to the General Ledger and to the Accounts Receivable Subsidiary Ledger.

Accounts Receivable Subsidiary Ledger

General Ledger

Philbin, Inc.

Date	Ref	Debit	Credit	Balance
Mar 4	S3	2,700		2,700

Karen's Cousins

Date	Ref	Debit	Credit	Balance
Mar 12	S3	3,600		3,600

Casper's Corners

Date	Ref	Debit	Credit	Balance
Mar 22	S3	1,300		1,300

Patrick & Deal

Date	Ref	Debit	Credit	Balance
Mar 30	S3	1,100		1,100

Cash No. 101

Date	Ref	Debit	Credit	Balance

Sales No. 410

Date	Ref	Debit	Credit	Balance
Mar 31	S3		8,700	8,700

Accounts Receivable No. 130

Date	Ref	Debit	Credit	Balance
Mar 31	S3	8,700		8,700

Sales Discounts No. 420

Date	Ref	Debit	Credit	Balance

Notes Receivable No. 120

Date	Ref	Debit	Credit	Balance
Bal				3,000

Interest Revenue No. 440

Date	Ref	Debit	Credit	Balance

8-12. (Recording in the Cash Payments Journal)

During the month of October, 1995, Golden's Nursery made the following cash payments:

Oct   2   Check number 126 to Filadora's Flowers in payment of invoice
          number F1234 dated September 24, $2,300, terms 1 10, N 30.

      5   Purchased merchandise from Adam's Gold for $500, check
          number 127.

      8   Check number 128 to Mueller Gardens in payment of invoice
          number M1217 dated September 10, $1,950, terms 2 10 EOM, N
          30 EOM.

     11   Check number 129 to Super Supply for supplies, $370.

     12   Check number 130 to McGrath Farms in payment of invoice
          number MC1011 dated September 30, $4,100, terms 2 15, N 30.

     16   Purchased merchandise from Fall Colors for $630, check
          number 131.

     17   Check number 132 to Salmeri Sunflower in payment of invoice
          number S3345 dated September 17, $2,100, terms N 30.

     28   Check number 133 to Super Supply for supplies, $400.

     31   Check number 134 to Westlake Power for utilities, $295.

     31   Check number 135 to Acme Services for maintenance, $700.

Required: a.   Record the above transactions in the Cash Payments Journal.

b.   Total the amount columns of the Cash Payments Journal. Prove that
     total debits equal total credits by completing the following table:

Column	Debit	Credit
Cash		
Purchase Discounts		
Accounts Payable		
Purchases		
Supplies Expense		
Other Accounts	_____	_____
Totals	=====	=====

c.   What additional accounts would be included in the Cash Payments Journal if the
     perpetual inventory system were used?

8-12 Working Papers

Cash Payments Journal   Page 2

Date 1995	Check No.	Payee	Cash Cr.	Ref	Purch. Discount Cr.	Accts. Payable Dr.	Purch Dr.	Supplies Expense Dr.	Other Accounts	Amount Dr.

8-13. (Recording in the Cash Payments Journal)

Selected cash payments for Rosa & Company during the month of December, 1995, are shown below.

Dec 2   Check number 318 to Floria General in payment of invoice number F409 dated November 26, $1,600, terms 2 10, N 30.

    8   Purchased merchandise from Orville's for $1,500, check number 319.

    9   Check number 320 to Maria, Inc. in payment of invoice number M233 dated November 13, $3,200, terms 1 10 EOM, N 30 EOM.

  10   Purchased merchandise from Greenacres for $1,300, check number 321.

  12   Check number 322 to Computer City in payment of invoice number C289 dated November 29, $4,600, terms 2 15, N 30.

  15   Check number 323 to Super Supply for supplies, $250.

  16   Check number 324 to Stevens Limited in payment of invoice number S327 dated November 16, $1,575, terms N 30.

  18   Check number 325 to Clean House for maintenance, $1,200.

  30   Check number 326 to Super Supply for supplies, $420.

  31   Check number 327 to Northern Power & Light for utilities, $375.

Required: a.   Record the above transactions in the Cash Payments Journal.

          b.   Total the amount columns of the Cash Payments Journal. Prove that total debits equal total credits by completing the following table:

Column	Debit	Credit
Cash		
Purchase Discounts		
Accounts Payable		
Purchases		
Supplies Expense		
Other Accounts	_____	_____
Totals	══════	══════

Cash Payments Journal   Page 2

Date 1995	Check No.	Payee	Cash Cr.	Ref	Purch. Discount Cr.	Accts. Payable Dr.	Purch Dr.	Supplies Expense Dr.	Other Accounts	Amount Dr.

8-14. (Posting from the Cash Payments Journal)

Required:

Using the information from Problem 8-13:

a. Indicate how each of the column *totals* of the Cash Payments Journal should be posted.

Column Total	How Posted D = DEBIT C = CREDIT N = NOT POSTED
Cash	
Purchase Discounts	
Accounts Payable	
Purchases	
Supplies Expense	
Other Accounts	

b. How are the *individual* Accounts Payable entries posted?

How are the *individual* Other Accounts posted?

c. Post from the Cash Payments Journal to the General Ledger and the Accounts Payable Subsidiary Ledger. The balance in the Cash account before posting is $50,000.

Accounts Payable Subsidiary Ledger

Maria, Inc

Date	Ref	Debit	Credit	Balance
Nov 13	P11		3,200	3,200

Stevens Limited

Date	Ref	Debit	Credit	Balance
Nov 16	P11		1,575	1,575

Floria General

Date	Ref	Debit	Credit	Balance
Nov 26	P11		1,600	1,600

Computer City

Date	Ref	Debit	Credit	Balance
Nov 29	P11		4,600	4,600

General Ledger

Cash — No.101

Date	Ref	Debit	Credit	Balance

Accounts Payable — No.230

Date	Ref	Debit	Credit	Balance
Nov 30	P11		10,975	10,975

Purchases — No.510

Date	Ref	Debit	Credit	Balance
Nov 30	P11	10,975		10,975

Purchase Discounts — No.520

Date	Ref	Debit	Credit	Balance

Supplies Expense — No.610

Date	Ref	Debit	Credit	Balance

Utilities Expense — No.620

Date	Ref	Debit	Credit	Balance

Maintenance Expense — No.630

Date	Ref	Debit	Credit	Balance

8-15. (Using Special Journals and Subsidiary Ledgers)

Transactions for Torby Limited during the month of December, 1995, are listed below. All purchases and sales on account are on terms of 2 10, N 30. The gross method is used for recording both purchases and sales.

Dec 1   Purchased $1,000 of merchandise on account from Kendrick Company, invoice number K654.

2   Purchased $600 of supplies; check number 101 was issued to Super Supply.

3   Purchased equipment for $10,000 on account from Tonawanda Equippers. The equipment has a residual value of $1,000 and a life of 5 years.

5   Returned $100 of the merchandise purchased on December 1 to Kendrick Company for credit.

9   Paid Kendrick the balance due, using check number 102.

12   Made cash sales of $15,000.

13   Sold merchandise of $6,000 on account to Saia Sound, invoice number 4446.

15   Paid $466 to Niagara Edison for utilities, check number 103.

16   Saia Sound returned $300 of merchandise for credit.

20   Received payment in full from Saia Sound.

24   Sold merchandise of $4,500 on account to Scrivanni Cyberspace, invoice number 4447.

26   Sold merchandise of $2,000 on account to Teresa & Tracy International, invoice number 4448.

27   Received $1,120 on a note receivable of $1,000 plus interest of $120.

28   Purchased $1,750 of merchandise on account from Tamara Tram, invoice number T777.

29   Purchased $3,000 of merchandise on account from Kyle Outfitters, invoice number KO237.

30   Paid wages of $8,600, check number 104.

31   An inventory of supplies at the end of the month shows $225 supplies on hand. Made an adjusting entry to reflect this.

31   Recorded depreciation for one month on the equipment purchased on December 3.

(REQUIREMENTS FOR THIS PROBLEM ARE ON THE NEXT PAGE.)

Required:

    a.   Record the above transactions in the appropriate journals provided on the following pages. Make any necessary postings to the Accounts Receivable and Accounts Payable subsidiary ledgers as the transactions are recorded.

    b.   Add the columns in the special journals to assure that debits equal credits.

    c.   Post all the journals to the general ledger.

    d.   Prove that the subsidiary ledgers agree with the balances of the control accounts.

8-15 Working Papers

	General Journal			Page 1
Date	Description	Post Ref	Debit	Credit

Date 1995	Customer	Ref	Amount

Sales Journal   Page: 1

Accounts Receivable Subsidiary Ledger

Saia Sound

Date	Ref	Debit	Credit	Balance

Scrivanni Cyberspace

Date	Ref	Debit	Credit	Balance

Teresa & Tracy International

Date	Ref	Debit	Credit	Balance

General Ledger

Accounts Receivable   No. 130

Date	Ref	Debit	Credit	Balance

Sales   No. 410

Date	Ref	Debit	Credit	Balance

Purchases Journal			Page: 1		
Date		Supplier	Invoice Number	Ref	Amount

Accounts Payable Subsidiary Ledger

Kendrick Company				
Date	Ref	Debit	Credit	Balance

Tamara Tram				
Date	Ref	Debit	Credit	Balance

Kyle Outfitters				
Date	Ref	Debit	Credit	Balance

Tonawanda Equippers				
Date	Ref	Debit	Credit	Balance

General Ledger

Accounts Payable			No. 230	
Date	Ref	Debit	Credit	Balance

Purchases			No. 510	
Date	Ref	Debit	Credit	Balance

Cash Receipts Journal   Page 1

Date 1995	Account	Ref	Cash Dr.	Sales Discounts Dr.	Accts. Rec. Cr.	Sales Cr.	Other Accounts Cr.

Cash Payments Journal   Page 1

Date 1995	Check No.	Payee	Cash Cr.	Ref	Purch. Discount Cr.	Accts. Payable Dr.	Purch Dr.	Supplies Expense Dr.	Other Accounts	Amount Dr.

General Ledger

Cash No.100

Date	Ref	Debit	Credit	Balance

Equipment No. 150

Date	Ref	Debit	Credit	Balance

Supplies Expense No.610

Date	Ref	Debit	Credit	Balance

Depreciation Expense No. 640

Date	Ref	Debit	Credit	Balance

Purchase Returns No. 530

Date	Ref	Debit	Credit	Balance

Utilities Expense No. 620

Date	Ref	Debit	Credit	Balance

Accumulated Depreciation No. 160

Date	Ref	Debit	Credit	Balance

Sales Returns No. 430

Date	Ref	Debit	Credit	Balance

Wages Expense No. 630

Date	Ref	Debit	Credit	Balance

Purchase Discounts No. 520

Date	Ref	Debit	Credit	Balance

Supplies No. 140

Date	Ref	Debit	Credit	Balance

Sales Discounts No.420

Date	Ref	Debit	Credit	Balance

Interest Revenue No. 450

Date	Ref	Debit	Credit	Balance

Notes Receivable No. 135

Date	Ref	Debit	Credit	Balance

SUBSIDIARY LEDGERS AND SPECIAL JOURNALS